THE SECOND CHILD

NEW PERSPECTIVES ON FAMILY

Published in cooperation with the National Council on Family Relations

NCFR

Series Editor: **Linda Thompson**
University of Wisconsin, Madison

Books appearing in New Perspectives on Family are either single- or multiple-authored volumes or concisely edited books of original articles on focused topics within the broad field of marriage and family. Books can be reports of significant research, innovations in methodology, treatises on family theory, or syntheses of current knowledge in a subfield of the discipline. Each volume meets the highest academic standards and makes a substantial contribution to our knowledge of marriage and family.

THE SECOND CHILD

Family Transition and Adjustment

Robert B. Stewart, Jr.

Published in cooperation with
the National Council on Family Relations

SAGE PUBLICATIONS
The International Professional Publishers
Newbury Park   London   New Delhi

To Andie, Ian, and Jessa, for having patience while Dad was a little crazy with this project, and to the two Bobs, for showing me how to think systemically.

Copyright © 1990 by Sage Publications, Inc.

For information address:

 SAGE Publications, Inc.
2455 Teller Road
Newbury Park, California 91320

SAGE Publications Ltd.
6 Bonhill Street
London EC2A 4PU
United Kingdom

SAGE Publications India Pvt. Ltd.
M-32 Market
Greater Kailash I
New Delhi 110 048 India

Printed in the United States of America

Library of Congress Cataloging-in-Publication Data

Stewart, Robert B.
    The second child : family transition and adjustment / Robert B.
  Stewart, Jr.
      p.   cm. — (New perspectives on family)
    May 1990.
    Includes bibliographical references and indexes.
    ISBN 0-8039-3519-6. — ISBN 0-8039-3520-X (pbk.)
    1. Second-born children.   2. Family—Psychological aspects.
  I. Title.   II. Series.
  HQ777.22.S74   1991
  306.874—dc20   90-43949
                                                                        CIP

FIRST PRINTING, 1990

Sage Production Editor: Diane S. Foster

Contents

Series Editor's Foreword

Although most researchers know that they should be doing theory-based, multimethod, longitudinal work on whole families, few seem to have the courage or stamina to do it. Robert Stewart does it. The research project Stewart presents in *The Second Child* is exemplary: It offers readers important substantive findings and shows them how good research is accomplished. It is the powerful combination of Stewart's insightful information about the family's transition to the birth of the second child and his innovative, thorough way of doing research that makes this book worthy of sponsorship by the National Council on Family Relations.

Stewart's focus on the birth of the second child is rare and overdue after decades of research on the transition to first parenthood and a handful of studies that contrasts first-time parents with all other parents. Stewart followed 41 middle-class families from before birth through the first year of the second child's life. Mother, father, and firstborn child were all interviewed on five occasions. In a remarkable way, Stewart monitored the family system as it progressed from three to four members. Using a mingling of systems and stress theories for guidance in the study of family transition, he considered marital, parent-child, and sibling relationships. Stewart has something important to say about the development of men as fathers, division of labor between women and men, sources of stress and support for mothers and fathers, firstborn children as active family members, and much more.

The research design and process, however, are almost as remarkable as the content of this project. Stewart used many methods of data collection—observations of family interaction, interviews with each family member, assessments and questionnaires. I particularly liked the notion of interviewing firstborn children, whose average age was three. The longitudinal nature of the project is also noteworthy. I was especially impressed by the sense of collaboration that pervaded the research project. Robert Stewart's colleagues were undergraduate researchers who were actively involved in every aspect of the study. And the final chapter of the book describes what happens when Stewart and his student colleagues present their interpretation of findings to the parents who participated in the study. The ensuing discussion between researchers and the researched is marvelous.

The New Perspectives on Family Series allows researchers to present their projects in all their complexity and detail. Authors do not have to reduce a larger vision to journal-size glimpses. Stewart's book illustrates how useful it can be for students and more seasoned scholars to read about whole projects and the process by which such work is achieved.

Robert Stewart traces the birth of this research project to the birth of his second child, Jessa. Although researchers are loathe to admit it, many research projects are born of similar personal experiences. Thanks, in part, to Jessa, we now have a book that helps us understand the mysteries and miseries of second-time parenthood.

—*Linda Thompson*
University of Wisconsin
Madison

Preface

A very wise mentor once taught me that a preface is not a casual before-the-fact statement—made after the fact, of course—describing what the following volume is about. Instead, he explained that the preface should be skillfully employed to disarm most critics by carefully and clearly stating what the book is not about. With his words in mind, I would like to indicate that this book is not intended as a conceptual bridge between psychology and sociology, between child development and family therapy, or even between the child development and family relations disciplines. Such bridges are sorely needed, and the contents of this book might be useful in encouraging others to work toward their construction, but what is offered here should not be viewed as a bridge over these long-existing chasms.

On the other hand, what is presented here is a description of the collaborative efforts between me and a number of undergraduate researchers who, at the time of their involvements, did not hold particularly strong allegiance to any discipline. These students viewed the relative insularity of social science disciplines as being maintained by artificial barriers that could be crossed easily if a common vocabulary and theoretical foundation were agreed upon. To them, the deep chasms seemed more like wide plateaus that could be traversed if one were willing to put forth the effort. These students were introduced to general systems theory before the comforts provided by our more traditional reductionistic methods had a firm hold on them. The notions of interlocking and interdependent social systems of influence and effect appeared to be a useful means for studying family development, and the transitions and adjustments the family experiences at the birth of a second child provided an interesting, and relatively unexplored, phenomenon to which we could apply our integrative efforts.

These students also were introduced to Robert McCall's (1977) "Challenges to a Science of Developmental Psychology." Our discussions of this article indicated that his arguments made intuitive sense to this group

9

of students, but they were somewhat surprised to find that interdisciplinary, multivariate, longitudinal studies were not the norm in developmental research. Although they quickly learned why many of us shy away from such designs, they recognized that answering McCall's challenges remains an important goal for the discipline.

It is customary for an author to accept full responsibility for whatever deficiencies and shortcomings his book may have, while at the same time asserting that the strengths and virtues of his work, if any, are the direct result of thoughtful colleagues, eager students, and a patient family. There are deficiencies in this work, and there are things that I certainly would do differently if only I could turn back the hands of time. Still, the contents of this work should be of interest to those seeking a systemic understanding of family development, and perhaps they will be able to avoid some of the pitfalls we encountered.

The research project presented here could not have been completed without the contribution of three of my students. Linda A. Mobley, Susan S. Van Tuyl, and Myrna A. Salvador contributed approximately two undergraduate years each to all phases of this project—from its initial planning to the final series of data analyses. When they graduated and left Oakland University they had more research experience and more refined research skills than many of the graduate students I have known. To say that their departures were bittersweet is indeed an understatement, and during the two years of preparing this manuscript I have realized repeatedly just how valuable their individual and collective contributions had been.

I would also like to thank Pauline Behmlander, Nanette DesNoyer, Carin Medla, Lori Oresky, and Deborah Walls for their assistance with data collection. These five women were responsible for maintaining the interest and cooperation of their respective subject families over the course of this project so that complete data might be obtained. The fact that no family withdrew from the project prior to its completion is evidence enough that these interviewers/observers were successful, and I am deeply indebted to them for their hard work and dedication.

I especially want to thank Wanda C. Bronson for her careful reviews and critiques of earlier drafts of this manuscript. Deborah Szobel's accurate and perceptive critiques of the final drafts of the manuscript, and her gentle suggestions for editorial changes, clarifications, and improvements are especially appreciated. Moreover, Laurie Gottlieb, Susan Haworth-Hoeppner, Debra Meyer, and Jennifer Rashid provided assistance during the preparation and revisions of this manuscript. Linda Thompson, editor of the Sage New Perspectives on Family series, and her reviewers provided numerous insightful comments and suggestions that greatly improved the quality of this project; I am indebted to them for their assistance. Finally, I would like to acknowledge the 41 families who volunteered to participate in this project and thank them for their outstanding cooperation. This project was supported in part by a Faculty Research Grant from Oakland University, by a Biomedical Research Grant (S07RR07131) from the National Institutes of Health, and by an Undergraduate Research Grant from the Oakland Alumni Association awarded to Linda A. Mobley and Susan S. Van Tuyl.

—*Robert B. Stewart, Jr.*

PART I

The Problem

The events surrounding the births of our two children were quite different. My wife and I were calmly watching a movie on television when it became apparent that our first experience with labor and delivery was about to begin. We briefly continued our ongoing debate concerning just how one was supposed to time the contractions—from beginning to beginning or from beginning to end—as we wondered whether we would have time to finish watching the movie. My MG-B would not start, but very pregnant women probably should not even try to sit in such a car, so I drove my wife's car. To this day she teases me for driving so slowly to the hospital. Actually, I drove at exactly the speed limit simply because I did not want to be associated with the comic stereotyped scene of the slightly crazed, confused husband racing to the hospital only to pace the floor with other expectant fathers. Besides, the hospital was only a mile away.

The second labor and delivery, approximately two years later, was a nightmare. The pronouncement that it was time to go to the hospital came during dinner, and by then we had resolved our debate concerning the proper timing of contractions (it is from beginning to beginning). Because both of our families lived hundreds of miles away, we had prepared a list of names and phone numbers of people who had volunteered to come at a moment's notice to stay with our son. I began with the first name and worked my way down to the last without reaching a single one. My wife was growing more than just a little uncomfortable and anxious, and our son was showing clear signs of concern as his dad was beginning to lose his cool. I was later amused at the realization that the transition to parenthood certainly was not limited to the birth of a first child. Our second arrived safely, and with her the plans for this research project.

This project represents a synthesis of the methodologies of developmental psychology, family sociology, and systems theory to obtain detailed observational, interview, and assessment data describing familial role adjustments following the birth of a second child. Adjustments in

parent-child, sibling, and marital relations were analyzed using a longitudinal design. The first assessments were obtained during the third
trimester of the second pregnancy, and subsequent assessments were
made throughout the first year of the second child's life. Even though this
project was not developed to test specific hypotheses, a number of
questions guided its orientation. Among these were the following:

(1) Is the birth of a second child perceived by parents to be a stressful event,
    and do mothers and fathers differ in their perceptions of the magnitude or
    sources of the stress associated with it?
(2) How do the members of the family adjust to the new role definitions and
    demands incurred after the birth of a second child?
(3) Do parents alter the division of their child-care, infant-care, or household
    maintenance responsibilities following the birth of the second child?
(4) Do parents seek a wider social support network following the birth of a
    second child, and is there an intrafamilial pattern of preferred sources of
    support, or do mothers and fathers seek and utilize divergent support
    networks?
(5) How do various aspects of the parents' support networks and their satis-
    faction with their adjustments to the second child act to mitigate the stress
    associated with this period of familial adjustment?

Chapter 1 presents a synopsis of the models serving as theoretical
foundations for this project. First, a brief introduction to the central tenets
of general systems theory is provided (e.g., Bertalanffy, 1968; Buckley,
1967). This introduction is followed by a more detailed presentation of
the primary principles of systems theory (e.g., P. Minuchin, 1985). Examples are drawn from child and family development literature to illustrate
these principles. Next, some of the ways other researchers have incorporated systems thought into their studies of families are briefly summarized
(e.g., Belsky, 1981; Kaye, 1985; Sameroff, 1983). Finally, the chapter
closes with an introduction to the classic ABCX model of family stress
(Hill, 1949) and McCubbin and Patterson's (1982, 1983) elaboration of
this model. This model will serve to guide our exploration of family
transitions associated with the birth of a second child. Readers already
familiar with general systems theory, its application to the study of
families in general, and the study of familial adjustment to stress in
particular may wish to go directly to Chapter 2, which provides a summary
of empirical literature relevant to this project.

A brief summary of the literature concerning the transition to parenthood introduces Chapter 2 (e.g., Hoffman, 1978; Rossi, 1968), and then a detailed discussion is presented of six studies that were especially important in shaping this project. These studies include the Shereshefsky and Yarrow (1973), Grossman, Eichler, and Winickoff (1980), and Entwisle and Doering (1981) studies of the first pregnancy, and studies of early parenting conducted by Cowan and Cowan (1987), LaRossa and LaRossa (1981), and Belsky and his associates (e.g., Belsky, Spanier, & Rovine, 1983). Because these projects approached the transition to parenthood from different theoretical and methodological perspectives, a simple integration of their common findings is not appropriate. Instead, a detailed summary of their unique contributions is offered. Speculations concerning how familial adjustment to the birth of a second child may be qualitatively different from that of the initial transition to parenthood are then presented. Two primary themes are addressed in this section of the chapter: (a) the issue of potential increased paternal participation in the family (e.g., Baruch & Barnett, 1986; Crouter, Perry-Jenkins, Huston, & McHale, 1987; Kreppner, Paulsen, & Schuetze, 1982), and (b) the role of the firstborn child in familial adjustment following the birth of a second child who is also his or her sibling (e.g., Dunn, Kendrick, & MacNamee, 1981; Nadelman & Begun, 1982; Stewart, Mobley, Van Tuyl, & Salvador, 1987). The chapter closes with a summary of the primary research objectives of the project.

1

A Systems View
of the Family

Evidence of interest in reuniting the disciplines of family sociology, developmental psychology, and family therapy through the integrative strength of general systems theory is found in Patricia Minuchin's (1985) introductory article to a special issue of *Child Development*. Her review presents a reformulation of concept and method in studying family and individual development that is based, in part, on Ludwig von Bertalanffy's (1968) description of general systems theory. In this approach the family is regarded as an organized, open system, and each individual as a unique, contributing member of that system. General systems theory has come to describe a level of theory somewhere between pure mathematics and the specific theories of various disciplines, and is now considered the fifth in a set of world hypotheses (Pepper, 1942). Specifically, general systems theory is considered to be a form of "selectivism" based on the root metaphor of the purposeful, self-regulating system. In its actual application, however, general systems theory primarily serves "as neither a formula nor a doctrine, but as a cluster of strategies of inquiry; not a theory but an organized space within which many theories may be developed and related" (Berrien, 1968, p. 13). Salvador Minuchin's (1974) structuralist theory of familial therapy may be viewed as an illustration of a general systems approach in that his concept of family structure is defined in terms of self-regulation, hierarchical organization, and the differentiation of the family into subunits.

Patricia Minuchin (1985) indicates that a general systems orientation supports certain research emphases, such as observational techniques and the description of recurrent patterns, and challenges others, such as correlational studies that do not permit one to determine how systems may self-correct over time. Observational methodology and the description of recurrent patterns of behavioral interaction are techniques employed by many disciplines, including family therapy, ethology, and developmental psychology. The primary goal of this project was to identify the recurrent patterns of action and interaction, patterns of systems self-correction and self-organization, and the critical points of system development through the use of naturalistic observation, open-ended interviews, and specific indices of family functioning as families reorganize themselves following the birth of a second child. These data should prove to be invaluable to family therapists and researchers of family or individual development who seek an empirically derived description of the range of response in this normative life event.

This project therefore represents an attempt to study the entire family as a system composed of numerous interdependent subsystems as it develops and achieves a new state of equilibrium following the birth of a second child—a normative life event that has not yet been the focus of much empirical inquiry. In presenting this work, I will integrate literatures such as the transition to parenthood work of family sociologists and psychologists (e.g., Cowan, Cowan, Coie, & Coie, 1978; Cowan et al., 1985; Entwisle & Doering, 1981; Goldberg, Michaels, & Lamb, 1985; Isabella & Belsky, 1985; Kreppner, Paulsen, & Schuetze, 1982; McHale & Huston, 1984, 1985; Rossi, 1968), work on the interdependence of family subsystems (e.g., Belsky, 1979, 1981; Belsky, Spanier, & Rovine, 1983; Cox et al., 1985; Pedersen, 1975), and studies of the sources of parental stress (Abidin, 1979, 1983) and of support networks (Cohen & Wills, 1985; Crnic, Greenberg, Ragozin, Robinson, & Basham, 1983) with that of family therapy (Hansen & Johnson, 1979; McCubbin & Patterson, 1982, 1983; S. Minuchin, 1974; Olson, Sprenkle, & Russell, 1979). Of course, I am aware that in making such an integrative attempt it will be extremely difficult to avoid contradictions in the underlying theoretical assumptions of the numerous disciplines. Furthermore, I know that such an integration is likely to be somewhat unsatisfactory to some readers, as I have had to make hard decisions concerning what materials to include and what to exclude.

GENERAL SYSTEMS THEORY

General systems theory is a discipline concerned with the general properties and laws of "systems." The formal origin of general systems theory is usually attributed to Ludwig von Bertalanffy (1968), who described an interdisciplinary set of principles and models that apply to systems in general, irrespective of the particular elements and forces involved. The basic quest of general systems theory has been to develop a body of systematic theoretical constructs that would enhance interdisciplinary communication between specialists previously isolated from one another. Indeed, Boulding (1956), an early proponent of general systems theory, remarked that if specialization within science continued to make communication across disciplines more difficult, each scientist would become a walled-in hermit able to mumble in a private language that only he or she could understand.

A *system* is defined as a complex of components operating in concert, and the purpose of general systems theory is to develop a set of principles that applies to systems in general. Among the features essential in the definition of a system are multivariate interaction, maintenance of wholes in the counteraction of component parts, and the multilevel organization of these wholes into systems of increasingly higher order. Issues such as differentiation, centralization, regulation, evolution toward higher, more adaptive organization, and goal directedness in various forms also are fundamental to the understanding of systems theory. Bertalanffy viewed most scientific disciplines of his time as trying to isolate phenomena into simpler and simpler units of analysis (i.e., mechanistic reductionism), with the assumption that this analysis was the sole and proper approach to understanding. A primary goal of general systems theory has been to provide a framework for the generalization of scientific concepts so that disciplines such as biology and the behavioral sciences might be able to address issues pertinent to their phenomena—such as development, evolution, functional analyses of behavior, adaptation—that had not been addressed in the physics-based system of scientific inquiry. General systems theory, therefore, is a general science of "wholeness" that, until the writings of Bertalanffy, was considered a vague, hazy, and semi-metaphysical concept.

Bertalanffy argued that to understand any phenomenon scientifically, one needed to understand not only the phenomenon's elements in isolation from one another but, more important, their interrelations. Specifically, Bertalanffy argued that it was necessary not only to study parts and processes in isolation, but also to solve the decisive problems found in the organization and order unifying them. Organization and order are assumed to result from the dynamic interaction of the parts of the system, thus making the behavior of parts different when studied in isolation than it is with the whole. Traditionally, the primary goal of science has been to split reality into ever smaller units, to isolate individual causal links, and to establish an explanatory and predictive system of laws similar to those found in theoretical physics. It is Bertalanffy's position that this scheme has been insufficient, and that we must learn to think in terms of systems of elements in mutual interaction. More recently, the biological, behavioral, and social sciences have come into their own and have realized that an application of physics is not sufficient or even feasible for many of their most pressing areas of inquiry. For example, it was noted that the living organism possesses a structural and functional order: an organization, maintenance in continuous change, regulation, and apparent teleology. When considering human behavior, goal seeking and purposiveness cannot be ignored even by those accepting a strict behavioral position.

This basic change in perspective has evolved into a more contemporary *general systems framework*, a broad set of approaches to complex phenomena based on the metaphor of the purposive, self-regulating system that naturally grows in complexity (often referred to as "negative entropy"). Traditional concepts of one-way causality, of the relationship between "cause" and "effect," or of the linear predictability between a pair or among a few variables, have been quite useful in a wide range of scientific endeavor. Nevertheless, many problems in biology or the behavioral and social sciences are multivariate in nature, and unidirectional conceptualizations of causality are simply inappropriate. Realizing this, Bertalanffy proposed a less restrictive conceptualization of causality by introducing the concept of *equifinality*. The classical principle of causality holds that similar conditions produce similar effects, and, consequently, that dissimilar results are due to dissimilar conditions. Equifinality holds that an open system is capable of reaching its final normal state by any number of routes. For example, a growing organism might reach its final end state, conceptualized as a certain species-specific body size, from different initial sizes at birth, or after various disturbances or individual differences in timing or duration of growth spurts throughout its life.

In its most basic form, general systems theory rejects the classic notions of independent and dependent variables and instead places a greater emphasis on the interdependence of variables and the organization of phenomena. It tends to focus on contextual hierarchical structures and fluctuating processes rather than on basic elements and static entities. As such, it rejects the reductionism model so prevalent in psychology and instead encourages researchers to consider a more holistic perspective. Berscheid (1986) argues that "abandoning the reductionistic faith does not necessarily mean abandoning the analytic method." She argues that the systems approach may hold some important benefits for researchers and theorists if it is employed discriminatingly. Among these benefits are the likelihood that questions of process will receive more attention and that questions of static structure will be regarded as less interesting than they have been traditionally. Moreover, by assuming a broader perspective, researchers should be better able to identify the variables that have important implications for the system. As a caveat, Berscheid notes that the investigator who truly assumes the systems approach may easily drown in his or her data, as too many variables suspected to be important to the system might be considered.

Aspects of general systems thought can be found throughout psychology and sociology as numerous researchers and theorists have grown dissatisfied with reductionism and its mechanistic models of human behavior (e.g., Homans, 1950; Miller, Galanter, & Pribram, 1960; Parsons, 1951). Buckley (1967) has provided an integrated summary of many of these works by addressing the broader issue of the study of the complex process, or adaptive system, model. Borrowing from such allied fields as information or communication theory and cybernetics, Buckley describes complex adaptive systems as self-regulating, self-directing, and self-organizing. He suggests that the behavior of complex, open systems does not result as a simple and direct function of impinging external forces, but instead that mediating processes (such as decision-making or negotiating procedures) intervene between the external forces and the resultant behavior. As the adaptive system grows progressively more complex, these mediating processes are assumed to become more autonomous or independent as they adjust the system to external contingencies, direct it toward more satisfactory environments, or permanently reorganize aspects of the system so as to derive more efficient means of interacting with the environment.

Buckley points out that concepts such as "self-regulation" may be somewhat misleading because they tend to include connotations that may overemphasize the independence of the system at the expense of the environment. To avoid this problem, Buckley suggests two more neutral descriptions of the basic processes of adaptive systems: morphostasis and morphogenesis. *Morphostasis* refers to those processes that tend to preserve or maintain a system's given form, organization, or state. *Morphogenesis* refers to those processes that tend to elaborate or change a system's given form, structure, or state. For example, homeostatic processes might be considered forms of morphostasis; evolution and ontogenetic development are examples of morphogenesis.

To introduce the discussion of how the principles of general systems theory can be applied to the study of family systems, I would first like to provide a summary of each of the primary principles defining open and adaptive systems. In this summary I will draw extensively from Laszlo's (1972) descriptions of living systems, from Patricia Minuchin's (1985) review paper, in which she outlines a number of basic principles of structural family theory and their relationships to developmental psychology, and from Marvin and Stewart's (1990) discussion of the utility of a family systems framework for the study of attachment. Six primary principles defining open and adaptive systems will be discussed:

(1) *Wholeness and order:* Any system is an organized whole, and elements within the system are necessarily interdependent.

(2) *Circular causal relationships:* Patterns of effect or causality within a system are circular rather than linear.

(3) *Maintenance of invariant relationships:* To maintain order, some relationships—either within the system or within its interplay with the environment—must remain invariant.

(4) *Adaptive self-regulation:* Evolution and change are inherent in any open system, and homeostatic properties exist to assist the system's adaptation.

(5) *Adaptive self-organization:* When the change imposed upon the system is sufficiently large, the adaptive system will reorganize itself to establish a new balance.

(6) *Subsystems and boundaries:* Systems are composed of subsystems separated by boundaries.

Each principle will be illustrated with an example drawn from the literature concerning parent-child relations, Minuchin's (1985) comments concerning family therapy, or common daily experiences within families. It should be pointed out that the general systems principles described below are equally applicable at the individual, dyadic, or family level. Furthermore, this set of principles itself constitutes an interrelated system within which each principle contains elements of, or implies, each of the others. Therefore, no single principle is necessarily more important than any other, and all must be considered to some degree if a systemic perspective is to be obtained.

Wholeness and Order

This first systems property refers to the notion that the whole is more than the sum of its parts by noting that the whole includes the property of relationships among the parts. The concept of wholeness escapes its metaphysical connotations in a general systems framework by directing attention to issues such as hierarchic structure, stability, differentiation, steady state, and goal directedness. The essential thrust of this principle is that no individual, or that individual's behavior, can be understood outside of the context in which he or she is functioning. Rather than attempt to understand the individual by relying solely on a reductionistic form of analysis (i.e., understanding that individual's component parts), the systems researcher will attempt to describe and understand patterns in the larger organizations that constitute both the individual and the system of which that individual is a part. While studying these patterns, systems researchers can either describe the structure of the individual or treat the individual as a "black box" without violating conceptual or methodological rules (Berrien, 1968, p. 32).

An excellent example of the application of this principle at an individual level can be found in the work of Ainsworth and her associates focusing on the interplay among the three behavioral systems of attachment, fear/wariness, and exploration (e.g., Ainsworth, Blehar, Waters, & Wall, 1978; Bretherton & Ainsworth, 1974). It has been argued on conceptual as well as empirical grounds (e.g., Bretherton & Ainsworth, 1974; Sroufe & Waters, 1977) that the large group of attachment behaviors and the other behaviors in the infant's repertoire could be categorized into four complex, interrelated systems of behavior: the attachment, affiliative, fear/wariness, and exploratory systems. Stewart and Marvin (1984) later added a fifth system, that of caregiving, so as to establish a coding system that could be utilized in dyadic situations. Behavioral systems might overlap with one another in a number of ways. For example, a single behavior might serve two or more systems that are not themselves conflicting, as when a child backs away from a stranger (signaling wariness) while approaching the mother (demonstrating also an attachment behavior). The interplay of behavioral systems might be observed as two conflicting systems are evoked simultaneously and produce a "blend response," as when the wariness and affiliative systems interact to create a coy, flirtatious response in the child. Finally, the interplay of systems might be sequential and cyclic, such as when the child moves away from the mother to explore the environment, then seemingly notices that the mother is too far away and races back to her side before repeating the process of exploring away from the secure maternal base. This particular interplay of systems of behavior yields a complex behavioral pattern that is certainly more than the sum of its parts, and that would not have been discovered if Ainsworth and her associates had maintained a strictly linear, reductionistic analytic approach.

At the family systems level of analysis this principle of wholeness and order suggests that to understand the relationship between infant and mother fully one must have sufficient information concerning the infant-father and mother-father relationships. A thorough understanding would be obtained by having further information concerning not only the relationships among all members—that is, the structure of the family as a whole—but also the functional outcomes of each member's interactions, which are crucial in establishing and maintaining the integrity and coherence of the family. Berrien (1968) suggests that it is useful to conceptualize the role as being the basic unit of a social system (cf. Parsons & Shils, 1951, p. 190). The role therefore is considered to be a sector of the individual actor's total system of action. When considering larger social systems, one may conceive of functional roles to be assigned to separate people or to specialized divisions within the organization (cf. Miller, 1965). This would lead the systems researcher to expect that the variability of a social system and its success in dealing with a variety of tasks will depend upon the ease with which the members of that system can assume various roles as they are needed. For example, the husband who is able to adopt the role of emotional supporter may facilitate the success of the entire family system by enhancing his wife's ability to nurture their child. Although researchers trained in the traditional methods of reductionism might wish to know whether maternal incompetence in feeding was the cause or the result of marital tension and conflict, those adopting a systems orientation have another conceptualization of causality that renders this question less interesting.

The systemic concept of wholeness and order implies the existence of certain patterns of interaction and expectations that serve definable outcomes and maintain the coherence of the family as a system. Kaye (1985) describes this demonstration of a shared purpose derived from a shared history as being an important criterion in distinguishing a social system from any collection of people. One of the primary means through which family coherence is maintained is that of shared expectations and plans, or "working models" (Bowlby, 1969, 1973) of how the members of the family cooperate to organize physical proximity and contact. Families certainly vary in the manner in which they interact to maintain various definitions of familial order, but each member of a family (beyond a certain developmental point) will have a working model of his or her and the other members' contributions to those patterns.

Circular Causal Relationships

The traditional Cartesian-Newtonian model of causality has probably done more to hamper progress within the field of developmental and social psychology than any other single concept. (Those interested in reading more on this topic might begin with Ellen Berscheid's (1986) eloquent and humorous discussion of the issue.) Historically, psychologists have searched for a single cause for a single effect, or at best for multiple causes for that effect. The belief that cause-effect relationships are linear—that they "go" in one direction—has interfered with many aspects of the field. In the search for these simple causal relationships the field has largely abandoned its descriptive phase and has ignored the fact that "effects" often feed back and become their own "causes" (cf. McCall, 1977). On the other hand, within a general systems framework, "causal" relationships are viewed as complex, often circular, feedback loops, and where the observer begins the causal analysis is largely arbitrary. The process of this causal interaction might be described as involving a spiral of recursive feedback loops rather than a straight line of influence. Within this framework, a causal analysis amounts to a careful, temporal description of the interactive pattern under consideration and of the contributions made by each element (e.g., person) within the pattern. Certainly some of the elements of a social system may have more "power," or degrees of freedom, within the pattern than others, but it is difficult to imagine that the output of one element simply constitutes the "cause" of the structure or functioning of the other.

The studies of Brazelton, Koslowski, and Main (1974) and Stern (1974) on the reciprocal control of early infant-mother face-to-face interaction are good examples of systemic causal analysis. Indeed, Brazelton et al. (1974) indicate that in their research the strength of the dyadic interaction dominated the meaning of each member's respective behavior such that each member's behavior became part of a cluster of behaviors that interacted with a cluster of behaviors from the other member—no single behavior could be separated from the cluster for analysis without losing its meaning in the sequence. Stern (1974) characterizes as a "waltz" the mutually regulatory actions of the infant and mother, who constantly made readjustments in their behavior. These studies have culminated in detailed temporal descriptions of the steps involved in this complex, mutually regulatory, circular interaction, and of the contributions to the pattern made by each participant. As to what "caused" this complex pattern—it only makes sense to ascribe the cause to the pattern itself.

Almost any other attempt to formulate a causal statement will return one to a temporal description of the pattern.

The adoption of this orientation provides family researchers with at least three major types of questions regarding causality: those concerning moment-to-moment interaction, those concerning ontogeny at either the individual or the systemic level, and those focusing on maladaptive behavior (Marvin & Stewart, 1990). An example of a systemic causal analysis of the first type may be found in the negotiations and rituals between parents and children at bedtime (Green, unpublished data). In such a situation, the child's objective is to remain up and awake as long as possible, while the fatigued parents' goal is to get the child to bed with the least amount of conflict so that they can shift their focus from issues of the parental subsystem to those of the spouse subsystem. Permitting small diversions such as one more story, another drink of water, and then another trip to the bathroom therefore would be purposeful only as a means of decreasing the probability of overt confrontation. Each participant in the ritual recalls a similar shared history, employs a similar working model, and has a similar expectation of what specific behaviors are required of each to get the child to bed. Questions of causality framed in a linear manner become hopelessly confounded if one acknowledges that this pattern of interaction is being caused or shaped by parents, children, and spouses, and that it is perpetuated because all members of the family gain a sense of predictability concerning the behaviors of the others in this context. If so simple a situation as a child's bedtime ritual requires a circular form of systemic causality to be understood properly, then certainly even more complex situations such as ontogenetic changes in families or their members, or the development of maladaptive behavior or patterns of interaction, would require systemic analyses (Marvin & Stewart, 1990).

Maintenance of Invariant Relationships

This proposition states that, in order to function, there must be order, or constraint, both within the system and within its interplay with the environment. In a complex system it is not necessary that all relationships with the environment be invariant, but rather that in certain essential respects—which respects depend on the particular system-environment coupling being considered—particular aspects of that coupling must be maintained within specific limits (Ashby, 1956, 1962). This becomes particularly important in the case of complex open systems such as the child as a system, the child-caregiver dyad, or the family as a whole, where information received by the system, or certain parts of that system, alters its state or organization. If the change resulting from this information extends beyond some necessary invariant limit, the organization of the system will be disturbed or destroyed. Bowlby (1969) employs this principle in speaking of the "predictable outcome" (invariant) of infant-mother proximity as functioning to protect the infant from danger.

The concept of exploration from a secure base mentioned above and studied naturalistically by Anderson (1972) also might serve to illustrate this principle. Anderson observed mother-child dyads in a park setting and noted that the children were free to explore the environment and move away from their mothers as long as the mothers did not move from the bench on which they had been sitting. As the children explored the park setting they would return occasionally to their mothers in a sort of "checking in" manner before returning to their discoveries. Older children were able to abbreviate this return behavior such that they were required only to look back at their mothers and make eye contact, or simply note that their mothers remained on the bench. The distances the children moved from their mothers and the amounts of time the children devoted to exploration without returning to these secure bases increased with age and, presumably, the security the children felt while exploring.

Family theorists employ this principle in describing how both normal and maladapted families must maintain certain variables within set limits or face disturbance or destruction, or how children often are "chosen by the family" to play a major role in this process. Indeed, Kaye (1985) has pointed out that even those families that appear to be "closed" in the sense of being overly rigid, insular, or enmeshed (cf. Olson et al., 1979) often function as open systems with even greater intensity than do "normal" families, in that they constantly adapt to outside influences so as to perpetuate their own maladaptive rules of interaction.

This principle implies that any controlling system must possess a greater degree of complexity and variability than the system that is controlled. When applied to social systems, Ashby (1956, 1960) suggests, it means that a person or organism possessing a greater variety of role behaviors would be able to control persons or organisms with fewer behaviors at their command. (The interested reader should see Ashby, 1956, 1960, for a detailed discussion of his "law of requisite variety.") Furthermore, Ashby suggests that in complex social systems a point may be reached where a subsystem becomes so adaptive, versatile, or self-sufficient that it no longer depends upon the suprasystem for support. When such a point is reached, the subsystem may break out of its earlier controls and instead become a component of a suprasystem collateral with its former "parent" system.

Consider for a moment a situation in which two systems, such as young boy and his immediate environment, potentially influence one another. If certain variables must be maintained within certain limits, then only the system with the greater variety (i.e., the greater range of possible "moves" or degrees of freedom) can reduce, limit, or control the amount of variety in the coupling of the two. For example, if the child is subject to dangers, and if he is unable to protect himself (less variety in himself than in the environment), then in order to maintain his "essential variables" within certain limits he must be coupled with (attached to) another system of more complexity—in this case a caregiver. This caregiver may in turn need to be coupled to another system, be it a spouse or extended family, to deal completely with the wide, dangerous variety in the environment. This coupling must be maintained until the child possesses the necessary variety (knowledge and skills) within himself and/or can become coupled to another system (a peer group, older sibling, or so on) that can provide the necessary variety (cf. Marvin, 1977). In a sense, the argument is that the biological function of attachment might be described as the protection of the child from various sources of danger while that child is developing the skills necessary to assume that protective function him- or herself (Marvin & Stewart, 1990). In our own species, as well as in many others, this mother-child system tends to be coupled with others (e.g., spouse, other children, extended family) to form an even larger system with yet more variety, thus substantially increasing the entire family system's chances of survival.

Adaptive Self-Regulation

This fourth property refers to a cybernetic stability that self-regulates a system to compensate for changing conditions in the environment by making coordinated changes in the system's internal values (Sameroff, 1983). This proposition formally presents the logic by which the system maintains those essential variables discussed above. The basic unit of such self-regulation is the negative feedback loop, through which the organism acts to reduce the effects of deviation from a standard (which may or may not be represented internally). This corrective feedback can be initiated by any individual or subsystem within the overall system.

This property is typically summarized by noting that systems possess the capability of *homeostasis*, which technically implies the continual restoration of a steady state. Kaye (1985) points out that the term *homeostasis* implies a truly static condition. He suggests, therefore, that *equilibration* is a better word to describe this property because it does not imply that the end state will be the same as the former state; *equilibration* instead suggests a balance between opposing forces rather than the return to any given condition. In this sense, the term is employed much as Buckley has used *morphostasis*.

Attachment researchers already are familiar with this principle in a number of contexts, the most obvious being that of "goal-corrected proximity seeking." The young child compensates for changes in the environment (e.g., mother leaving the room) by activating a self-corrective behavior system, and terminates that system when feedback from his or her activity indicates that deviation from an internal standard (e.g., contact with mother) no longer exists. At a dyadic level, a slightly more complex example occurs when both mother and child alter their internal settings (e.g., from visual to a rapidly and mutually established physical contact) when both notice some startling change in environmental conditions (e.g., a large dog approaching the child).

An illustration of this systemic property is found in the results of my master's thesis research (R. Stewart, 1977). Mothers, fathers, and babies were observed in a modification of the Strange Situation procedure devised by Ainsworth and Wittig (1969). I noticed that fathers interacted very little with their babies when the mothers were present in the room. Instead, fathers tended to engage in solitary activities such as reading a magazine or newspaper. However, when the mothers left the room, most fathers ceased this solitary activity and immediately engaged the baby in playful activity as if to distract the baby from any distress that might be initiated by the mother's departure. The fathers tended to remain engaged with their babies throughout the mothers' absences, and even the entrance of a stranger, male or female, had virtually no effect on the fathers' interactions with their infants. In contrast, mothers decreased their interactions with their babies when another adult entered the room, even to the point of breaking off conversations in the middle of a sentence. When the mothers returned, the fathers immediately returned to their solitary activities, and the mothers assumed primary responsibility for interacting with their babies. The fact that the babies displayed only brief, almost casual greetings to their mothers and then returned to exploration suggests that the families already possessed smoothly operating self-regulatory strategies in which they anticipated disturbance and planned for it before the babies became distressed.

As Patricia Minuchin (1985) states, when this principle is operating at a family level, the self-regulatory mechanisms reside in the family rather than in the individual. In most instances these processes are adaptive, as when one parent assumes responsibility for feeding the baby in the middle of the night so that the other can get a full night's sleep. However, family therapists deal regularly with families in which there is much unresolved conflict between the spouses, and in which the integrity of the family is self-regulated through parental focus on some "symptomatic" behavior of a child. When a therapeutic change is induced in this kind of family (e.g., when the parents begin to resolve their conflicts or the child decreases his or her symptomatic behavior), other family members typically behave in a way that has the "predictable outcome" of returning the family to its former, maladaptive state.

Adaptive Self-Organization

The fifth property concerns a reorganization that alters the parameters within the system when the system is subjected to a new constant in the internal or external environment. That is, a new event acts upon the internal constraints of the system and the system reorganizes itself, establishing a new homeostatic or equilibrated balance. In a successful self-organizing system, this reorganization takes place in a way that continues to maintain the system's essential variables within limits necessary for its survival. Adaptive self-organization differs from adaptive self-regulation in that the latter allows the system to resist temporary disturbances and return to the previous steady state without permanent changes being imposed. It should also be noted that while many instances of self-organization refer to developmental, or "stage" changes, others are nondevelopmental (e.g., changes in residence, occupation, or financial status, or occurrence of a physical disability). This property represents those processes described by Buckley as morphogenic.

At an individual level, some of the best-known examples of systemic reorganization are those of cognitive developmental changes (e.g., Flavell, 1985; Piaget, 1970). Strong arguments have been made that family systems undergo formally similar, discontinuous developmental changes (e.g., Carter & McGoldrick, 1980; Haley, 1986). At these transition points in the process of family development, the family as a whole must reorganize its familiar patterns of interaction. There is often a period of instability as the family members experiment with and negotiate new patterns for maintaining important variables within certain limits. Eventually, the family again will experience a period of stability once these newly negotiated patterns of family interaction (i.e., a new shared working model) become familiar and more established. At that point in its development the family will return to making ongoing self-regulatory adjustments until it again is forced to reorganize when it encounters its next "crisis."

The research of Entwisle and Doering (1981) and of Cowan et al. (1978) illustrates this principle of self-organization at a family level. Both studies found that families in their samples moved toward traditional role structure and differentiation of household responsibilities soon after the birth of the first child, in spite of previously held egalitarian beliefs and practices. This new division of labor and role structure often was established without regard to whether the mother returned to the work force after a maternity leave. Much the same conclusion can be inferred from studies of families with physically handicapped children (e.g., Kazak & Marvin, 1984). Perhaps the strain and uncertainty associated with the acquisition of a new role prompts parents to seek comfort in more traditionally defined role behavior.

Subsystems and Boundaries

This principle states that any system is composed of subsystems, and that any system constitutes a subsystem for a yet larger or more inclusive system. Formally, subsystems within a system are distinguished from one another by differences in the rules by which they are governed and self-regulated. The differences in the rules therefore constitute the boundaries separating the subsystems. Communication or interaction across these boundaries is also governed by rules that maintain their integrity. In many biological systems, these boundaries are not always firm, and one member of a system can belong to different subsystems either coincidentally or at different times. However, membership in different subsystems still implies different sets of operational rules for membership in each subsystem.

The subsystems typically attributed to families are the spouse subsystem, the parenting subsystem (which may or may not be occupied by the same members as the spouse subsystem), the parent-child subsystem, the sibling subsystem, and other subsystems composed of specific alliances within the family, grandparent relations, and the like. Each of these subsystems is characterized by its own set of operating rules and rules for communication with other subsystems. Individuals often are interchangeable from one subsystem to another—the father is also a husband, a member of a friendly alliance of "boys against girls," and so on. This flexibility of subsystem membership is usually adaptive, but it can become maladaptive when individuals are forced into two conflicting or contradictory subsystems simultaneously, when they occupy a developmentally inappropriate subsystem for too long, or when an appropriate member is excluded while an inappropriate member is included. For example, an older girl can be a member of a parenting subsystem for short periods of time only as long as she is given the power as well as the responsibility of the role, and as long as she is also given adequate membership in the sibling subsystem. A young boy can enjoy some intimacy with his mother only as long as his father is not excluded from the spouse subsystem and clear boundaries are drawn as to when the boy is excluded from that subsystem. When these boundaries or rules are "violated," one or more individual or familial essential variables are at risk.

The rules that constitute the boundaries around subsystems, and individual membership in these subsystems, are established by recurrent patterns of interaction among all family members. These rules undergo changes when a family member, or the family itself, reaches a new developmental transition, and/or when some significant internal or external event, such as divorce or economic change, affects the family. Healthy families will realign boundaries and subsystem memberships to reflect these new realities. It is when families are too fearful or resistant to make these changes that they become maladapted, static, and symptomatic, and require therapeutic intervention.

FAMILY SYSTEMS PERSPECTIVE

The importance of studying the family as the socializing unit finally has received recognition (Belsky, 1981; Bronfenbrenner, 1979; Kantor & Lehr, 1975; Parke & O'Leary, 1976; Pedersen, 1975). Bronfenbrenner's (1979) conceptualization of the ecology of human development as a series of ever-widening systems of experience and/or influence often is cited by developmental psychologists interested in assuming a systems perspective. Briefly, Bronfenbrenner describes the immediate setting experienced by a developing person as the "microsystem" and the system of such systems as the "mesosystem." A system composed of this higher-order mesosystem and other systems not directly involving the individual as a participant but still affecting and affected by his or her development is referred to as the "exosystem." Finally, the overall culture or subculture affecting all lower-order systems is known as the "macrosystem." With regard to family development, the microsystem could be represented by the family unit itself, the mesosystem by the parents' work experiences or by their social lives outside their roles as parents, the exosystem by the network of social supports sought or maintained by the parents, and the macrosystem by the current cultural dictates concerning family-life activities.

Kantor and Lehr (1975) have adopted many of Buckley's arguments in developing their systemic study of family processes. They define the family as a social system that involves almost continuous interchange, not only within the system but across the boundary between the system's inner and external environments. They suggest that families evolve networks of interdependent causal relations that are governed primarily by means of feedback control mechanisms, thus making the relations among the component parts of the family circular, or reciprocally influenced. Families are conceptualized as open, adaptive, information-processing systems that can change their action patterns or structure in accordance with the demands of prevailing circumstances. On the basis of their observations of families, Kantor and Lehr have proposed that the information-processing function of families operates primarily in a distance-regulation manner: Family systems operate to inform their members of what constitutes proper or optimal distance (the parameters governing when, where, how, and why to move or act) as relationships among members fluctuate. By focusing on the positive and negative feedback loops operating within the family and between the family and its surrounding environment, Kantor and Lehr sought to discover the processes by which family members move toward specific targets or goals.

A means for integrating the disciplines of family sociology and developmental psychology, and thus for advancing the study of infancy and early experience, has been presented by Belsky (1981). In his scheme, the two disciplines' respective literatures on parent-infant relations (e.g., Ainsworth, 1973; Lamb, 1977) and the transition to parenthood (e.g., LeMasters, 1957; Russell, 1974) are coupled with an emerging literature linking marital relations and parenting (e.g., Belsky, 1979; Pedersen, 1975). The study of the family system through this scheme encourages one to consider the family triad, composed of marital and parent-infant relations, as the basis for socialization. Parke, Power, and Gottman (1979) have presented a similar scheme for considering numerous types of influences within the triadic family system. Among these familial influence effects are (a) *transitive* influences, such as when one family member has an influence on another member of the triad through the remaining individual (e.g., the father has a transitive influence on the infant when he kisses the mother and she in turn caresses the infant); (b) *circular* influences, such as when one member of the triad is the source of behavior as well as the recipient of the consequences of that behavior (e.g., poor marital relations may affect parenting behavior, which in turn influences the infant's functioning, which, coming full circle, affects the marital relationship); and (c) *parallel* influences, such as when one member of the triad imitates the actions of another when interacting with the third member. Belsky's model takes Parke et al.'s taxonomy one step further by extending the notion of triadic transitive influences to show that the effects of one party on the relationship that exists between the other two can be both direct and indirect. For example, an infant can have a direct effect on the marital relationship of his or her parents, which in turn can affect their parenting activity. In short, Belsky's (1981) transactional framework draws our attention to "the fact that parenting affects and is affected by the infant, who both influences and is influenced by the marital relationship, which in turn both affects and is affected by parenting" (p. 3).

Belsky (1981) provides a review of these literatures to demonstrate how this transactional framework might further our understanding of early experiences in human development. In this review he notes that family sociologists generally have failed to consider individual differences between infants as a factor affecting marital relations, and that developmentalists have failed to consider marital quality as a moderator of infant effects. The organizing scheme offered by Belsky is presented in a modified form at the top of Figure 1.1. This figure was developed to emphasize familial relationships and roles, rather than simply the three family members as individual social agents (cf. Feiring & Lewis, 1978). Belsky recognized that this scheme mixed different levels of analysis in its attempt to assess the interdependence of behavioral domains such as "infant behavior and development" with dyadic relationships such as "marital relations." He also was well aware of the dilemma presented by the study of interpersonal interactions in conjunction with an analysis of interpersonal relationships (cf. Hinde, 1982). Moreover, one might recognize that the so-called parenting domain includes both maternal and paternal parenting behaviors. Even though some researchers have encouraged us to focus upon the combined or joint influences of mother and father rather than on each separate parent-child relationship (e.g., Belsky, 1980; Pedersen, Yarrow, Anderson, & Cain, 1978), others have demonstrated qualitative as well as quantitative differences between maternal and paternal parenting (e.g., Clarke-Stewart, 1978; Kotelchuck, 1972; Main & Weston, 1981).

In short, Belsky's scheme might be viewed as an interesting, though somewhat simplistic, illustration of how family development might be described from a systems perspective. Although he limits his discussion to family triadic situations so that clarity might be obtained, he notes that families with more than one child also could be studied through this transactional scheme. The study of familial adjustment to the birth of the second child demands that Belsky's transactional scheme be expanded to include at least two additional elements—firstborn child behavior and development (contrasted with the second-born infant domain) and sibling relations. His triangular model originally was depicted with six single-headed arrows indicating all possible unidirectional influences. This figure has been modified to emphasize the bidirectionality of effect among these components of the family by replacing the single-headed arrows with three two-headed ones. This triangular model then was expanded by including the second child and the implied relationship between the siblings in a two-child family to become a pentagon with ten such two-headed arrows. This model is presented at the bottom of Figure 1.1.

Such a scheme certainly would be useful to researchers interested in normative familial transitions. For example, research on the effects that the transition to parenthood has on marital satisfaction has revealed different patterns for wives and husbands. Several studies have reported that when marital satisfaction decreases after the birth of a first child, the magnitude of the decline often appears to be greater for wives than for husbands (Belsky et al., 1983; Glenn & McLanahan, 1982; Waldron & Routh, 1981). This sharper decline may be due, in part, to the fact that wives typically have higher prebirth satisfaction scores than do husbands and, due to their greater involvement in child-care tasks, may be more vulnerable to the negative effects of the baby (e.g., Waldron & Routh, 1981). An alternative explanation may be found in considering that the initial transition to parenthood constitutes distinctly different events for husbands and wives with respect to their life cycles. Questions such as these cannot be addressed through our traditional linear approaches to

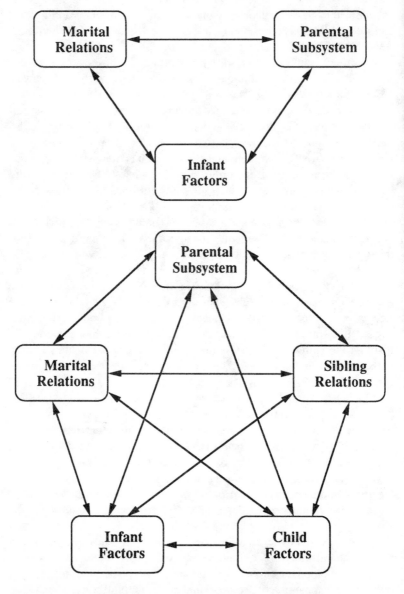

Figure 1.1. Belsky's Scheme for Integrating Family Sociology and Developmental Psychology (top) and Its Elaboration When Applied to Family Transition at the Birth of a Second Child

SOURCE: The top portion of this figure is adapted from Jay Belsky, "Early Human Experience: A Family Perspective," *Developmental Psychology, 17*(1). Copyright 1981 by the American Psychological Association. Adapted by permission.

causality. On the other hand, systems theory, with its assumption of circular rather than linear causality, may consider such questions.

Sameroff (1983) has described a general systems theory of development and has specifically applied it to the process of socialization. His model appears, in some respects, to be superior to Belsky's transitional scheme. Where Belsky's scheme might be described as merely another presentation of the interactionist position that one cannot examine the bits and pieces of behavior in isolation, Sameroff's model is more closely tied to Bertalanffy's (1968) discussion of general systems theory. Recall that Bertalanffy's position is that to understand a given phenomenon one must understand not only the elements but, more important, their interrelations. The concept of wholeness, which often has been treated as some metaphysical notion, is to be operationalized through the use of such concepts as hierarchic structure, stability, teleology, differentiation, steady state, and goal directedness (Sameroff, 1983). Sameroff's model incorporates each of the basic systems properties discussed above, and also includes the notion of dialectic movement to suggest that an organism changes its environment through its functioning and thereby creates a new adaptive situation that requires further changes in the organism.

Aspects of this model already can be found in many of the psychological and sociological literatures. For example, the suggestion that the transition to parenthood might represent a "normal crisis" that has long been a part of the family sociology literature (e.g., Rossi, 1968) might be viewed as an illustration of the principle of adaptive self-organization. The principle of hierarchical structuring is seen clearly in Salvador Minuchin's (1974) structuralist theory of family therapy in that he defines structure in terms of the hierarchical organization and differentiation of the family into subunits. In the case of the transition at the birth of a second child, the family can be viewed as an organized system that changes its own environment by electing to increase the number of its members, and then enters a period of transition as the subsystems within the familial suprasystem seek a new equilibrium in response to this change.

Kaye (1985) comments on the application of systems theory to the developmental study of families and makes a number of critical observations. As developmentalists broadened their definition of interaction, they recognized that parent-child interactions—indeed, all interpersonal interactions—were bidirectional. They soon after recognized that social interactions were more than bidirectional. Kaye points out that relationships are organized so as to achieve certain goals; that is, they possess a *demonstrated shared purpose* that the members would be unable to achieve on their own. In studying the family as a system, Kaye suggests that two kinds of descriptions are necessary: process models and competence models. The process model describes how the system seems to work in real time, while the results that system is capable of producing are described by a competence model. Kaye points out what he labels a "locus problem" in applying each of these models to family systems because "it is not families that perceive, act, remember, or possess energy, motivation or identity; it is people who do so" (p. 48). Each person in a family is an intact organism that is physically detached from the others in both space and time—individual members of a family may enter and leave the system at different times, but somehow the identity of the family is maintained. In a related discussion, it is interesting to note, Kaye points out that it is a mistake to consider an individual person as a subsystem of the family. He bases this opinion on the assumption that the person's self—the sum total of the person's skills, values, goals, attitudes, and so on—is not entirely within the person but is instead constructed and internalized by all the members of the family system.

Patricia Minuchin (1985) begins her discussion of family systems theory by noting that developmental psychology and family therapy have a great deal in common. While this is certainly true, it is also important to consider Kaye's observation that family therapy is not family psychology. Kaye (1985) points out that clinicians have different goals (the development of better methods of intervention, improvement of diagnosis, and efficient intervention), while developmental psychologists tend to direct their attentions to well-functioning families. He argues that the important question is not whether families with serious problems are normal (they are) or whether normal families have problems (they certainly do), but whether families seen clinically provide an adequate and representative data base for understanding normal family processes. He argues, as have Kantor and Lehr (1975), that the observation of well-functioning families is a crucial part of the overall task of developmental psychologists if we are to obtain an adequate description of family interaction.

In applying the general systems model to this study of the family, I would suggest that the family represents an "open system" in that it is a structure that maintains its organization and goal directedness despite changes in its composition. This is to be contrasted with a "closed system," which has a structure that can be specified and an operation reducible to a few mechanistic principles. Of course, one may choose to represent the family as a closed system, and then attempt to explain the interactions of family members by applying an approach such as the exchange and interdependence theories of Thibaut and Kelley (1959; Kelley, 1979; Kelley & Thibaut, 1978) for describing the operation of small groups. Indeed, such an approach would be extremely useful in obtaining detailed descriptions necessary for the development of process models of familial interaction. Unfortunately, such a strategy could not adequately describe the dynamics of family transition, adjustment, and development. On the other hand, the conceptualization of the family as an open system, when combined with concepts of other disciplines through the rubrics of general systems theory, appears better equipped to produce a thorough representation of family functioning and development. Both Minuchin's and Sameroff's descriptions of systems approaches have presented primarily at the level of what Pepper (1942) refers to as a "world hypothesis." A more empirically based theory is needed to guide our research, but this theory must be highly eclectic if it is to address each of the six primary principles of systems thought.

FAMILY STRESS THEORY

General systems theory has long provided an integrative framework for research and theory formation in the study of marital and familial dynamics in the face of stress (Hansen & Hill, 1964; Hansen & Johnson, 1979; Hill, 1949, 1971; McCubbin & Patterson, 1982, 1983). One of the major contributions in this area, the ABCX family crisis model, was developed by Hill (1949) in his study of war separation and reunion. In its simplest presentation, Hill's model states that a stressor event (A) interacts with a family's existing resources (B), and this in turn interacts with the family's perception and definition of the stressor event (C) to create a crisis situation (X). This model was expanded and refined by McCubbin and his associates (McCubbin et al., 1980; McCubbin & Patterson, 1982, 1983) in an attempt to identify the variables that account for the observed differences among families in their positive adaptations to stressful situations. Based on their observations of families that had husbands/fathers held captive or unaccounted for in the Vietnam War, McCubbin and Patterson (1982, 1983) describe the Double ABCX model and the Family Adjustment and Adaptation Response (FAAR) model as a multistaged process whereby families become aware of and subsequently adapt to a wide range of stressors. The Double ABCX model builds upon Hill's (1949, 1958) ABCX model by redefining precrisis variables and adding postcrisis variables in an effort to describe (a) the additional life stressors and strains prior to and following a crisis-producing event, (b) the range of outcome of family processes in response to the "pileup" of stressors associated with this event, and (c) the intervening factors that influence the course of family adaptation. The FAAR model describes family adaptation to change as a function of the pileup of demands, family resistance, and adaptive resources, and the family's perception and appraisal of the stressful situation. Their model, presented in Figure 1.2, can easily serve as a framework upon which to organize this study of familial adjustment to the stress inherent in the birth of a second child.

Stressors, the a factor, are defined as discrete life events or transitions affecting the family and having the potential to produce change in the family system. The most common practice in family research is to classify stressors as normative and nonnormative events (McCubbin et al., 1980). *Normative* life events are so classified because they are expected, scheduled changes involving entrances into or exits from social roles, or are associated with developmental role changes and task realignments. *Nonnormative* stressor events are those that occur unexpectedly, such as natural disasters, death (if not associated with old age), and war. It is important for this discussion to make clear the distinction between stress and strain. Strain is usually defined as a condition of felt tension or difficulty. Unlike stressor events, strains do not have a discrete onset; rather, they emerge more subtly within families either from unresolved tension associated with a prior stressor or from ongoing interpersonal relationships. The changes produced by stressors may be conceptualized as affecting various aspects of familial structure and function, including boundaries, goals, roles, patterns of interactions, and values. Family hardships are defined as those special demands on the family that are specifically associated with the stressor event. Given such a definition, a stressor might be conceptualized as a trigger initiating some form of adaptive self-organization within a family system.

The b factor, the family's resources for meeting the demands of stressors and/or hardships, are described as the family's ability to prevent an impending change from creating a disruption within the system (Burr, 1973). Family adaptability and integration, as well as the presence of a sufficient social support network, are prominent examples of existing resources. Personal resources such as knowledge, self-esteem, and skills that are applicable and available to the family in times of need are also included within this factor. Familial attributes such as cohesion, adapt-

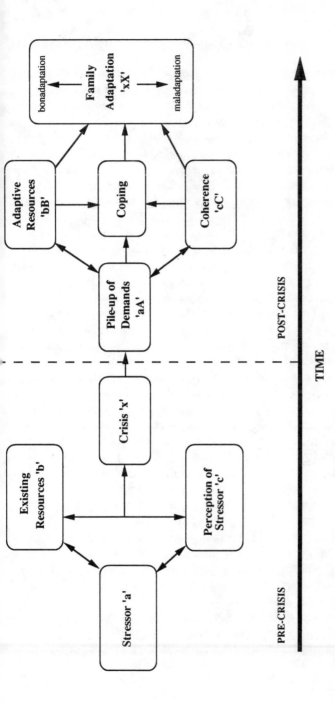

Figure 1.2. The Double ABCX Model of Adjustment and Adaptation

SOURCE: Adapted from Hamilton McCubbin and Joan Patterson, "The Family Stress Process: The Double ABCX Model of Adjustment and Adaptation," in H. McCubbin, M. Sussman, and J. Patterson (Eds.), *Social Stress and the Family: Advances and Developments in Family Stress Theory and Research* (Vol. 6). Copyright 1983 by the Haworth Press, Inc. Reprinted by permission.

ability, and communication are important factors as well (Olson et al., 1983).

McCubbin and Patterson (1983) describe the c factor as the subjective definition the family makes of the seriousness and meaning of the stressor, ranging from the positive outlook of the event as an opportunity or challenge for growth to the negative perspective of the event as an uncontrollable prelude to the demise of the family. It reflects a degree of a sense of acceptance and understanding of the situation, and further provides a framework on which the family members base their perceptions of their overall adjustment. Finally, the crisis, or x, factor is conceptualized as being a continuum representing the amount of disruption or disorganization in the family system (Burr, 1973). It is important to note that crisis is distinct from stress (conceived as a demand-capacity imbalance) in that it is characterized by the family's inability to restore stability, and by the continuous pressure to make changes in the family structure and patterns of interaction (McCubbin & Patterson, 1983).

In their observations of the familial adaptation over time, McCubbin and Patterson note four additional factors necessary to supplement the Hill ABCX model. First, they note a pileup of additional stressors, factor aA, following the initial stressor that often includes other normative transitions occurring as the family adjusts to the initial stressor, prior strains, strains associated with the consequences of familial efforts to adjust, ambiguity in terms of uncertainty concerning the future, current or future boundaries, and prescriptions for acceptable or proscriptions for unacceptable methods of crisis resolution at both familial and societal levels. In addition to the original existing resources available to the family, a new set of adaptive resources, factor bB, also exists. These include the already-existing resources and the expanded resources, which include additional social support sought or obtained in response to the demands emerging from the initial crisis situation, newly obtained knowledge or skills, and newfound patterns of familial adaptability. The subjective familial response to the original stressor and its subsequent pileup of demands at times modifies the meaning the family gives to the crisis-adaptation situation. Factor cC is conceptualized to represent the family's continued experience with the new demands and the family's continued redefinition of the situation itself.

For example, consider the events described in the opening paragraphs of the introduction to Part I of this volume. My need to find someone to stay with our firstborn when my wife began her second labor represents the aA factor in that additional stressors were beginning to pile up as we entered this transition phase. There simply was no need to arrange for a sitter at the time of the firstborn's birth. On the other hand, some of the names on our list of potential sitters were those of other parents from our son's day-care center, and thus represent the bB factor—new adaptive resources. Finally, our subjective appraisal of the entire situation was qualitatively different from that of the first labor and delivery; at least we were less anxious about the labor itself and could remember how to time the contractions properly.

McCubbin and Patterson (1983) have found that coherence is an intervening factor between the stressful crisis event and familial adaptation because it acts as a facilitator of the family's adaptive resources. The coping strategies employed by the family to eliminate stressors, manage hardships, maintain systemic functioning, acquire or develop resources to meet demands, or implement structural changes to the family system to accommodate new demands then become the focus of attention as researchers attempt to describe the patterns of interaction and organization associated with family adaptation, the factor xX. Specifically, McCubbin and Patterson advise researchers to focus their attention on the interplay of these four additional factors as they interact to affect family adaptation. Adaptation does not mean that disorganization or change in the system has not occurred; instead, it implies that the system has resumed its routine level of operation after having to cope with change, or that some new organization has been derived to enable the family as a system to maintain certain relationships invariant. Their conceptualization of this balance is less restrictive than Hill's former notion of crisis, in that McCubbin and Patterson recognize that disruptions of familial patterns of functioning might be perceived as opportunities to renegotiate intrafamilial relationships (cf. Hansen & Johnson, 1979). Indeed, just as systems theorists have pointed out that living systems evolve toward greater complexity, families might initiate situations requiring adaptive self-organization.

Differences between families in their subjective appraisal of similar life events or transitions, the cC factor in McCubbin and Patterson's model, may be due, in part, to interfamilial differences in initial resources (the b factor) or expanded resources (the bB factor). Cohen and Wills (1985) conducted a review of the research reporting a positive association between social support and well-being, and have concluded that social support factors may intervene between a stressful event and a stress reaction by attenuating or preventing a stress appraisal response. Specifically, they suggest that the perception that others can and will provide necessary resources may either redefine the potential for harm posed by a stressful situation or increase one's perceived ability to cope with the imposed demands, thus preventing a particular situation from being appraised as stressful. Moreover, social supports may alleviate the impact of the stressful situation by providing a solution to the problem. Cohen and Wills conclude that when social support is conceptualized in terms of the perceived availability of interpersonal resources (esteem support, informational support, social companionship, instrumental support) that are responsive to the needs elicited by a stressful event, this support can act as a buffer to mitigate the stressful effects of that situation.

These observations in turn lead to a further elaboration of the Double ABCX model by McCubbin and Patterson (1982, 1983) into a process model called the Family Adjustment and Adaptation Response. This model can be briefly summarized by noting that the FAAR processes occur in two distinct phases: the Adjustment Phase, in which the family makes a response to the initial stressor or stressors, and an Adaptation Phase, in which the family resolves the crisis situation. McCubbin and Patterson further describe the Adjustment Phase as one where the family employs an initial adjustment or coping strategy to avoid, eliminate, or assimilate the demands of the stressor. The outcome of these coping strategies is defined as adaptation, which varies along a continuum from bonadaptation to maladaptation. The Adaptation Phase can be conceptualized as two subphases of family accommodation over time. The earlier level of familial accommodation, Restructuring, involves first an awareness by at least one family member that the existing family structure and modes of functioning are not adequate to meet the new set of demands. This is followed by an initial restructuring process as the family members search for and implement structural changes that they believe will solve the problem of demands as they have defined it. Thus the first level of accommodation constitutes what systems theorists describe as adaptive self-organization.

Once this change in the family structure has been initiated, the family enters the second level of accommodation, Consolidation, where it attempts to mold this new structure into a coherent and effective whole. Specifically, the second level of accommodation draws attention to the fact that, if the structural changes made in the earlier subphase are to be integrated as a viable and stable component of the system, additional changes, adjustments, or fine-tuning will be necessary before these changes can be consolidated. This adaptive self-stabilization process focuses on concomitant changes in the family system so that a coordinated, stable, congruent system of functioning might be derived from the tandem processes of assimilation and accommodation inherent in the Consolidation subphase of family adaptation (McCubbin & Patterson, 1982, 1983).

McCubbin and his associates have begun presenting empirical evidence in support of the Double ABCX model of family stress and adaptation (e.g., Lavee, McCubbin, & Olson, 1987; Lavee, McCubbin, & Patterson, 1985). Their findings support the position that a pileup of demands in previous family life events is significantly associated with postcrisis strain. Moreover, they note that intrafamilial system resources such as family cohesion, adaptability, and supportive communication prove to be part of the family's adaptive power in that they directly enhance overall familial adaptation. On the other hand, social support factors such as community or friendship support or community activity appear to have a buffering role in that they reduce postcrisis strain. Their findings further suggest that the family's coherence and meaning are influenced by its experience of demands and resources, and that external factors such as the positive experience of perceiving social support or the negative experience of the perceived pileup of demands are more influential than the family's internal resources. Although family strain negatively affects marital adjustment and perceived well-being, it is somewhat paradoxically associated with a more optimistic or cohesive appraisal of the situation. On the other hand, when the level of marital adjustment is controlled, these researchers' results indicate that strain actually functions to enhance the family's sense of coherence.

The McCubbin and Patterson Double ABCX model is not, however, without its weakness. Walker (1985) points out that the model requires the identification of an initial event to begin the crisis process, and that an adequate model of family stress will not exist until we attend to the multiple interdependent levels of the social system—individual, dyadic, familial, social network, community, and cultural/historic. This requirement is not especially problematic if one is interested in studying family adaptation in response to a clearly defined, normative, life-course event such as the birth of a child, but it is quite troublesome if one wishes to focus on the daily interaction patterns of families. Walker is indeed correct when she points out that many of our daily individual behavior and social interactions are directed toward coping with stress (or perhaps strain associated with a stressful situation). Furthermore, she is correct when she notes that an event-initiated stress model would assume that behavioral, familial, and social patterns are homeostatic, and that stressful events would disrupt this homeostasis and require action so that homeostasis can be restored.

Lavee et al. (1987) respond to Walker's critique by suggesting that researchers adopt a salutogenic paradigm rather than the traditional pathogenic paradigm when seeking to understand familial stress. Specifically, they encourage researchers to focus on identifying those conditions that are associated with family health and well-being rather than on the causes of illness and maladaptive situations. They argue that researchers might profit by considering disorder and the disruption of homeostasis in families to be the normal state of affairs, and that they might then direct their attention to describing and understanding the "mystery of well-being" rather than states of dysfunction. Such a suggestion is certainly interesting and well within the scope of a systems framework, but it is not sufficient, and another response to Walker's critique is needed.

You may recall from the previous discussions that adaptive systems possess both self-regulating and self-organizing properties. The former property is concerned with the issue of homeostasis, or, to use Kaye's term, equilibration. McCubbin and Patterson (1983) have consistently defined stress as events or transitions that have the potential to produce change in the family system. One might ask whether they define this change as the type that could be illustrated by a temporary loss of equilibrium or something more substantial, such that a new system of order or a new type of organization is required so that the system as a whole will be able to maintain its important functions. Just as developmentalists make a clear distinction between the terms *age difference* and *age change* when describing the effects of ontogenetic development on behavior (Baltes, Reese, & Nesselroade, 1977), such a distinction ought to be made concerning the ontogenetic development of a system. Not all stressors result in permanent changes to the system; some produce merely brief periods of disequilibria, and in these cases the contextual model described by Walker is indeed a better choice than the Double ABCX model. On the other hand, when the stressful event is such that the system itself becomes reorganized, and in a sense becomes a new system, then McCubbin and Patterson's framework is quite useful. Walker remains correct in drawing our attention to the multiple interdependent levels of the social system, but we would first like to focus our attention on the individual, dyadic, and familial levels of analysis before attempting any study at the social network, community, or cultural/historical levels.

One final corollary issue must be mentioned before closing this section on family stress theory. The use of the concept of crisis has led to a great deal of confusion within the family development literature. Hill (1949) has defined *crisis* as any sharp or decisive change for which old patterns are inadequate. However, one must recognize that not all disruptions of family functioning need be viewed as exigent. Hansen and Johnson (1979) suggest that high levels of disorganization might be essential to the maintenance of family relationships and, further, that such situations may even push families to creative solutions in problem solving. Therefore, Hansen and Johnson prefer to view crisis as one end of a stress continuum, with *stress* itself defined as a condition of "heightened ambiguity" in family roles. Indeed, they suggest that stress be viewed as a process involving a complex set of changing conditions that have a history (in the case of families, a shared history) and a future, rather than a short-term, single stimulus. The response of the family to such ambiguity is to start experimenting with other interaction patterns to see what can be modified and still achieve role fit among members. Moreover, Hansen and Johnson note that since developmental events can be anticipated, the family can start experimenting with the new patterns slowly while maintaining the comfort of old patterns.

SUMMARY

Ludwig von Bertalanffy's general systems framework provides a means of generalizing the literatures from a number of interrelated disciplines such that the familial process of adapting to the birth of a second child might be studied systemically. In applying Patricia Minuchin's family system model to the study of family adjustment to the birth of a second child, I suggest that the family represents an "open system" in that it is a structure that maintains its organization and goal directedness despite changes in its composition. This is to be contrasted with a "closed system," which has a structure that can be specified and an operation reducible to a few mechanistic principles. Furthermore, I suggest that families are multivariate in nature, and that unidirectional conceptualizations of causality are simply inappropriate when describing such open systems. Bertalanffy's "equifinality" principle of causality thus is critical in the study of family adjustment in that we would expect that an open system is capable of reaching its final normal state by any number of routes. Finally, I wish to suggest that McCubbin and Patterson's Double ABCX model can be employed heuristically to focus our attention on a number of key issues pertinent to familial adjustment following a stressful event. In particular, I wish to focus upon the pileup of demands associated with the birth of a second child, the family's adaptive self-stabilizing and/or self-organizing processes for coping with these demands (in particular the obtainment of additional resources, or the utilization of potential resources not yet employed), and the subjective appraisals each family member might have concerning this overall adjustment process. In the next chapter I will briefly summarize the literatures concerning the initial transition to parenthood in order to extrapolate how familial transition associated with the birth of a second child might be qualitatively different.

2

The Family
in Transition

THE TRANSITION TO PARENTHOOD

In the area of family development, the eight stages described by Duvall (1977) have constituted one of the most frequently employed systems for categorizing major family transitions. These stages were established with reference to family life events involving changes in family size, developmental stage of the oldest child, and the work status of the breadwinner. The eight stages are as follows:

- Stage 1: married couples without children
- Stage 2: childbearing families (oldest child less than 30 months of age)
- Stage 3: families with preschool children (oldest child less than 6 years old)
- Stage 4: families with schoolchildren (oldest child 6-13 years old)
- Stage 5: families with teenagers (oldest child 13-20 years old)
- Stage 6: families launching young adults (oldest child gone through youngest child leaving home)
- Stage 7: middle-aged parents (empty nest through retirement)
- Stage 8: aging family members (retirement through death of both spouses)

This categorical scheme assumes a high degree of interdependence among the members of the family in that each time one or more members are added to or leave the home, or each time the oldest child changes in his or her individual developmental stage, the rules governing interpersonal interactions change, thus requiring some redefinition of the family members' roles vis-à-vis other members. Furthermore, such a stage theory allows one to view the processes of family development in phases, and to concentrate on role reciprocities and conflicts at different periods of family development. As a descriptive theory, such a framework enhances our understanding of families by generating descriptions of typical family functioning at various points along a family career continuum. Unfortunately, its focus on structural stability within stages also places severe restrictions on the framework, and these limitations need to be recognized.

The single major deficiency of such a stage-discrete family development model is that it does not provide insight into the developmental change processes by which the family members differentiate and transform their interaction structures. Moreover, the framework seems to imply that the various stages are relatively long and enduring, while the transitions that delineate them are merely short periods of disorganization followed by reorganization. This may contribute to the tendency among many researchers to focus upon the stability within each of the major stages while ignoring the dialectic processes involved in making the transition from one stage to another. One must be careful not to state the assumptions of the family development framework too strongly, so as to imply that structural change will be uniform and consistent and that each role structure will be different from stage to stage. Indeed, one must consider not only what changes from stage to stage, but what remains stable across points of transition (cf. Mederer & Hill, 1983).

Finally, the family development framework is limited in that it deals primarily with developmental events and changes such as childbirth and retirement, which are predictable and ubiquitous. It does not deal with changes brought about by idiosyncratic family characteristics, cohort or historical differences, or other nondevelopmental stressors. Neugarten and Hagestad (1976) argue that major stresses are caused by unanticipated events that upset the expected sequence and rhythm of family life, and that the events used in this framework to delineate each of the stages are so thoroughly expected and anticipated and have been vicariously experienced so often that their stress-inducing potential may have been neutralized. They further argue that changes in one role are unlikely to affect other relationships uniformly, because family roles allow for improvisation and negotiation by individual family members. Although the family development model is limited by its tendency to focus on descriptions of family functioning within stages rather than on the processes through which families progress from one stage to another, by its tendency to ignore variations in the initial levels of family organization prior to transitions, and by its failure to consider the concept of interfamilial differences in the "ease of role transitions" (Burr, 1972), more recent work in family development has begun to address these weaknesses (e.g., Mederer & Hill, 1983; Menaghan, 1982).

It has long been assumed that transitions that produce a change in household structure, through either the addition of a new member or the departure of an established one, would be particularly stressful to the family unit (Hill & Rodgers, 1964). Family developmental theorists adopting a life-span perspective have assumed that role transitions—that is, events signaling the assumption of new social position or responsibility—would be expected to have major impact on the individual's experience in related roles and on his or her overall psychological well-being. Hill (1949), in particular, has suggested that the addition of a family member would precipitate a "crisis" for married couples in that this event would render established patterns of interaction inadequate, and would necessitate some immediate changes in the family's means of functioning. Certainly it is well established that a three-person group, whatever its nature, is inherently less stable than a two-person group (Simmel, 1950; Stryker, 1964), but when that third person is a baby for whom the parents may not yet know how to care, the situation is potentially even more stressful.

Many sociologists have commented on birth as a life-cycle event by noting that parenting is a role for which our society offers little preparation and that there is no period of apprenticeship to parenthood analogous to premarital courtship (Hill & Aldous, 1969; Hobbs, 1968; Rossi, 1968). For a very large majority of adults, the birth of a child and the transition to parenthood are among the most salient changes in life. Rossi (1968) has stated that the major transition from adolescence to adulthood, especially for women, is not marriage or the obtainment of a career, but parenthood. Hill and Aldous (1969) have even described parenthood as the event that signifies full entrance into adult society, with all the responsibilities that such status carries. Indeed, Hoffman (1978) surveyed a national sample and found that parents of both sexes most often indicated that "becoming a parent" was the most important life event in defining adult status in that it was "the end of carefree existence" and the beginning of a new status characterized by being responsible for others and less egocentric (p. 344). The salience of this event is all the more important when one considers that there is little formal socialization, education, or training for first-time parents, although becoming a parent is one of the most complex and challenging of life's major role transitions.

The first birth and the transition to parenthood have been described as constituting a pivotal, or critical, life event (Hobbs, 1965; LaRossa & LaRossa, 1981; LeMasters, 1957). Many researchers interested in the transition to parenthood have concerned themselves primarily with the degree to which "crisis" is experienced by couples following the birth of the first child. Although some studies indicate that the birth of the first child does disrupt the marital relationship (Dyer, 1963; LeMasters, 1957), other data indicate that the adjustment to parenthood is only mildly stressful (Beauchamp, 1968; Belsky, 1981; Feldman & Rogoff, 1968; Russell, 1974). Most research has indicated that the wife generally experiences a greater amount of stress during this period than her husband (Belsky, Spanier, & Rovine, 1983; Glenn & McLanahan, 1982; Hobbs & Cole, 1976; Power & Parke, 1984; Russell, 1974). Indeed, Fein (1978) reports that most first-time fathers are adjusted to postpartum life within a few weeks. The combination of the father's lower stress levels and shorter periods of stress has no doubt contributed to the tendency of many researchers to view the father's contribution during this phase of family development as that of providing support for his wife to ease her transition and enhance the development of her maternal skills (Grossman, Eichler, & Winickoff, 1980; Parke, 1979; Pedersen, Yarrow, Anderson, & Cain, 1978).

Hobbs and Cole (1976) and Rossi (1968) have argued that the mother has to make the greatest adjustment because the maternal role typically is defined as that of primary caregiver. The greater adjustment demanded of mothers also may be due in part to the fact that the mother's parenting role is defined in our society more rigidly than is the father's (see Russell, 1978). This position has been supported by reports from Cowan, Cowan, Coie, and Coie (1978), Cowan et al. (1985), and Entwisle and Doering (1981) of a shift toward a more traditional, sex-differentiated division of roles and instrumental behavior following the birth of a first child, regardless of both the type of division a couple has established previously and the mother's current employment status. This shift is most pronounced in household tasks; lesser effects have been noted with family decision-making roles and child-care tasks. It appears that first-time fathers assume primary economic support responsibilities as their chief means of fulfilling their role as parent, while household chores and child care become more exclusively the wives' domain. Indeed, Gutmann (1975) extends Rossi's (1968) observation that pregnancy, more so than marriage, may be viewed as the true departure point to adulthood, because the birth of a child includes a perceived "parental imperative." In addition to the normative increases in nurturant behavior associated with women's transitions to parenthood, Gutmann observes that new fathers display greater responsibility, selflessness, and moderation, as their new roles are efined chiefly in terms of supportiveness. Still, it is important to note the range of expressions of the men's characters. A number of studies have revealed that fathers who receive experience or training in child care are more involved with their children (e.g., Kotelchuck, 1976; Parke, Hymel, Power, & Tinsley, 1980; Pedersen, Zaslow, Cain, & Anderson, 1980).

The literature on stress theory has been useful in describing parental reactions to the first pregnancy and birth. For example, Levy and McGee (1975) applied Janis's (1958) model of normal stress to describe parental reactions to the birth of a first child, and found this model to be useful in describing not only the mother's but also the father's reaction to the experience. Janis's model of normal stress behavior suggests that three phases of stress management exist: the threat phase, the danger impact phase, and the postimpact victimization phase. With respect to childbirth, these phases may be seen to refer to pregnancy (threat), labor and delivery (danger and impact), and postpartum recovery (postimpact), with Levy and McGee's results suggesting that most parental concern is focused upon the labor and delivery stages (cf. Entwisle & Doering, 1981).

LeMasters (1957) conducted the first study to assess Hill's (1949) position that the transition to parenthood constitutes a family crisis. He found, as did Dyer (1963) a few years later, that the majority of middle-class couples experience "extensive or severe" crisis when the term *crisis* is defined as a "sharp change for which old patterns were inadequate" (Hill, 1949, p. 51). LeMasters notes that the birth crisis forced a reorganization of the family as a social system in that "roles had to be reassigned, status positions shifted, values reoriented, and needs met through new channels" (p. 352). Because the transition to parenthood is typically perceived as a normal life event rather than a deleterious situation, Rapoport (1963) suggests the term *normal crisis* be used instead. These studies were soon followed by reports that focused more on couples' reactions to the changes associated with parenthood than on the changes to behavioral patterns per se. These reports have found much lower levels of "crisis" among new parents (Beauchamp, 1968; Feldman & Rogoff, 1968; Hobbs, 1965, 1968; Russell, 1974). In her classic paper summarizing the literature addressing the transition to parenthood, Rossi (1968) writes that it is "time . . . to drop the concept of 'normal crises' and to speak directly, instead, of the transition to and impact of parenthood" (p. 28).

Rossi continues her review by illustrating how the parental role differs structurally from other primary adult roles, and by specifying the phases in the development of parenthood. Chief among the distinguishing features is the fact that it is irrevocable. As Rossi states, "We can have ex-spouses and ex-jobs but not ex-children" (p. 32). Rossi questions the level of preparation of American couples for parenthood by noting the following:

(1) Our education system is dedicated primarily to the cognitive development of the young, and probably a majority of American mothers, and certainly the fathers, approach parenthood with no previous child-care experience beyond sporadic baby-sitting; furthermore, this lack of relevant experience undoubtedly leads to unrealistic expectations that later may trigger disappointments.

(2) Pregnancy provides a limited opportunity for preparation and/or learning through reading, discussions with spouse, and a nesting phase as the house is prepared for the infant.

(3) The abruptness of the transition to parenthood is unlike the gradual transition associated with the assumption of new duties and responsibilities in, for example, a new job or profession.

(4) Few or no specific guidelines exist for parent prescriptions.

Following Rossi's suggestion that researchers focus attention on the positive and negative impacts of parenthood on young adult men and women, Russell (1974) asked couples who had recently experienced the birth of their first child to complete a checklist describing their reactions to the transition to parenthood. Most of the mothers (58%) and fathers (75%) reported a "slight" crisis, with the mothers' mean score being significantly higher (i.e., more stressful) than that of the fathers. More interesting, the respondents also were asked a number of questions related to the "gratifications" of becoming parents rather than to the "crises" typically associated with this transition. Among the items were "more things to talk to spouse about" and "pride in baby's development." Russell reports that both mothers and fathers checked more gratification items than crisis items, and concludes that the behavioral changes associated with new parenthood are extensive, but that most new parents are only slightly or mildly bothered by these changes, and that a large number actually report gratification arising from first parenthood.

In a similar vein, Sollie and Miller (1980) asked parents to write brief positive and negative comments on the impact of becoming parents. Four general positive and four general negative themes were identified in the parents' responses. The four positive themes included emotional benefits resulting from the love, joy, happiness, and fun that routinely accompanied child care and especially play with the child; the self-enrichment and personal development experienced when parental responsibilities and obligations were assumed; a sense of family cohesiveness, especially concerning a strengthening of the couple's marital vows; and a sense of identification with and pride in the child. On the negative side, the themes tended to focus on issues such as the physical demands (including loss of sleep) associated with caring for a child; strains on the husband-wife marital relationship; emotional stresses (including self-doubts) experienced by the parents as they began to realize the weight of parental responsibilities; and adjustments made by the parents in terms of the loss of opportunity and income and the increase of restrictions on personal freedoms.

Menaghan (1982) obtained subjective appraisals of family transitions (e.g., the birth of a first child, births of later children, child starting school, child becoming a teen, child leaving home) by asking married couples whether anything about each transition was especially bothersome, pleasant, or exciting; whether it changed their lives in some manner; and whether it changed how they felt about themselves. Not surprisingly, the birth of a first child was reported as the most salient event in terms of its being the most bothersome, being associated with the greatest pleasure or excitement, causing the greatest changes in the lives of both men and women, and leading to changes of self-perception. Somewhat more surprising were the revelations that the births of later children, while viewed as being less pleasant or exciting, were nonetheless perceived as being bothersome, and were effective in changing the lives and the self-perceptions of both men and women to a degree that was not significantly different from that of the birth of a first child.

Research on the social and psychological concomitants of pregnancy, birth, and the transition to parenthood in normal, well-functioning adults was relatively rare until the early 1970s. Since then, several detailed reports have appeared of longitudinal, systemic research on families who have passed the perinatal and transition-to-parenthood periods. Six of these projects, three focusing primarily on pregnancy, birth, and the perinatal experience, and three focusing on early parenthood, will be described in detail. Because these projects have approached the transition to parenthood from different theoretical and methodological perspectives, each will be described individually so as to highlight its unique contributions, and then an integrative summary of their conclusions will be provided. In each case it is important to recognize that the transition to parenthood experience has direct and indirect effects not only on mothers and fathers individually, but also on their relationships with each other.

STUDIES OF PREGNANCY, BIRTH, AND PERINATAL EXPERIENCE

Shereshefsky and Yarrow on the Psychological Aspects of a First Pregnancy

Shereshefsky and Yarrow (1973) conducted a multidisciplinary study of 62 young, predominantly middle-class families during pregnancy and early parenthood. The mothers underwent psychological testing and psychiatric interviews beginning at the end of the first trimester of pregnancy and continuing until six months postpartum. Home visits and interviews with the husbands were carried out, but the primary emphasis was on the data obtained from the wives, thus limiting the usefulness of these data if a family systems perspective is desired. Indeed, these data are severely dated by changes that have since occurred in the cultural climate. For example, Shereshefsky and Yarrow report that, of the fathers in their study, not one was present for the delivery of his child, and that several fathers fainted when told of the birth (p. 109)!

Throughout the period of study, couples indicated a significant decline in marital quality, but because of the rather global nature of the design, specific conclusions were difficult to obtain. Shereshefsky and Yarrow report that a woman's adaptation to the first pregnancy was predicted by several personality characteristics, such as nurturance and ego strength, as well as by her capacity to visualize herself as a mother. Moreover, the woman's perception of being mothered suggested that the memory of her own mother as warm, empathic, and happy in her mothering role was positively related to the new mother's self-confidence and negatively related to her sense of anxiety about the pregnancy. Shereshefsky, Liebenberg, and Lockman (1973), using the same sample, found that a factor called "woman's confidence," consisting of confidence in maternal role, reaction to pregnancy fears, and perception of being mothered, was positively correlated with the husband's responsiveness to the parental role. It was interesting to note that the mothers of male infants reacted to their maternal roles with greater variation than did the mothers of girls. Shereshefsky (1973) summarizes this study by noting that her multidisciplinary research team came to see that *pregnancy-as-crisis* could have different connotations. On the one hand, if the term *pregnancy-as-crisis* was used to mean a stress involving a threat or loss and requiring resources beyond the ordinary, then their data suggested that the first pregnancy was not a crisis. On the other hand, if the term was used to denote a turning point, then their subjects were indeed involved in a crisis. The first pregnancy made "substantial demands for change in current routines of living" and in terms of inner reality, as both mothers and fathers became aware of their "intrapsychic selves" (p. 245).

Grossman, Eichler, and Winickoff and the Boston University Pregnancy and Parenthood Project

Grossman, Eichler, and Winickoff (with Anzalone, Gofseyeff, and Sargent) (1980) collaborated to conduct the Boston University Pregnancy and Parenthood Project. Initially, 100 women and 90 of their husbands participated in this longitudinal project, which began with interviews conducted near the beginning of the pregnancy. Two- and five-year postpartum interviews also were conducted, with more than half the subjects still participating at the two-year follow-up. Approximately half the parents were expecting their first child, with the rest expecting their second, third, or fourth. Grossman et al. report that their subjects experienced "increases in stress and strain in the marriage" as reflected in lower marital adjustment scores (p. 201). They note that for most of the parents, and for the men in particular, the birth of the child appeared to displace the marriage as a focal source of gratification. By one year postpartum, they report that the "marriage had regained its place in the women's lives as important, but it never seemed to retain the absolute centrality that it had before the first child was born" (p. 247). On the other hand, Grossman et al. indicate that first-time fathers reported a sense of "being more of a family" (p. 200), and that mothers reported that their "overall life satisfaction seemed to increase" (p. 132), indicating that although the birth of the child may have had some deleterious effects on the marriage, most couples felt that having a baby enhanced their marital relationship.

As noted by Shereshefsky and Yarrow (1973) before them, Grossman et al. found that couples experiencing their first childbirth shifted toward a more traditional division of household labor soon after the birth of the child, despite the fact that many of the couples had enjoyed more egalitarian relationships prior to the birth. One year later, these first-time mothers reported higher levels of anxiety, perhaps due to the fact that they were unable to fulfill the traditional expectation that a new mother should be able to manage her child and house with little or no direct assistance from her husband (p. 129). Indeed, Grossman, Pollack, and Golding (1988) have continued the analysis of the data from this sample, and report that women who were more autonomous during their pregnancies tended to have husbands who were less involved with their 5-year-olds. They suggest that these women, whose sense of a separate self was more developed, seemed to be monopolizing the job of parenting with their first child, possibly in an attempt to satisfy some "supermom" ideal (p. 89). This recalls the notion of the "complementarity of parenting": When the mother is willing to care for the child and is able to do it well, the father tends to concentrate less on parenting tasks (Grossman et al., 1980, 1988; Pollack & Grossman, 1985).

On the other hand, complementarity is not the entire story. Grossman et al. (1980) had reported earlier that the fathers told them that they had learned to parent from their wives. When comparisons were made of spouses' parental behavior, Grossman et al. (1988) found that the levels of husbands' parenting skills correlated with those of their wives. These two findings suggest the existence of complementarity, which allows the man to function as a parent to his children in ways that are quite different from his wife's, and identification, which allows the man to accept the role of learning how to be a good parent by modeling his wife.

Entwisle and Doering and the
Johns Hopkins Study of the First Birth

Entwisle and Doering (1981) conducted the third of the longitudinal studies of pregnancy and the transition to parenthood that will be described in this section. Their project involved 120 wives, 60 with their husbands, who were experiencing first pregnancy and childbirth. Approximately half the sample was described economically as middle-class, and half was lower-class. The major points of contact included an interview with the wife during the sixth or seventh month of pregnancy, interviews with the wife and husband at the ninth month, interviews with the wife immediately postpartum, interviews with the wife at two to three weeks postpartum, and interviews with the husband at four to eight weeks postpartum. The purposes of the project were to provide a detailed description of couples as they became first-time parents and to examine associations among variables that linked pregnancy, the birth crisis (labor and delivery), and the ensuing period of parenthood. In attempting to establish these causal links between circumstances and events during pregnancy and their later effects on psychological and social functioning, Entwisle and Doering found that prior preparation helped couples to cope better with pregnancy, labor, and delivery and to have more realistic expectations about the process of child rearing. Social support from family, friends, and community also seemed to help the couples adjust to parenthood.

Entwisle and Doering applied Janis's (1958) model of normal stress to describe parental reactions to the birth of a first child, and found this model to be useful in describing not only the mother's but also the father's reaction to the experience (cf. Levy & McGee, 1975). Janis's model of normal stress behavior suggests that three phases of stress management exist: the *threat phase*, occurring when the individual becomes aware of the impending crisis; the *danger impact phase*, when the actual crisis has occurred; and the *postimpact victimization phase*, when the individual adapts and adjusts to the consequences of the crisis event. Janis interviewed patients before and after surgery and noted that three clear-cut groups emerged. One group denied the existence of the impending crisis and then became belligerent when it arrived. Another group vacillated between a panicked response and total disregard of the crisis. The third group experienced moderate anticipatory fear, admitted some anxiety, and then sought information concerning the event and strategies for adjusting to it. Interestingly, this third group experienced the least amount of trauma from the surgery and the easiest recovery.

With respect to childbirth, these phases refer to pregnancy (threat), labor and delivery (danger and impact), and postpartum recovery (postimpact). Doering and Entwisle (1975) applied Janis's model to women undergoing childbirth and found that mothers who had sought knowledge beforehand required less medication during labor and delivery. Moreover, their degree of preparation for childbirth was linked to the amount of medication they required during delivery, and even the most minimal preparation was better than none at all. Most important, the prepared women experienced significantly more positive feelings for their infants at their first meeting, and these initially positive reactions were associated with better early mothering. The results of both Levy and McGee's (1975) and Entwisle and Doering's (1981) studies suggest, however, that most maternal preparation is focused upon the labor and delivery stages.

Level of preparation thus was a primary factor in partitioning the Entwisle and Doering sample for between-groups analyses. The women's "preparation level" was evaluated by combining information measuring the final level of preparation achieved by the time of the birth. It included the women's knowledge about labor and delivery obtained from books, magazines, movies, and organized classes. Three levels of preparation were derived, ranging from nothing and/or pregnancy or childbirth manuals, to hospital-based classes plus manuals, to Lamaze training with manuals. Preparation level was found to be related to the wife's education level, the quality of the couple's communication, and the woman's desire for an active role in childbirth and child care.

Overall, Entwisle and Doering found that many of the women in their sample had unrealistic expectations in several areas related to childbirth and parenting. Even though they typically expressed confidence in their abilities to care for their newborns unaided, considerably more than half the mothers had no previous experience with baby care. Entwisle and Doering found that over half (57%) of the mothers in their sample had no experience in caring for a child under 6 weeks old. They suggest that this lack of relevant experience may have led to unrealistic expectations on the parts of these mothers such that they would be vulnerable to later disappointments. For example, Entwisle and Doering report that over half the mothers in their sample expected their babies to sleep through the night before they were 8 weeks old (p. 35). This inexperience in caring for young infants turned out to be a major source of social stress for the couples involved in the study.

The men in this sample experienced preparation that varied widely, but in levels that correlated highly with that experienced by their wives. This preparation provided the men with fuller participation in the birth, which helped them cope with the birth event and accentuated their contribution to the quality of the wives' birth experience. While none of Shereshefsky and Yarrow's husbands was present at delivery, 84% of the husbands in the Entwisle and Doering (1981) sample were present during labor and 64% were present at delivery (a variety of birth complications limited the participation of some husbands). In an earlier study, Doering, Entwisle, and Quinlan (1980) had noted that the husbands' participation at the delivery improved the quality of the birth experience for women who delivered vaginally. Similar to the fathers in the Grossman et al. (1980) sample, the fathers here indicated that participation in the birth of their first child was the most thrilling and profound event in their lives so far. Indeed, fathers who were present at the delivery scored higher on fathering measures than fathers who were absent by choice. Interestingly, those fathers who were absent against their will tended to score even higher than those who were present, thereby suggesting that motivation, rather than actual presence at the birth, may be the key causal element for fathers.

Regardless of social class, preparation for childbirth increased the woman's awareness at birth and improved her overall birth experience. In general, the women who delivered vaginally showed a strong positive correlation between their level of preparation and how they rated their childbirth experience. Subsequent analyses revealed that the major causal impact of preparation on the woman's birth experience was her increased level of awareness, and hence self-control, during the birth itself, which in turn acted to increase the quality of the experience. Moreover, the husband's participation in the delivery exerted both direct and indirect effects, again through increasing maternal awareness, on the quality of the wife's birth experience. The wife's positive experience was found to contribute reciprocally to the husband's birth enjoyment, thus suggesting that the nature of the couple's experience at delivery is affected in a circularly causal fashion. Maternal levels of preparation also influenced women's subsequent feeding behavior, but this effect varied with social class, in that preparation increased the likelihood that middle-class mothers would elect to breast-feed and then would persist in breast-feeding once this decision was reached. Middle-class fathers played a role in encouraging their wives to breast-feed, while lower-class fathers encouraged persistence in, but not necessarily selection of, this domain. These findings about father involvement are consistent with other reports concerning the father's regard for the mother and its relationship to her feeding competence and her overall ability to provide good mothering (Pedersen & Robson, 1969).

A major contribution by Entwisle and Doering is found in their study of the fathers' preparation. The women's preparation level helped the women to have positive birth experiences; moreover, their husbands' participation in the birth made a separate contribution to the quality of the women's experience. Entwisle and Doering (1981) point out that "young fathers find themselves expected to measure up to fathering standards they have no role model for. They are expected to be a different kind of father from their own father" (p. 256). Father preparation may be just as important as mother preparation, particularly in light of the finding that the father's participation at delivery has both direct and indirect effects on the quality of the mother's birth experience.

Entwisle and Doering's project also raises important questions about the type of preparation classes made available to prospective parents. It has been well established that attendance at most preparation classes will not help in the adjustment to parenthood (Parke & O'Leary, 1975; Wente & Crockenberg, 1976). Despite their preparation, many of the parents in the Entwisle and Doering sample did not know how to respond to or care for their infants after birth. Indeed, the parents were described as being so involved with the pregnancy and upcoming labor and delivery that they were unable to think past these events so as to have concerns about parenting issues.

Collectively, these three longitudinal studies of couples' adjustment to pregnancy and the early transition to parenthood suggest that, for the couples involved, childbirth is a critical turning point in their lives. The critical nature of this turning point can become even more stressful if the couple has a "romanticized" view of parenthood (LeMasters, 1957, p. 55), are tyrannized by the "myth of parenthood" (Grossman et al., 1980, p. 254), or maintain "unrealistic expectations" about parenting and are "unable to think past the birth event" (Entwisle & Doering, 1981, pp. 35, 257). On the other hand, the term *crisis* in its usual connotation is not appropriate in describing this normative life event. Perhaps the best way to summarize this literature focusing upon the couple's reactions and responses to pregnancy, labor and delivery, and the transition to parenthood is to note that the events involve for most couples modifications to their previously established patterns of interaction. Most parents are only mildly bothered by these changes; many of them find the changes gratifying and fulfilling.

STUDIES OF EARLY PARENTHOOD

Cowan and Cowan and the Becoming a Family Project

Carolyn and Philip Cowan and their associates have been directing the Becoming a Family Project throughout the past decade. Their primary goals have been to assess the impact of the transition to parenthood on men, women, and their marriages; to assess the effectiveness of preventive intervention on the couple's adjustment to parenthood; and to examine the impact of the quality of the couple's relationship on the development of young children. A five-domain model of family structure has been developed to provide a theoretical rationale for the choice of variables in a project of such scope (Cowan & Cowan, 1987; Cowan et al., 1985). In particular, the following five domains illustrate how the family system might be analyzed from different levels:

(1) the characteristics of each individual in the family
(2) the husband-wife relationship
(3) the parent-child relationships
(4) the relation between the nuclear family and the family of origin (i.e., the intergenerational view)
(5) the balance between external sources of stress and support, including social networks and jobs or careers

In the preliminary study leading toward this longitudinal project, Cowan and Cowan were joined by Lynne and John Coie in an exploratory effort to identify the important variables affecting the couple's relationship during the transition to parenthood, and the potential that this early family growth process might be facilitated through educationally helpful and supportive intervention (Cowan et al., 1978). Eight couples, selected via a quota sampling procedure, participated in ongoing groups of four expectant couples and a leader/facilitator couple leader, and four other expectant couples not participating in group discussions served as a comparison group. Weekly meetings began during the third trimester of pregnancy and continued until the fourth month postpartum; the comparison group couples were interviewed late during the pregnancy period and at approximately six months postpartum. Conflicts over the use of time alone and as a couple and over the adjusted division of labor were the most salient issues at the follow-up assessment. The most dramatic finding of the project was that, regardless of the type of division of roles employed by the couple prior to the pregnancy, by the time of the follow-up assessment, all eight couples indicated a shift toward a more traditional division. The shift was most pronounced with household tasks, and least pronounced with baby-care items (cf. Shereshefsky & Yarrow, 1973).

In addition to this shift to a traditional division of labor, most of the couples reported a radical alteration in the amount of time being allocated to particular tasks, an alteration that had been anticipated by the couples during pregnancy. Interestingly, the anticipation of the change did not protect the couple from sensing the stress often associated with such a change. Cowan et al. report that the couple spending the highest number of hours in home and baby care seemed to be experiencing the most distress, while the couple spending the fewest hours in these activities seemed most content. Accompanying these changes was an increasing discrepancy between partners in their perceptions of mutual roles. Even though the couples had agreed during the latter stages of pregnancy in their descriptions of who did what around the house, by the follow-up stage each parent, especially mothers, perceived that his or her share of baby-care tasks was greater than the spouse perceived it to be.

This shift toward traditionalism and the spouses' perceptions of their relative contributions has continued to be a focus through the various phases of the Becoming a Family Project. In addition to the report that each parent tends to rate self-participation in family tasks as slightly greater than the spouse gives him or her credit for, Cowan and Cowan (1981) have found that in every case where discrepancies exists between actual and ideal assessments of role arrangements, the mean ideal rating is a step closer to an egalitarian division of role responsibility. The lack of fit between a practiced traditional role division and the egalitarian ideal is associated with lower role satisfaction for these couples. Men and women with low role satisfaction tended to have the most traditional role divisions, and the women tended to have lower marital satisfaction as well. Cowan and Cowan suggest that it is not the baby per se that affects parental satisfaction negatively, but the trend toward role imbalance between the spouses that leads to partner dissatisfaction.

In another study, Cowan and Cowan (1983) provide another report of the Becoming a Family Project and address the issue that a well-functioning relationship during pregnancy and soon after birth should be a strong predictor of the woman's positive adjustment to birth and early parenthood (see Grossman et al., 1980; Shereshefsky & Yarrow, 1973). In particular, they focus on parenting stress defined not only in terms of the characteristics of the child and the new demands placed on the parent, but also on the stress of parenting on the individual person and his or her marriage. Cowan and Cowan used the Parenting Stress Index (PSI) developed by Abidin and his associates (Abidin, 1979; Burke & Abidin, 1980) to assess the parental stress experienced by the couples in their study. The PSI is a self-report instrument designed to identify parent and child systems that are under stress, and in which deviant development of the child or family is likely to take place, or where dysfunctional parenting is likely to occur. They found that marital satisfaction during pregnancy and soon thereafter was not predictive of later parenting stress for fathers. Instead, the fathers' high parenting stress at 6 months postpartum was predictive for both lower marital satisfaction and lower self-esteem at 12 months and 18 months postpartum. For mothers, parenting stress at 6 months postpartum did not predict future marital dissatisfaction, but higher marital satisfaction did appear to be an antecedent of lower parental stress. Mothers' satisfactory feelings about themselves and their marriages before the birth predicted lower parenting stress when the baby was both 6 and 18 months old. Furthermore, maternal self-esteem and role satisfaction with respect to the division of household and child-care responsibilities at 6 months predicted lower parental stress at 18 months postpartum. On the other hand, maternal stress in parenting appeared to be associated with the mother's feelings about herself and her marriage during the pregnancy, and her parenting stress did not appear to be associated with future levels of marital satisfaction.

Parental stress associated with the transition to parenthood has been assessed by numerous researchers employing the Parenting Stress Index. Awalt (1981) used the PSI with mothers and fathers in her study of the transition to parenthood and found that maternal role satisfaction was associated with postpartum marital satisfaction, and she further found parental stress to be associated with lower marital satisfaction in both men and women following the birth of a first child. She also reports that marital satisfaction ($r = -.58$ for mothers and $-.44$ for fathers) and parental role satisfaction ($r = .53$ for mothers and $.36$ for fathers) are significantly related to parenting stress after childbirth. Crnic, Greenberg, Ragozin, Robinson, and Basham (1983) studied the effects of social supports on maternal stress; they report that intimate support (from spouse/partner) has the most positive effect in lessening the impact of stress and in improving mothers' attitudes toward and behavioral interaction with their infants. A similar effect was noted by Pedersen, Anderson, and Cain (1977) in their report that the husband's esteem for the wife as a mother is positively related to her skill in feeding the infant. Green (1980) also employed the PSI in a study of the transition to parenthood, and reports that the mothers of "difficult" infants are more likely to be stressed and in need of their husbands' support. Moreover, the fathers of such infants are less likely to provide supportive child care, thus resulting in a highly stressed family system. In using the PSI to study the transition from triadic to tetradic family system, one need only add another domain to assess the effects of the newborn as a source of stress. Such a domain can simply replicate the existing questions of the Child domain, since this instrument has been normed on a sample of 534 families with children between the ages of 1 month and 10 years (Abidin, 1983).

In the next report from their ongoing project, Cowan and Cowan (1985) examined the effect of parents' work patterns on marital and parent-child relationships. At this point in the longitudinal project the children were 3 to 4 years old. Observations of parent-child interaction were made in a semistructured situation in which the two were asked to work together to complete a number of tasks. Cowan and Cowan found that the more hours fathers of boys worked outside the family, the more stress and anxiety were observed in their sons, even though these same boys appeared more relaxed with their mothers. These mothers, however, tended to be warmer and more responsive to their sons than were the mothers whose husbands worked less time. A different pattern was noted with daughters of fathers who worked more hours; these fathers tended to be less engaging and to provide less structure for their daughters, who in turn were more anxious, less warm, and less task oriented than daughters of fathers who worked less. The indirect positive effect noted with mothers and sons was not found with daughters of fathers who worked more hours, as these girls remained less warm and task oriented with their mothers as well.

With more than 50% of the mothers in their project employed, correlates of maternal employment became an important issue for the Becoming a Family Project. Cowan and Cowan report that the more hours mothers of boys were employed, the more engaged and less frustrated their sons tended to be with the tasks. Moreover, the daughters of such mothers tended to be less anxious and to have higher scores on cognitive and role-taking tasks. Collectively, these results suggest that long hours of paternal employment outside the home are somewhat detrimental to parent-child relationships, while long hours of maternal employment are associated with positive consequences. This is supported further by the finding that when fathers worked more outside the home they tended to report higher levels of depression and associated symptoms, while for mothers the opposite was true. Indeed, higher levels of father involvement in child rearing were associated with lower levels of depression and associated symptoms and higher levels of self-esteem, even though these higher levels of involvement seemed to have some negative effects on the mother-daughter relationship. Specifically, the wives of husbands who were highly involved in child rearing tended to be less warm, responsive, and permissive with their daughters, who in turn were more frustrated and angry with their mothers. Not surprisingly, Cowan and Cowan report that those parents who were most satisfied with their marriages before becoming parents tended to be the happiest with their relationships four years later.

Cowan et al. (1985) integrated the preliminary reports they had presented at various professional conferences into a contribution to a special issue of the *Journal of Family Issues* devoted to the transition to parenthood. In this work, they indicate that men's psychological involvement as parents increased over the period of the longitudinal study, but that their involvement in this domain remained small in comparison to that of their wives. The women tended to stop working outside the home, or at least cut their hours drastically, while men spent more time at their jobs. Indeed, the men tended to see themselves as good providers and therefore contributing directly to the welfare of their wives and children, while their wives interpreted these actions as pulling away from the family at a time when the men were needed most. This discrepancy, and other factors, contributed to the decline in marital satisfaction reported from pregnancy to 6 months postpartum; this decline was noted even more sharply by the second year of parenthood. Indeed, Cowan et al. report that marital satisfaction declined moderately from 6 to 18 months postpartum for mothers, but that it plunged steeply for fathers over this time. They suggest that the impact of becoming a parent is felt first by the mother, and only later by the father—the largest discrepancy between maternal and paternal evaluations occurs at 6 months postpartum; a year later the discrepancy is no larger, but the decline in marriage satisfaction has increased as now fathers too have begun to feel the impact of parenthood. For both men and women the only significant correlation with declining marital satisfaction is increasing marital conflict. Research by Levenson and Gottman (1983) suggests that husbands and wives may attempt to cope with their differences and resolve their conflicts in very different ways that may, in and of themselves, further escalate the sense of conflict between the couple.

Cowan et al. (1985) have summarized their project by noting that husbands and wives experience different paths in their transitions to parenthood. Men experience the transition much more slowly, first becoming actively involved in their role as provider for the child. They do not become as involved in child care during the first year as they had expected to prior to the birth, but their involvement does continue to increase over the first few years of the child's life. Women experience the transition in a much more radical way, as many abandon jobs and/or careers and devote a significantly larger portion of themselves to the care of the baby. Collectively, the couple experiences the transition by having the parental aspects of their respective roles expanded, by having the partner/lover aspects of their relationship reduced, and by having the conflict in their marriage increased as they are forced to cope with more issues. This has led Cowan and Cowan to rephrase Jesse Bernard's (1974) description of marriage so as to suggest that there are three transitions to parenthood—his, hers, and theirs.

LaRossa and LaRossa on
How Infants Change Families

A second longitudinal study of the transition to parenthood and early parenting both replicates and supplements many of the findings of Cowan and Cowan and their associates. LaRossa and LaRossa (1981) conducted a sociological investigation of the transition to parenthood by longitudinally studying the experiences of 10 couples expecting the birth of their first child and 10 expecting the birth of their second. Conjoint interviews were conducted at three, six, and nine months postpartum. The data derived from these interviews allowed LaRossa and LaRossa to develop a *conflict sociological model* to describe the process of the transition to parenthood. The conflict orientation of their model implies an assumption that when people are "confronted with a choice under conditions of real or perceived scarcity, most people will be inclined to choose themselves over others" (Sprey, 1979, p. 132). The resource assumed to be scarce during the transition to parenthood is "free" or "down" time, when the parent is free from the responsibilities of child care and is able to pursue a career or leisure activities. Indeed, from their very first report of the pilot research in this area, Cowan et al. (1978) have provided evidence to support this assumption by noting that conflict over the use of time alone is one of the most salient issues affecting the transition to parenthood.

LaRossa and LaRossa's conflict sociological model begins with a recognition of the helplessness of the human infant and the infant's dependence upon the parents for survival. This helplessness places the couple in the position of having to arrange for continuous coverage for the infant. This coverage results in a loss of free time, which in turn leads to a conflict of interest between the husband and wife. A number of "contingency propositions" are suggested to mediate the causal relationship between contiguous steps along the model. For example, the link between the helplessness of the infant and the need for continuous coverage is mediated by the relative degree of protectiveness of each of the parents. Protectiveness is assumed to be a continuous variable extending from complete protectiveness (hence total subordination of self to the perceived needs of the child) to complete disregard (hence a total lack of interest in the child). Although both parents might share in providing care for the child, it is safe to assume, and indeed it has been found by Entwisle and Doering (1981), that in most families the mothers will shoulder the lion's share of these responsibilities regardless of her individual level of protectiveness.

The link between the need for continuous care and the consequent scarcity of free time is mediated by the couple's degree of interchange-ability or impersonalization of coverage for the infant. This suggests that providing care for the infant is viewed as a zero-sum situation, whereby one person's "winning" (being free to pursue his or her own goals) implies that the other must "lose" (forgo his or her own goals). The perceived value of the free time gained or lost certainly acts as a mediating factor affecting the path from the scarcity of time to the couple's conflict concerning that scarcity. Finally, the perceived legitimacy of the division of labor established by a husband and wife is conceptualized as an important qualifying factor affecting their response to the conflicting goal situation.

In discussing the processes utilized by couples as they negotiate and legitimate a division of labor, LaRossa and LaRossa point out that most fathers are periodically willing to assume primary responsibility for the care of their infants, thereby enabling their wives to obtain some down time. It is interesting to note that most of the fathers in their study perceived this activity to be "helping their wives" rather than sharing in parental responsibilities. Pleck (1976) has also found that most husbands and wives do not believe that men should do more family work, and that there are more men than women among those who do feel that men should contribute more to the family. Collectively, these findings suggest that women may "want" to remain chiefly responsible for the house and for the children, though LaRossa and LaRossa are quick to emphasize that the rationale behind this so-called want may vary widely. In particular, they note that the women may not trust their husbands to do a good job, that they may have learned that their husbands' assistance is more trouble or costly than it is worth, or that they may feel threatened because their husbands' involvement might undermine their own identities.

In describing the negotiations between the husband and wife as they plan to maintain the continuous coverage for their newborn child, La-Rossa and LaRossa make an important distinction between the quantita-tive (clock time) and qualitative (subjective perception of desirable and undesirable tasks to be performed) aspects of time. The negotiations of divisions of labor within a family certainly involve both aspects of time; however, the rules of the clock and the values of particular times and tasks are not as clearly or formally defined as they typically are in the workplace. Indeed, in most family settings the rules of the clock are far more flexible and the values of times and tasks are ambiguous at best. This makes negotiations within the family considerably more problematic (i.e., more overt, conscious, and intense) than those of the workplace (LaRossa & LaRossa, 1981). It is interesting that none of the couples in the LaRossa and LaRossa sample were striving in their negotiations to establish a role-sharing arrangement that was based on principles of equality, defined as a parity of activities in terms of a quantitative conception of time. Instead, the couples sought equity in their negotiations, defined in terms of a parity of opportunity and constraints using a qualitative conception of time, or in what they personally saw as a just or fair arrangement. Thus LaRossa and LaRossa characterize the couple's negotiations over the division of labor during the transition to parenthood as being essentially concerned with the distribution of resources and constraints emerging from their interactions. These interactions are assumed to be preceded by individual computations of equity as each spouse compares his or her own situation with those of other new parents (the CL, comparison level, in Thibaut & Kelley's, 1959, terminology) and with those of adults in alternative relationships or positions (the CLalt in Thibaut & Kelley's terminology).

As these comparisons are made by each of the spouses, conflicts will arise as the spouses become aware of discrepancies or misalignments between what they say they do (or want) and what they actually do. These discrepancies will need to be realigned if these conflicts are to be resolved. LaRossa and LaRossa describe a number of aligning actions (e.g., excuses, justifications, appeals of various types) that couples utilize either collectively or individually as they seek a form of balance. The important distinction in this approach to the transition to parenthood is that the focus is not on the behavioral changes experienced by the couple, but instead on their attitudes toward these changes. On a short-term basis these aligning actions serve to reduce the stress associated with conflict by permitting egalitarian beliefs to continue despite contradictory evidence. Aligning actions such as excuses, justifications, and rationales can be made for behaviors (or the lack thereof) and they can be evaluated by the other party in the negotiation so that the couple can, in effect, avoid recognizing the discrepancy between belief and behavior. For example, the egalitarian husband and wife who find their conduct becoming more traditional after the birth of their first child can make excuses for this misalignment and still maintain their commitment to egalitarian ideals.

On a long-term basis these aligning actions serve to change the relationship of the couple by allowing their beliefs to drift in the direction of the misaligned conduct. In this case the couple who have been making excuses for their failure to live up to egalitarian ideals can gradually adjust their beliefs so as to fit their behavior.

LaRossa and LaRossa (1981) detect a shift toward traditionalism not only in the divisions of labor adopted by the couples, but in their patterns of communication as well. They suggest that this "traditionalization" of the couple may be the key to the consistent finding that middle-class mothers experience significantly more difficulty during the transition to parenthood than do middle-class fathers. LaRossa and LaRossa conceptualize traditionalization as an organizational transformation rather than simply a behavioral change, because they view the transition to parenthood as the beginning of "a systemic level change in the marriage toward a more traditional social organization" (p. 95). Rossi (1977) has argued both that hormonal changes during pregnancy, birth, and nursing may establish a biological base predisposing mothers to make greater investments in the child and that early child socialization practices tend to establish traditional sex-role behaviors long before the individual becomes a parent (Rossi, 1968). LaRossa and LaRossa find both these arguments insufficient to explain the couple's shift toward traditionalism following the birth of a child, and instead argue that the process is both sociohistorical and interactional as revealed through the process of negotiating a division of labor. In short, the important points are that, from the perspective of the couple, the division of labor is a problem of equity, based on a qualitative conception of time, and that the characteristics and forms of this division of labor will be interactive and emergent as the couple seeks some systemic form of reorganization so as to meet the needs of their child.

Belsky and the Pennsylvania
Infant and Family Development Project

The third of the longitudinal studies focusing on the transition to parenthood and early parenting has been conducted by Jay Belsky and his associates. The Pennsylvania Infant and Family Development Project is probably the most ambitious longitudinal project undertaken in this area. The primary goals of this three-cohort longitudinal study, which ultimately plans to follow 250 families from the last trimester of pregnancy through their infants' first year of life, are to obtain a detailed description of the change in the marital relationship across the transition to parenthood and to identify those factors and processes that account for the observed variation in marital change. Furthermore, the project was designed to assess the changing nature of the relationship between marital and parent-infant interaction and to identify the determinants of competent parenting.

Belsky (1984) has proposed a general model of the determinants of parental functioning that organizes and integrates the many familial and extrafamilial factors hypothesized to influence parental functioning. His model entails a developmental analysis of the determinants of parenting and suggests that parental functioning is influenced by a variety of factors. The three major determinants of competent parenting are as follows: (a) the personality/psychological well-being of the parent, including the temperament style, adopted sex-role orientation, and developmental history of the parent; (b) the characteristics of the child, including the gender, developmental status ("age"), and temperament style of the child; and (c) contextual sources of stress and support, specifically including aspects of the marital relationship, social support network, and occupational experiences of the couple. Belsky and Vondra (1985) point out that the determinants of competent parenting across the transition to parenthood are "multiply, reciprocally, and even hierarchically organized" (p. 547). Indeed, they argue that factors such as the timing of the first birth in terms of the life courses of the individual parents and their marital relationship, the division of labor selected by the couple, the emotional and instrumental support received from friends and family, and the demands and satisfactions that the parents derive from their parental and professional or career roles must be considered collectively in understanding the determinants of parenting.

The Pennsylvania Infant and Family Development Project was designed to further our understanding of early human experience by examining the ontogeny of parenting from a family systems perspective. This project, and the model upon which it is based, obviously builds upon Belsky's earlier suggestion that to understand parenting and its influence on child development, attention must be devoted to the marital relationship (Belsky, 1981). In particular, this project was designed to assess, among other things, the stability and change in marriage and social network contact across the transition to parenthood (Belsky et al., 1983; Belsky, Lang, & Rovine, 1985; Belsky & Rovine, 1984), the changing nature of the relationship between marital and parent-infant interaction over the first year of the infant's life (Belsky, Gilstrap, & Rovine, 1984), the development of the mother-infant relationship and the influence of parenting on infant development (Belsky, Rovine, & Taylor, 1984; Belsky, Taylor, & Rovine, 1984), the role of violated expectations on adjustment to the transition to parenthood (Belsky, 1985; Belsky, Ward, & Rovine, 1986), and the role of sex typing and the division of labor as determinants of parenting (Belsky, Lang, & Huston, 1986).

In one of the first papers to come from this project, Belsky et al. (1983) focused on the marital adjustment of the 72 couples constituting the first cohort of the study. Of these couples, 41 were bearing a first child, and 31 a second or later-born. Interviews were conducted with the couples jointly at the beginning of the third trimester of pregnancy, and at three and nine months postpartum, to obtain couples' assessments of their household and child-care division of labor, their joint leisure activities, and their characterizations of their marriage in terms of its being a romance, a friendship, and a partnership. The spouses completed individual questionnaires at each session. In order to assess self-reported marital quality, the Spanier (1976) Dyadic Adjustment Scale (DAS) was completed along with each spousal questionnaire. Home observations were obtained at one, three, and nine months postpartum under the premise that the observations focused on the routine experiences of the baby. Various marital interactions were coded in terms of spousal interactions related to and independent of the infant, and a global reciprocal engagement rating was obtained to assess the extent and intensity of the couple's interaction.

Belsky et al. found that the couples' overall marital quality (dyadic adjustment) declined significantly at each time of measurement. Moreover, marital cohesion and affectional expressions declined significantly between the prepartum and postpartum assessments. Wives scored significantly higher than their husbands on prepartum cohesion, and displayed a far more significant decline after the birth of the child. The wives also reported significantly higher marital quality than did their husbands, and primiparous couples scored higher than multiparous couples on all scales except consensus. Significant time and parity effects were noted with the various characterizations of the marriage. In particular, primiparous couples tended to characterize their marriages as more of a romance than a partnership, while multiparous couples did just the opposite. All couples revealed declines in their romance scores over the course of the study (though not to a significant degree), and partnership scores increased significantly from the three- to nine-month postpartum sessions. Couples having their first child reported more joint leisure activity than did their multiparous counterparts, but all couples reported a decline in these activities from the prepartum to the postpartum sessions. With regard to marital interactions, the primiparous couples displayed more behaviors than the multiparous couples in every category that involved the parenthood role and the demands of the baby. Significant declines in the amounts of positive affect and baby-related interactions were noted for all couples over the course of the study. Especially interesting was that, regardless of the measure employed, individual spouses and couples tended to maintain their relative rankings throughout the periods of the study; wives tended to be somewhat more stable than their husbands, though both husbands and wives were reliably stable.

In a report of data obtained from the second cohort of the project, Belsky et al. (1985) presented more differentiated assessments of the marital relationship and replicated this pattern of decline in marital quality across the transition to parenthood. This replication involved 67 Caucasian couples, each of which was expecting the birth of their first child, and included a substitution for the DAS that more sufficiently discriminated distinct dimensions of the marriage, such as feelings, interpersonal behaviors, and attitudes (cf. Huston & Robins, 1982). The schedule of measurements, interviews, and observations employed with the first cohort was utilized again. New questionnaires were employed to obtain information about marital activity, mood, and attitudes by having both spouses evaluate the positive and negative interpersonal events/activities of their relationship, their levels of conflict and maintenance, their feelings of love and ambivalence, their characterization of the marriage in terms of romance, friendship, and partnership, and their overall marital satisfaction.

Once again the decline in marital quality was more evident among wives than among husbands, and was largely observed in the first six postpartum months. Individual differences remained quite stable, suggesting consistency in the face of change. Both husbands and wives were found to be increasingly dissatisfied with the positive behaviors of their partners; both wished that their spouses would display more positive behaviors. Specifically, husbands who were dissatisfied with the level of interpersonal activities with their wives wanted their partners to direct more positive behavior toward them. Instead, these husbands tended to have wives who decreased their spousal efforts to work at the relationship. For both husbands and wives, satisfaction and love declined linearly over time, though the decline in degree of change was greater for wives. The couples' senses of romance and friendship decreased over time, while the sense of partnership increased. Interestingly, the decline in the sense of omance was greater for husbands, and the increase in the sense of partnership was greater for wives. Collectively, these results suggest that he marital relationship becomes focused more on instrumental functions nd less on emotional expression after the birth of a first child. With egard to marital interaction, significant declines in all measures of nterpersonal interaction, baby-related interaction, and overall engagement were seen throughout the postpartum assessments. As was the case vith the previous cohort, individual spouses and couples tended to maintain their relative rankings across the periods of the study on all measurements. Within-family correspondence between husbands and wives was lso found to be high, and it increased over the course of the study.

Belsky and Rovine (1984), using the data from the primiparous and multiparous couples of the first cohort, assessed the impact of having a child on the social support networks of these couples by obtaining information concerning each couple's social network contacts and level of family support throughout the transition period. They discovered that contacts with extended family members, as well as with other parents of young children, increased over time, thus providing a concrete example of how the children might be able to "produce their own development" cf. Lerner & Bush-Rossnagel, 1981) by encouraging social contact to enhance parenting and thereby their own development. Moreover, they noted that emotional and material support were greater at three months postpartum than at other times, and that each was greater for primiparous han for multiparous parents. This observation clearly supports Power and Parke's (1984) suggestion that contact and support may vary as a function of stress and, therefore, with the particular phase of the transition process currently being experienced by the couple. Interestingly, couples that lived close to their families of origin and that lived in the community longer had more contact with their own parents, but did not receive any more material or emotional support. Consistent rank orderings of both couples and individual scores on all measures of contact and support were found across all time periods, suggesting that constancy in the face of change characterizes social network development across the transition period.

In the next phase of this project, Belsky, Gilstrap, and Rovine (1984) used the data of the first cohort to focus on the stability of mother-infant and father-infant interactions over the transition period. Unstructured home observations were conducted at each of the postpartum times of measurement, and maternal and paternal rates of interaction with the infants were recorded. A global rating of engagement defined as the extent and intensity of each of the three dyadic interactions also was obtained. As might be expected, all measures of infant functioning revealed significant changes associated with the time of assessment, hence the age of the infant. No significant infant gender or birth order effects were detected and no interindividual stability over time was noted. When the parent behaviors were analyzed, significant age of child, mother versus father, and birth order effects were detected, but no significant differences were found in the mothers' and fathers' treatment of sons and daughters. Specifically, parental levels of overall engagement, caregiving, and positive affection declined as the child got older, while stimulating and responding to the child increased. Mothers were more engaging, responsive, stimulating, and affectionate at all ages observed, while fathers tended to read or watch television more. Interestingly, the differences between the mothers and fathers in levels of engagement, caregiving, and affection declined over time, suggesting that the fathers became more involved as they gained more experience or as their wives spent less time breast-feeding.

Across all age levels, primiparous parents interacted more with their infants in all recorded categories, and, especially with stimulation, the difference increased with time. This birth order or parity effect was stronger for fathers than for mothers, though it is possible that multiparous fathers did not interact with their infants as much as their primiparous counterparts because they were busy taking care of the older children in the family. It is unfortunate that the behavior of these older children and their interactions with their parents and younger siblings were not recorded by Belsky, Gilstrap, and Rovine (1984). The existence of the older children has been reduced to simply the unitary designation "multiparous parents." (Perhaps the design for the third cohort of the project will assess this aspect of family development more adequately.) Individual stability of parental behaviors was found to be stronger between the three- and nine-month sessions than between any other two sessions, and somewhat greater stability was noted with mothers than with fathers.

Belsky, Gilstrap, and Rovine (1984) addressed the issue of developmental changes in the interrelationship of the marriage, parenting, and infant behaviors by correlating, within each age level, the summary engagement ratings of each dyad with the infant measures of fuss/cry, smile/excite, and explore. They found that high levels of father involvement with the infant covaried positively with high levels of marital interaction, and that high levels of marital interaction were associated with low levels of maternal involvement with the infant. It is unclear from hese data whether marital interaction is the cause or the product of father nvolvement, but it is clear that high levels of father involvement go ogether with high levels of marital communication, regardless of the age f the infant or the experience of the parents. Finally, it was noted that requencies of fussing and crying were independent of maternal, paternal, nd marital engagement at every age, but that smiling was positively orrelated with both maternal and paternal involvement by the nine-nonth postpartum assessment. This led Belsky et al. to suggest that father nvolvement is "yoked" to marital interaction in that the father's parental nd spousal roles seem to be more fused than the more easily distinguish-ble roles of mother and wife (p. 703).

Belsky (1985) and Belsky, Ward, and Rovine (1986) have examined, sing the data from the second cohort of primiparous couples, the issue f how prenatal expectations and the potential violation of these expec-ations might influence the couple's transition to parenthood. It has long een known that parents-to-be tend to romanticize the ways in which ecoming parents will affect their lives (LeMasters, 1957) or to have nrealistic expectations concerning the ease of caring for an infant (Ent-visle & Doering, 1981). Belsky, Ward, and Rovine (1986) assumed that he underestimation of the difficulties or stressful experiences and the verestimation of the benefits associated with the birth of a child would xacerbate the difficulty of adjusting to the new parenting role and the lecline in marital satisfaction typically associated with this transition. At renatal and three- and nine-month postpartum sessions, parents were queried about six domains of individual and family life that were derived rom content analyses of open-ended interviews with parents in the first ohort of the project (marital conflict, marital relationship, personal pinion, relations with extended family, relations with friends, shared aregiving). Additional assessments of the marital relationship were ob-ained using standard scales (Braiker & Kelley, 1979; Huston & McHale, 1984). Their analyses revealed that, overall, parents expected and expe-ienced small positive effects in their relationship due to having a baby. Specifically, the actual effect of having a baby turned out to be more ositive than had been expected, though the effect of the birth on the narriage turned out to be less positive than anticipated. Wives held a lightly more positive view than husbands concerning how the baby vould and did influence relations with friends and neighbors, and they xpected and experienced their husbands as being less involved in care-giving than did the husbands themselves.

Violations of expectations were identified by noting differences in scores across the two times of assessment. The presence of such violations did not appear to exert much impact on the husbands' appraisals of their marriages, but for wives, up to 25% of the variance in change in marital satisfaction was accounted for by noting the existence of such a violation. For both sets of spouses, the more family adjustment turned out to be less positive and more negative than anticipated, the more marital satisfaction and the efforts necessary to maintain a marriage declined, and the more feelings of ambivalence or confusion concerning the spouse increased. When events turned out less positive or more negative than wives antic-ipated, they experienced significant declines in their reported levels of marital satisfaction and in their efforts to maintain the relationship, and increases in their levels of marital conflict and in their ambivalence concerning their husbands. Neither the stress-enhancing effect of having an infant with a difficult temperament nor the stress-buffering effect of having a healthy, flexible personality was found to lessen the simple effect of experiencing a violated expectation. Belsky (1985) concludes that the woman's failure to anticipate accurately the nature of the change of life-style after the birth of the first child, her failure to recognize the baby's direct influence in this change, and especially her tendency to overestimate the positive aspects of this change were all associated with the greater negative change experienced in her marital relations.

Finally, Belsky, Lang, and Huston (1986) used the data from the wives of the second cohort of couples to address the effects of sex typing and the couple's negotiated division of labor on marital change. Previous to their work, Bassoff (1984) had found that new mothers who reported having more masculine sex-typed characteristics (i.e., instrumentality) were less likely to experience psychological distress than their more feminine (i.e., expressive) or undifferentiated counterparts. This finding is surprising, given Waldron and Routh's (1981) discovery that masculin-ity/instrumentality and femininity/expressivity did not predict change in couples' marital satisfaction across the transition to parenthood. Belsky et al. assessed the spouses' division of labor at the third trimester and the three-month postpartum sessions by jointly interviewing the couples and having them rate their relative responsibility for a list of five traditionally feminine household tasks, such as cooking and laundry. Data describing various aspects of the marital relationship were reported in the Belsky et al. (1985) replication effort, and were utilized here as well. The wives completed the Personal Attributes Questionnaire (Spence & Helmreich,

1978) to provide an assessment of their levels of instrumentality and expressiveness.

Their results indicated that women who scored high on masculinity/instrumentality experienced the greatest decline in the positive/affectional aspects of the marriage from the last trimester of pregnancy to the third month postpartum. Furthermore, those women who experienced increases in their relative levels of responsibility for household tasks experienced the most decline in the positive/affectional aspects of the marriage, as well as the sharpest increase in the negative aspects of that relationship. An interaction between femininity and the division of labor was also found to be significant in predicting both the positive and negative aspects of the marriage. Specifically, those women who were less traditionally feminine and whose household divisions of labor were especially traditional were the ones whose marriages suffered the greatest during the transition to parenthood. When femininity scores and change in division of labor scores were simultaneously split at their respective medians to produce four subgroups of wives, these nontraditional women enduring traditional divisions of labor scored the lowest on the positive aspects of the marriage and the highest on the negative aspects of the marriage even after adjusting for prenatal levels of marital quality. Belsky et al. commented on this interaction effect by noting that a woman with a low level of expressivity may be less inclined or able to meet the demand of nurturing a young infant. When this stressful situation is combined with the difficulty of coping with additional household responsibilities, the mother and homemaker roles may become overly taxed, thus leading to a decline in the quality of the marital relationship.

Overall, the general pattern of results coming from the Pennsylvania Infant and Family Development Project suggests that modest but highly reliable mean changes in the quality of the marital relationship, most of which would be regarded as somewhat unfavorable, occur during the transition to parenthood. Specifically, significant declines have been detected in measures assessing positive behavior, maintenance behavior, overall marital satisfaction, and feelings of love. Increases in feelings of ambivalence have been noted, and, in the case of wives, increases in conflict. The general characterization of the marriage relationship has shifted from romance to partnership. It is important to note that most of these changes took place in the time between the third trimester of pregnancy and the third month postpartum. Belsky et al. (1985) indicate that their data may underestimate the degree of real change in the marital relationship over the transition to parenthood because their samples consist primarily of well-functioning, middle-class, educated couples. Furthermore, Belsky, Ward, and Rovine (1986) conclude that because violated expectations seemed to exert such a damaging effect on marital relations, especially with wives, there is reason to suggest that opportunities ought to be developed to help parents-to-be adopt more realistic expectations about how having a child will affect their lives. The results of this project also provide us with a clue as to the next two important aspects of family functioning that need to be considered in our systemic study of the family in a transition—the involvement of the father with the firstborn child, and the adjustment of that child to the transition.

Summary of Longitudinal Studies

Despite the diversity of approaches taken, these longitudinal studies of adjustment at the transition to parenthood all find that this event is somewhat stressful to the couples involved. Each study found evidence that parents-to-be had unrealistic expectations of the positive effects of having a baby, or of their own or their spouses' ability to adjust to the demands of parenthood. Entwisle and Doering (1981) in particular found that mothers-to-be, because of their lack of preparation, were extremely unrealistic in their expressed confidence in their ability to care for their infants. Moreover, these mothers-to-be often were unable to consider issues of parenting prior to the births of their children because they were so overly preoccupied with the upcoming labor and delivery experience. Belsky and his associates have demonstrated how such unrealistic expectations might result in parents' experiencing violated expectations in the early postpartum months, and how this situation might lead to decreased marital satisfaction or increased marital conflict.

Each of the studies surveyed reports evidence of a shift toward a more traditional division of labor by the couple. This shift toward traditionalism often results in some degree of role imbalance, as even couples who espouse egalitarian ideals find themselves moving in directions that are not in accordance with their personal or mutual goals. Cowan and Cowan have indicated that while the burden of having to do the extra child-care tasks affects parental satisfaction negatively, the role imbalance leads even more to marital, or actually partner, dissatisfaction. These data support LaRossa and LaRossa's (1981) argument that the shift toward a more traditional division of labor within the household may be the key to the consistent findings of decreased marital satisfaction and increased conflict and/or ambivalence as the transition period proceeds. This shift toward traditionalism has been attributed to biosocial and physiological factors (Rossi, 1977), personality factors associated with early childhood socialization and sex-role learning (Rossi, 1968), and sociological factors as the couple seeks a new means of balancing the demands of the infant with their individual needs for free time (LaRossa & LaRossa, 1981).

Of course, a much simpler explanation can be offered. Family development theorists (e.g., Hill, 1949; Hill & Rodgers, 1964) would suggest that when previous response patterns fail to be effective for coping with new life circumstances, men and women search for role models from their own upbringing. Because their parents are likely to have arranged their roles more stereotypically than current ideology might dictate, contemporary men and women may find themselves falling back on older, more gender-differentiated patterns as they adapt to new parenthood. It is also important to remember that fathers today are being asked to measure up to standards that are not very well articulated in our culture. In the absence of clearly defined models, it is easy to see why couples may find it "more comfortable" to ease into the older, more traditional way of doing things. The process of aligning actions described by LaRossa and LaRossa is especially helpful in illustrating how this easing into traditionalism might be accomplished without the couple having to face the fact that they are, in fact, not living up to their own expectations.

Finally, each of these studies has indicated that wives and husbands respond differently to the birth of a child and to the transition to parenthood. Most of the studies have found that wives experience greater negative experiences associated with the transition, and that they experience these effects sooner than do their husbands. This may be due to the fact that the wife is far more involved with the pregnancy, labor, and delivery, and that she usually is what might be considered the aggrieved or exploited party in the traditional household. On the other hand, it might be due to the fact that the father's parental system of behaviors, feelings, and attitudes is buffered by the wife's experiences, or even that his adjustment to parenthood involves factors not yet considered by family researchers. It is logical to assume that role strain, from the father's perspective, might involve not so much a balance of responsibilities within the home as a balance of responsibilities between the home and the career. Cowan et al. (1985) have made a valuable contribution to the study of the transition to parenthood by drawing our attention to his, her, and their transitions.

ASSUMPTIONS CONCERNING
THE TRANSITION AT THE BIRTH
OF A SECOND CHILD

When one considers the adjustments required of the family at the birth of a second child, it may become necessary to qualify Rossi's assumption of the pivotal nature of the transition to parenthood and to recognize that the first and second births may have differential effects on husbands and wives. The source of this differential effect may be found in the perceived "parental imperatives" (Gutmann, 1975) experienced by each parent at each birth event. Specifically, it is logical to assume that the birth of a first child has a more pronounced effect on women, as they acquire the responsibilities of adulthood in general and parenthood in particular, given their immediate involvement with labor and delivery and with subsequent child-care responsibilities, and the fact that maternal parenting roles are more clearly and rigidly defined in our society than are paternal roles (cf. Hobbs & Cole, 1976; Rossi, 1968; Russell, 1978).

On the other hand, it would also seem logical to assume, given both the salience of the breadwinner role and the lack of clear guidelines concerning the expressive roles of fathers in the family, that first-time fathers would adjust to their emerging parenthood by assuming traditionally oriented role differentiations. Indeed, if these assumptions are tenable, then it might be expected that fathers would experience less family-related stress as they adjust to their new role of provider for mother and child by becoming more focused on job security (Gutmann, 1975). In order to assess the impact on fathers of the birth of a first child one might be well advised to employ a stress index specifically oriented to occupational stressors rather than familial issues.

In a similar manner, the birth of a second child may be conceptualized as an event that potentially affects men and women differently, and the event may be especially salient for men, as now they too have an imperative to assume parental activities. That is, the birth of a second child can be conceptualized as a normative developmental event that confronts the family with yet another period of role adjustment, but that may be qualitatively different from the first birth not only because of the presence of the firstborn child, but also because of the existence of new "parental imperatives" that may be perceived differentially by men and women. This period of role adjustment is potentially more complex in that now not only marital but also parent-child and the emerging sibling relationships must be considered. The second birth involves some degree of separation of mother and firstborn child. Distressful to the mother and the firstborn, the separation may also be especially stressful for the father, who may for the first time be asked to assume a more active or even a primary role in child care while serving as a liaison between hospitalized mother and the child at home. Researchers such as Robertson and Robertson (1971) and Bowlby (1969, 1973) have provided detailed descriptions of the emotional trauma experienced by the child when he or she is separated from the mother due to hospitalization, but little or no research has addressed the role of the father during this stressful time.

The period between the births of the first and second children might be conceptualized as a sort of on-the-job training for the father, so that he gradually acquires some definition of a parental role. Moreover, the period of time between the confirmation of the second pregnancy and the eventual delivery might be utilized to prepare the father for his eventual increase in child-care responsibilities. This preparation might be expected to impart minimal stress to the father, given the continued availability of reliable, established patterns of family functioning (i.e., the mother can assist the father should difficulties arise; see Hansen & Johnson, 1979). This suggests that fathers' assumption of greater responsibilities for caring for the firstborns, although perhaps not as stressful as that experienced by their wives at the first birth, constitutes a "new imperative" that places not only greater emphasis on their expressive, nurturant role rather than their supportive, provider role as breadwinner, but does so through a process potentially different from that affecting the mothers.

The second birth probably is experienced very differently by each parent, since the mystery and uncertainty associated with labor and delivery are not likely to be as great as at the first birth (Entwisle & Doering, 1981). In their longitudinal study of the first six months of parenthood, Entwisle and Doering report that, for middle-class couples, parental preparation classes were quite effective in aiding the initial adjustment to parenthood. This effectiveness is described as being due primarily to preparation for the birth experience itself, though preparation before birth did not appear to be very helpful in fostering role adjustment or integration. Entwisle and Doering interpret this situation by noting that during pregnancy the couple appeared to be unable to think beyond the birth event, hence any attempt to provide instruction concerning early parenting skills was rarely well received. Moreover, at the time of the second birth the parents simply had no time to contemplate the mysteries of labor and delivery because other needs and demands—the care of firstborn children—existed to divert their attention. The emergence of parental education programs designed to prepare parents and firstborn children for the birth of another child might be viewed as evidence of the parents' need for information on parenting rather than on the actual labor and delivery phases of childbirth.

Very few studies have addressed the issue of family development from a triadic to a tetradic system. Kreppner, Paulsen, and Schuetze (1982) describe numerous facets of familial development and interaction associated with the birth of a second child, and conclude that the father plays a crucial role at this point of intrafamilial dynamics because it depends on him whether the division of child care relieves the mother from being forced to "double" her existence for each child. These researchers describe the actual process of integrating the second child into the family as involving three phases: a *normalization* phase, lasting approximately eight months and concerning the reduction of the mother's preoccupation with the second child; a phase of *increased interest* on the parts of both father and firstborn child in the second child's development during the next eight months; and finally a *calming down* phase, lasting for the next eight months, as new family constellations of interaction are consolidated.

Kreppner et al. describe three primary strategies of role adjustment adopted by three-member families experiencing this process of integrating a new member: (a) The parents appear to be interchangeable and to double each other's activities; (b) the father looks after the firstborn child more regularly than before, thus allowing the mother to establish an intimate dyad with the new baby; or (c) the father takes more responsibility for household tasks and the mother takes primary responsibility for both children. The choice of strategy and the amount of time spent with the firstborn are determined in part by the parents' perceptions of the needs of the situation and of the second-born child in particular. It is important to note that each strategy serves to maintain family functioning following the birth of a second child by dividing the various tasks of child care and/or housekeeping between the parents. More important, each strategy entails a degree of reversal from the traditional division of responsibilities reported by Cowan et al. (1985), LaRossa and LaRossa (1981), Entwisle and Doering (1981), and Belsky, Ward, and Rovine (1986). The organization and consequences of these strategies over a two-year period have been described by Kreppner and his associates (Kreppner, 1986, 1987; Kreppner et al., 1982), and provide us with a detailed account of systemic fluctuations in both family constellations and dynamics, and of the father's role in "buffering" the mother as she works to integrate the new member into the family.

Although some of the longitudinal studies of maternal and paternal adjustment to pregnancy, birth, and parenthood described above included both primiparous and multiparous couples, a combination of factors potentially limit the interpretation of their results when one focuses on the issue of familial adjustment at the birth of a second child. Chief among these is the fact that Grossman et al. (1980) and Belsky and his colleagues (Belsky, Gilstrap, & Rovine, 1984; Belsky, Rovine, & Taylor, 1984; Belsky, Taylor, & Rovine, 1984) partitioned their samples into groups of first-time and experienced parents, with the latter imprecisely described as already having "from one to three children" or "a second or later-born child." Assuming that a new and salient "parental imperative" can be detected for fathers at the second birth, and that some shift toward shared responsibilities as described by Kreppner et al. might be found, I would hesitate to adopt such a design in order to detect it. Certainly the salience of each subsequent birth event, and the degree of role adjustment necessitated by the addition of more children, would diminish with each successive birth. Moreover, neither Grossman et al. nor Belsky et al. provide sufficient attention to the experienced fathers in describing their adjustments as being in any way different from that of primiparous fathers. For example, Grossman et al. report that at two months postpartum first-time fathers appeared to fulfill their fathering roles (defined in terms of quality of physical contact, degree of expressed affection, sensitivity and responsiveness, and acceptance of the infant) substantially better than did experienced fathers. The researchers suggest that this happened because experienced fathers were busy taking care of the older child(ren) at this stage, but no direct measures of paternal involvement or activity with older children were obtained. Even if we accept that these studies' definition of fathering in fact measures equivalent aspects in new and experienced fathers, one must be very cautious in interpreting these findings. In short, the potential increase in the fathers' participation in the family following the birth of a second child is an important issue that requires more careful scrutiny.

INCREASED PATERNAL PARTICIPATION

The results of the Kreppner et al. (1982) longitudinal study support the observation that men's family role participation has increased since the mid-1960s and early 1970s (Pleck, 1981). On the other hand, research focusing on fathers' involvement with their families has been equivocal to say the least. Recent studies have found that mothers attend to their infants more than fathers do even when the fathers are home from work (Parke & Tinsley, 1984), and even if both mother and father work outside the home (Coverman & Sheley, 1986). Although fathers have little contact with infants during the first few months after birth, they typically become more involved with them as they approach their first birthdays (Easterbrooks & Goldberg, 1984).

Even if fathers are beginning to increase their participation in the home, the consequences of this increased participation are mixed. Although it commonly has been found that increased participation brings fathers closer to their children and that this increase has a positive effect on the children as well as on the fathers (Baruch & Barnett, 1986; Gronseth, 1978; Hood & Golden, 1979; Radin, 1982; Russell, 1982), increased paternal involvement in child care often leads to increased tension and conflict associated with both the children and the wife (Hoffman, 1983; Lamb, Pleck, Charnov, & Levine, 1985; Russell, 1982; Russell & Radin, 1983). Much of this conflict is directly associated with the fathers' increased child-care and housekeeping activities in that mothers report dissatisfaction with the quality of the fathers' task performance. Russell (1982) has suggested that these conflicts may be due, in part, to mothers feeling that their traditional domains are threatened when fathers take over these tasks. Hoffman (1977) and Veroff, Douvan, and Kulka (1981) have made similar arguments in pointing out that motherhood is a major source of satisfaction and self-definition for women, and that, while most mothers desire more help from their husbands in child-care or housekeeping activities, an equal sharing of this role is quite threatening. This situation may be even more threatening for the modern mother who is not employed outside the home, and who may be suffering not so much from work overload as from anxiety about how valuable her contribution to the family may be in light of the trend toward increased maternal employment. In this case, increased paternal participation may heighten her fears that she is not a contributing member of the family who provides a unique and important service (Hoffman, 1979, 1983).

A number of factors have been identified that influence the father's potential to become more active in family life. Hoffman (1983) points to a general convergence of sex roles and notes that parents today are more flexible about divisions of labor, such that fathers' participation in traditional female child-care and housekeeping tasks is more widely acceptable (cf. Baruch & Barnett, 1981; Veroff et al., 1981). Radin (1981) suggests that the most important factor influencing paternal participation is that both spouses have grown up in families in which mothers were employed outside the home, especially when the wife found her own father's participation gratifying though not frequent enough. Russell (1982) found paternal participation highest in those families where the father could not obtain employment and the mother could, or where the couple felt that both incomes were needed and the best or only solution to the "child-care problem" was for the father to care for the children when the mother was at work.

Further support of this economic argument lies in the fact that fathers in dual-income families are more involved in housework and child care than are fathers in single-income families (Baruch & Barnett, 1981; Gold & Andres, 1978). This effect becomes even more pronounced when the mother is employed full-time (Hoffman, 1963), in families where the couples hold nontraditional attitudes concerning the roles of women (Baruch & Barnett, 1981), in only-child families where the child is a male (Barnett & Baruch, 1987), when there is more than one child (Walker & Woods, 1976), and when there are no other children (especially female) in the household old enough to assist in child-care activities (Hoffman, 1983). Barnett and Baruch (1987) also attempt to identify the determinants of fathers' participation in child-care and household chores. In doing so they identify five primary types of paternal involvement: total interaction time with child, solo interaction time, proportional interaction time, child-care tasks, and "feminine" household tasks. In families with employed mothers, the number of hours the wife worked per week was the strongest single predictor of the husband's participation in all forms except solo interaction and child-care tasks, where paternal participation could not be successfully predicted.

Crouter, Perry-Jenkins, Huston, and McHale (1987) conducted research focusing on the correlates of father involvement and found that fathers in dual-earner families performed twice as many solitary child-care activities as fathers in single-earner families. More important, their evidence suggests that different marital processes may underlie dual- and single-earner fathers' involvement with their children. Specifically, dual-earner fathers' involvement with child care was associated with lower levels of love and higher levels of negative interactions with their wives. It did not appear that the fathers were resentful of their wives' roles in the paid labor force; the more hours the wives worked, the more the husbands reported loving them. Instead, it appeared that their wives pressured them to become more involved in child care, and the negativism of the husbands was a reaction to this pressure. On the other hand, when single-earner fathers became involved it was probably because they felt comfortable with this activity. Perceived skill in child care was positively associated with involvement in child care with the spouse for single-earner fathers, but not for dual-earner fathers. These data indicate the importance of considering father involvement in the context of a family system.

Collectively, these findings suggest that paternal participation, especially in families with employed mothers, is less voluntary, less reflective of individual preference, and shaped primarily by the wives' employment-related demands. Unless the couple has resolved the issue of the wife's employment and already has adjusted and consolidated their roles and expectations, then one might assume that the consequences of the father's participation may be less positive, given Lamb et al.'s (1985) observation of an inverse relationship between the degree of choice a father has concerning his participation and the level of positive outcome from that participation.

Phyllis Berman and Frank Pedersen (1987) have greatly advanced our understanding of fatherhood in general and of men's transitions to parenthood in particular by collecting a number of studies of men's transitions to parenthood into a single volume. In addition to the contributions by Belsky, Cowan and Cowan, and Grossman, which continue to provide us with reports from their respective longitudinal projects, this volume includes reports from researchers such as Jane Dickie, Shirley Feldman, Frank Pedersen and his associates, Ross Parke and Edward Anderson, and Michael Yogman, all describing their own unique approaches to the study of familial, but especially paternal, adjustment to the transition to parenthood. These studies view the father in the context of the larger family unit and in relationship to other family subsystems, and emphasize the significance of the marriage relationship and the importance of wives' support for men's involvement with their infants.

Despite the diversity of approaches assumed by these researchers, a consistent pattern of results is found when their respective conclusions are compared. First, all of the researchers who compared the caregiving behavior of mothers and fathers found that mothers were far more involved in this activity than were fathers (Belsky & Volling, 1987; Cowan & Cowan, 1987; Dickie, 1987; Parke & Anderson, 1987). Cowan and Cowan add that this division of child-care responsibilities is far more traditional than either spouse had expected it to be. Dickie found that this disparity was often the source of considerable conflict between spouses. Interestingly, the absolute amount of father involvement was less important than how the parents functioned and how they ideally wanted to function. She reports that, although mothers and fathers wished ideally that fathers would participate more in all aspects of parenting, the mothers wanted even more father participation than the fathers did. The closer the father's participation was to his wife's perception of ideal, the more the wife felt supported in parenting. Cowan and Cowan provide an additional discussion of this theme by suggesting that the mother is often ambivalent about the father's role with the child. In particular, those mothers who have not yet fully developed career roles that can serve as a source of reward outside the family may have mixed feelings about increased paternal participation. Although the father's involvement might offer the mother some relief from the demands of primary caregiver for the infant, his efforts may be viewed as an encroachment upon the only domain that is solely hers.

Second, these studies provide evidence that it is important to consider the father's role as a parent and his direct interaction with his children, and to consider various forms of emotional support for competent fathering. In particular, these studies found that under conditions of low emotional support, fathers' parenting competence decreased disproportionately when compared with mothers' competence under similar situations. Fathers' parenting was found to be more dependent on spousal support than was mothers' parenting; indeed, the mothering system appeared to be more buffered or resilient than the fathering system. Belsky and Volling (1987) and Dickie (1987) in particular found that marriage and parenting were more closely related for men than for women, suggesting that the father's role is more sensitive to influence from marital factors than is the mother's role. Dickie (1987) suggests that changing cultural expectations are challenging the traditional emphasis on the father's provider role, and we are beginning to assume that men will assume more responsibility for the direct care of infants. She describes these men as entering parenthood "with 1980s demands and an upbringing that reflects values of the 1950s and 1960s" (p. 113). The wife's support of her husband then is viewed not only as a means of facilitating his child-care investment, but also as a means of lightening her own load.

In focusing upon the strains experienced by couples in general and fathers in particular, these researchers found that despite the pleasure and delight of becoming parents, many couples experience significant strain during the transition. Pedersen, Zaslow, Cain, Suwalsky, and Rabinovich (1987) found that fathers who reported feeling "the blues" interacted less with their infants than did a "no blues" group. Feldman (1987), in contrast, found a positive correlation between higher rates of infant caregiving and higher rates of perceived strain. It was interesting that men's reports of the adequacy of their marriages predicted their involvement with their infants, but not the strain associated with parenthood. Feldman suggests that it may be the case that the decision to accept more responsibility for parenting is experienced as discretionary by men more often than it is by women. She notes that while a nonsupportive marital relationship may lead to a father's disengagement from the child, he might not perceive it as a parenting strain, and that mothers may believe that they have no choice to disengage from the infant under such circumstances.

Finally, each of the studies found that phenomena such as strain and stress changed both qualitatively and quantitatively depending on the infant's age, and hence the parents' developmental changes with respect to the ontogeny of the family. Pedersen et al. (1987) suggest that no simple, single trajectory over time can be predicted from parental behaviors, attitudes, or self-reports during the prenatal phases to predict the course of the transition experience. Furthermore, Grossman's (1987) analysis of primiparous and multiparous fathers found that the experiences following the birth of a second child may change more radically for fathers than for mothers. In particular, she found that when a second-born child enters the family, the father often experiences an intensification of responsibility for the older child while the mother devotes herself more exclusively to the needs of the infant. (Note that this is identical to Kreppner et al.'s second pattern of adjustment observed in families experiencing the birth of a second child.) Grossman's observation of maternal and paternal differences in adjusting to first and subsequent childbirths further complicates the matter of making predictions from prenatal situations to postnatal behavior in that the father's and mother's behavior patterns must be considered in a complementary, systemic manner rather than in simple linear fashion.

THE FIRSTBORN'S ADJUSTMENT
TO THE BIRTH OF A SIBLING

The arrival of a sibling has been associated with marked changes in the behavior of firstborn children (Dunn, Kendrick, & MacNamee, 1981; Field & Reite, 1984; Henchie, 1963; Legg, Sherick, & Wadland, 1974; Nadelman & Begun, 1982) and with changes in the patterns of interaction between firstborn children and their mothers (Dunn & Kendrick, 1980; Kendrick & Dunn, 1980; Stewart, Mobley, Van Tuyl, & Salvador, 1987; Taylor & Kogan, 1973). Firstborn children are commonly found to exhibit distress during, as well as to derive benefits from, the changes in the family system surrounding the birth of a second child. This research generally supports the observation of Anna Freud (1965) that children sometimes show a rapid increase in developmental maturity during or after periods of stress. In particular, Nadelman and Begun (1982) found that, following the birth of a sibling, maternal ratings of many children either showed no changes or demonstrated improvement in specific behavior problems. Dunn et al. (1981) report that over 60% of the mothers in their sample indicated that their children showed signs of being more "grown up"—that is, more independent about feeding or toilet behavior, improved language ability, and so on—even though signs of "regression" also existed. Field and Reite (1984) detected an increase in fantasy play among preschool-age children who had new siblings. They interpret this play as an active form of coping with a new situation.

These findings suggest that the birth of a sibling represents a complex period of adjustment for the firstborn child. Dunn et al. (1981) acknowledge this complexity in suggesting that a single index of "disturbance" summarizing numerous different reactions is inappropriate because various reactions may differ in their prognostic implications. For example, increased withdrawal in the firstborn was associated with a poor relationship with the sibling at 14 months postpartum in their study, but increased negative or demanding behavior showed no such association. Dunn and Kendrick (1982) further report that children who frequently imitated the behavior of the newborn siblings were more likely to show warm, affectionate interest in their siblings over the next months, and that by 14 months postpartum the latter showed remarkably affectionate behavior toward them. They suggest that imitation of this sort should not be taken as a sign of regression, if this term is assumed to reflect disturbance and/or a poor prognosis for the child's familial relationships.

Dunn and Kendrick make it evident that one must be careful when employing the terms *dethronement, displacement,* or *regression,* which commonly have been associated with clinically based accounts of children's reactions to the birth of a sibling (cf. Black & Sturge, 1979; Petty, 1953). One also must recall that each of these terms possesses both a lay, or descriptive, connotation and a specific psychoanalytic meaning. In our previous longitudinal assessment of the firstborn's adjustment to the birth of a sibling, my colleagues and I used the term *regressive behavior* to refer to behaviors that parents typically mention as problems experienced with firstborn children as they adjust to a new sibling (Stewart et al., 1987). It is important to note that our (as well as Dunn & Kendrick's) use of this term is somewhat unfortunate if one assumes it necessarily to imply a psychoanalytically based defense process. Indeed, we suggest that greater insight into the process of the firstborn's adjustment to the birth of a sibling may be obtained by considering Trivers's (1974) concept of parent-offspring conflict. In describing what an offspring might do to deal with a parent who prematurely rejects, deserts, or weans the child, Trivers suggests that tactics such as mimicry or deception might be employed to make continued care of the first offspring attractive to the parent. That is, the offspring might revert to the gestures and actions of an earlier stage in order to induce continued investment on the part of the parent.

Trivers's notion of mimicry and deception (or "imitation," in Dunn & Kendrick's terms) is more fitting than the concept of regression in that it supposes an active search for a strategy to maintain or regain parental attention rather than reversal to a less mature stage of development. Logically, the strategy adopted would vary as a function of the child's gender, age, and even family interaction history. Indeed, from a family systems perspective, it is reasonable to suggest that the father's increased involvement in child-care activities following the birth of a second child (Belsky, Gilstrap, & Rovine, 1984; Grossman, 1987; Stewart et al., 1987) is, in part, a response to requests for care or interaction from the firstborn child seeking attention from sources other than his or her mother. Assuming this perspective gives us the opportunity to consider how the firstborn's behaviors and parental reactions to these behaviors might continue to shape one another, and hence the child's evolving strategy, in a circular manner (cf. P. Minuchin, 1985).

Stewart et al. (1987) interviewed 41 three-member middle-class families at 1 month prepartum and 1, 4, 8, and 12 months after the birth of a second child to assess the reaction and adjustment of firstborn children to this event. We also observed family members in a semistructured play session in order to obtain information concerning changes in familial interaction patterns. We found that the types and levels of responses displayed by the firstborn varied as functions of time elapsed since the birth and of the genders of both the first- and second-born children. Specifically, we found that the firstborn's initial responses were either imitations of the infant or confrontations with the mother or infant, whereas responses at 4 months postpartum were characterized by numerous anxiety behaviors but fewer imitations or confrontations, and later responses were primarily confrontations with the increasingly intrusive and independent infant. This pattern of change was conceptualized to be an alteration of strategies as the firstborn children sought to regain or maintain parental involvement within changing family conditions.

Furthermore, Stewart et al. found that a greater frequency of problematic behavior was reported by the mothers of same-sex sibling dyads, especially at the 1- and 8-month postpartum assessments. Observational data indicated that mothers dramatically decreased their interactions with the firstborn children over time, but that fathers tended to remain relatively stable in their frequencies of interaction. These data will be discussed in more detail in a later chapter.

Nadelman and Begun (1982) have addressed the issues of child gender and age and have provided evidence that, following the birth of a sibling, younger children, especially boys, show greater overall distress as identified by increased use of pacifiers, toilet accidents during the day, and increased wetting of the bed at night, whereas older children tend to show less distress and to express it through problems related to proximity maintenance (e.g., difficulty in being left with a sitter, following mother around the house, not playing well with other children). Dunn et al. (1981) have noted a similar age effect in that problems with increased clinging behavior were reported more frequently in younger children. Henchie (1963; cited in Moore, 1969) has reported effects related to both the gender and age of the newborn; according to her data, a male infant sibling evokes a more negative response from firstborn boys than does a female, whereas for girls, a male infant is more likely to be associated with a greater disturbance in the mother-child relationship. Additionally, Henchie found that older siblings' reactions to the new sibling tended to deteriorate somewhat as the baby grew into a "play-disrupting toddler." Although these age effects may seem meager when compared to the scopes of both the Nadelman and Begun and the Dunn and Kendrick projects, they suggest a potentially fruitful direction for further study of the firstborn's adjustment to the birth of a sibling.

The issue of individual differences in the firstborn's reaction and adjustment to the arrival of a sibling should not be ignored. Temperamental differences between the firstborn children assessed before the birth of a sibling have been linked to differences in the children's immediate reaction to the arrival of a sibling, and to the incidence of fearful worrying and anxious behavior during the subsequent year (Dunn & Kendrick, 1982). Specifically, Dunn and Kendrick report that children who were characteristically "negative in mood" on a temperament assessment were more likely to increase in withdrawal and to have more sleeping problems after the birth. Moreover, those children who were both "negative in mood" and "extreme in emotional intensity" were likely to respond by increased clinging to their mothers, and were more likely to experience increased and persistent fears and worries and to display ritualistic behavior. Children described as being extremely "unmalleable" tended to have feeding problems and to demand more attention from their mothers, and were more likely to protest the interaction between their mothers and the newborn siblings. Interestingly, these differences associated with the temperament of the firstborn child were found with measures of mother-firstborn interaction, but not with measures of sibling interaction, thus suggesting that the child's relationship with the mother is highly associated with his or her temperament style (cf. Dunn & Kendrick, 1982, p. 170).

SPECIFIC OBJECTIVES
OF THIS PROJECT

The purpose of the study reported in this volume was to assess, longitudinally, familial adjustment in general and parental role adjustment in particular following the birth of a second child, so that a more complete understanding of the transition to parenthood might be obtained. The Double ABCX model of family stress and the Family Adjustment and Adaptation Response process model of family adjustment and accommodation developed by McCubbin and Patterson (1982, 1983) have been utilized to organize this study of the parents' subjective appraisal of and response to this life event. The focus of the discussion will be on (a) the pileup of demands that family members experience during this transition period as they attempt to adjust (the systemic property of adaptive self-regulation) and maintain their way of living (the systemic properties of maintaining invariant relations, homeostasis, equilibration, or morphostasis), (b) the coping processes and/or changes the family members make to achieve this end (the systemic property of adaptive self-organization or morphogenesis), and (c) the new sense of cohesion acquired as the family members adjust to their new roles and newly adapted family system.

Specific objectives of this longitudinal study of familial adjustment following the birth of a second child might be thought of as pertaining to one of three aspects of family functioning. First are those areas pertaining to parental stress and support resources: (a) to compare maternal and paternal levels and sources of stress, as well as changes in these levels and sources, from the third trimester of pregnancy throughout the one-year period following the birth of a second child; (b) to compare maternal and paternal sources of support and levels of satisfaction with parenting over this time period; and (c) to assess the relationship among parental stressors, support, and satisfaction to determine how stress is buffered by support networks for each parent. Second, in the general area of family organization and functioning, the goals are (d) to describe parental role differentiations and adjustments adopted by the parents over this time period and (e) to describe changes in the structure of family organization over time. Third, the goals pertaining to the general area of parent-child and child-sibling relations include the following: (f) to assess the firstborn's adjustment to having a sibling and the parents' reactions to this process of adjustment, (g) to assess the role of initial differences in temperament on the firstborn's adjustment process and to note changes in the perceived temperament of the children over the transition period, and (h) to assess changes in the pattern or style of parent-child interaction over this transition period.

PART II

The Method

When I was a student at Penn State, one of my professors in human development and family studies described the eclectic theorist/researcher as someone who has one of each of his or her feet firmly planted on two clouds that are ever so slowly moving away from each other. The process of grounding a research project in systems theory might be described in much the same way. Our discipline's research techniques and analytic methods favor reductionism and independence rather than holism, interdependence, and circularity. While we were planning the data collection procedures for this project, one of the undergraduate research assistants questioned whether I knew my "causes" from the "effects"; this question occasionally has been raised by reviewers as well. Initially, I responded to such queries with some facetious, off-the-cuff remark, but now I feel much more comfortable simply saying, "You're absolutely correct, and I doubt you really do either!" The notions of cause and effect, and even of dependent and independent variables, take on new meanings in a systemic analysis.

Some researchers have attempted to realize the essence of systems theory by transforming their dependent variables into a composite score (a sum, a ratio, or a difference) to represent the overall or relative contributions of the various components of the system. Although this approach may be useful in particular instances (e.g., the couples' marital quality score used by Belsky, Spanier, & Rovine, 1983), it should not be used indiscriminately—there should be some reason for combining or transforming scores, some evidence that the two variables are systemically related prior to making the transformation. Given the exploratory nature of this project, I have purposely refrained from developing any such transformed scores and have instead decided to achieve a systemic nature in another way. Specifically, I have chosen to measure as many different aspects of family adjustment and functioning as my subjects and research assistants would tolerate, and to treat these measures both as dependent variables and, in subsequent analyses, as independent factors.

97

In this way any given measure might be conceptualized as an outcome or as the cause of other outcomes. The interdependence of variables and the circularity of causality thus would be ascertained across analyses, rather than within a single analytic procedure.

Linda Thompson, editor of the New Perspectives on Family series, suggested that I introduce the following chapter with a brief note describing the more subjective aspects involved in conducting this, or indeed any, long-term research project. This research effort was conducted at a small liberal arts university that holds a strong commitment to undergraduate teaching. Indeed, no graduate students were involved in this research project. Two of the students in my upper-level research design course collaborated to develop the basic design of this longitudinal effort. A small group of sophomores, not all psychology majors, were then recruited from my child development course and invited to join a team of student researchers in a two-year project. The two students who had worked to develop the basic framework for the overall project then focused their attention on the tasks of training the others to be interviewers and observers (Linda A. Mobley) and of continuing to conduct literature reviews and of developing interview protocols (Susan S. Van Tuyl).

When data collection began, we had trained five undergraduate students to conduct the interviews and observations. Individual members of this team assumed primary responsibility for various aspects of the overall project, with tasks typically defined with respect to the measurement involved, such as parental stress, familial division of task responsibility, and firstborn child adjustment. Regular meetings of this research team were scheduled so that leaders of each topic area could report the status of their efforts, and so that all team members could learn the statistical procedures that would be utilized in the months to come. When it became apparent that this group was becoming overwhelmed with data, another student (Myrna A. Salvador) was added to the team to function primarily as a data-base manager and data analyst.

Throughout the duration of this collaborative effort, all the members of the research team were involved in various interpersonal activities we referred to as the "Care and Feeding of Valued Researchers." In considering the longitudinal projects described in Chapter 2, one should take the time to recognize the administrative demands necessary to coordinate and conduct research of this scope. These projects involved not only the interdisciplinary collaboration of professionals, but also the long-term coordinated efforts of graduate research assistants and the mutual efforts necessary to sustain the interest and cooperation of both the subjects and researchers themselves. When we debate the virtues and methodological complexities of longitudinal research we rarely describe the "costs" imposed on the people involved in conducting those projects. Too often we focus all of our attention on the products of these research efforts and fail to recognize the important role of competent administration in the successful completion of these endeavors.

I have no doubt that most, if not all, longitudinal projects require such activities from time to time, but I never have found any discussion of the matter in any research methodology course or book. We teach design and analytic procedures, but issues of the interpersonal dynamics necessary for these procedures to work are often ignored. The students who worked on this project were novices when they began, but they were determined not to be "go-fers" who merely performed tasks; everyone wanted to know and understand every aspect of the project, and we took the time to make sure this opportunity was not missed. The approach greatly decreased the speed with which the project was completed, but provided a number of undergraduate students the opportunity to develop research skills not commonly found in their peers.

Methods sections tend to be notoriously boring, but methodological details are important to many readers. Chapter 3 and its associated appendices describe the families involved in this study and the procedures used to conduct this longitudinal assessment of their adjustment to the birth of a second child. Background information on each of the instruments employed is provided as well. Readers not interested in this detail can go directly to the presentations of our findings in Part III, Chapters 4 through 7.

3

The Families and Our Methods for Studying Them

SUBJECTS

Participants in the 15-month longitudinal study were 41 families who lived in the suburbs of a midwestern metropolitan area and who were anticipating the birth of a second child. Families were recruited through newspaper articles, appearances by the author on local television talk shows, advertisements on cable television, and posters placed in obstetricians' and pediatricians' waiting rooms. Some of the subject families were obtained through mother-to-mother referrals once an initial core of families had been contacted. All the mothers were in the third trimester of their second pregnancies, and were married to the fathers of their firstborn children. The average length of marriage for the couples was 4.24 years (SD = .8 years). The mean ages for the mothers and fathers at the beginning of the study were 29.4 and 30.8 years, respectively. Most of the parents had completed college (74% of the fathers and 61% of the mothers), and some held graduate-level degrees (20% of the fathers and 15% of the mothers). All the fathers and 41% of the mothers were employed at the beginning of the study.

Given our interest in considering the family as the unit of analysis and the fact that our sample included many families with both spouses working, we wanted to assess household socioeconomic status with a method that incorporated the status of both the husband's and the wife's occupations when both were employed. The Household Prestige Scale developed by Rossi, Sampson, Bose, Jasso, and Passel (1974) provides an index of household socioeconomic status that is derived from a linear combination of husband and wife occupational prestige scores and their respective education levels. Occupational prestige scores are based on Siegel,

Hodge, and Rossi's (1975) work with the National Opinion Research Center, which routinely rates occupational data on a 100-point scale in terms of the general public's estimate of social standing or prestige. These ratings then are grouped to create a hierarchy of nine levels of occupation. Differential weightings for husband and wife occupation and education levels have been empirically derived and have been found to be highly stable and reliable (Rossi et al., 1974). The mean household social prestige rating for the sample was 61.09 ($SD = 8.45$), with most families (64%) categorized as Level III, IV, or V, that is, upper-middle- to middle-class. Subjects whose household social prestige ratings placed them in Level III had occupations such as high school teacher, college professor, electrical engineer, automotive body design engineer, registered nurse, or attorney. Those with Level IV ratings had occupations such as police officer, sales manager, or accountant; those with Level V ratings had occupations such as graphic artist, office administrator, service manager for automobile dealership, or social worker.

Of the firstborn children, 25 were male and 16 were female. The mean age of the firstborns at the time of the birth of the second child was 36 months ($SD = 1.8$ months; mode and median also 36 months), with approximately equal numbers of 2-, 3-, and 4-year-olds. Of the second-born children, 20 were male and 21 were female; the resultant sex composition of the sibling dyads was 15 both male, 10 older boys with younger sisters, 5 older girls with younger brothers, and 11 both female. All second-born children were delivered without major unexpected complications (8 were planned cesarean-section deliveries). The breakdown of families by age of firstborn and dyad gender composition is presented in Table 3.1.

Nearly all the parents (95%) participated in some form of childbirth preparation classes prior to the birth of their first child, with Lamaze classes representing the most typical type of class utilized (97%). Over 90% of the fathers were present at the birth of the firstborn child, with only 4 fathers indicating that circumstances beyond their control prohibited their presence or participation. The number of families involved in prenatal preparation classes was slightly lower at the second birth, with only 80% of the families enrolled in classes. It is important to note that the majority of those electing to take the classes prior to the second birth did not merely repeat the same type of class as attended before. Instead, 85% of those taking any class elected to take an abbreviated Lamaze program that included a special section on preparing the firstborn child, and 9% attended hospital-based programs focusing on sibling prepara-

Table 3.1 Breakdown of Sibling Dyads by Age of Firstborn Child and Dyad Gender Composition

Age of Firstborn	Both Girls	Older Girl and Younger Boy	Older Boy and Younger Girl	Both Boys	Total
2-year olds $M = 23.19$ months $SD = 2.59$ months	4	1	2	6	13
3-year-olds $M = 36.43$ months $SD = 5.04$ months	3	4	3	5	15
4-year-olds $M = 51.73$ months $SD = 4.99$ months	4	0	5	4	13
Total	11	5	10	15	41

SOURCE: From R. B. Stewart, L. A. Mobley, S. S. Van Tuyl, and M. A. Salvador, "The Firstborn's Adjustment to the Birth of a Sibling: A Longitudinal Assessment, *Child Development, 58,* 341-355. Copyright 1987 by the Society for Research in Child Development. Reprinted by permission.

tion. When asked during the third trimester of pregnancy, all the fathers indicated that it was their intention to be present at the birth of the second child. None of the parents participating in this study knew the gender of their infant prior to delivery. When queried concerning their preferences for the gender of the second-born children, fathers were equally divided among those wanting males, those wanting females, and those having no preference; mothers, on the other hand, revealed a preference for daughters (43.9%) rather than sons (19.5%). A further analysis of these data revealed that fathers had a strong preference for wanting the second child to be of the opposite gender from the firstborn; that is, fathers wanted to have a child of each gender ($\chi^2 (2) = 11.18; p < .01$). Although mothers reported a strong desire for daughters if their firstborns were boys, they did not express a clear preference for sons if they already had daughters ($\chi^2 (2) = 9.14; p < .01$).

For these families, preparation for the birth of the second child involved more than just attending classes. Many parents indicated that their attendance of these classes had been mandated by various hospital policies so that the husbands would be allowed to be present during labor and delivery. Although a wide range of preparatory activities were reported across the sample of parents, reading books or magazine articles focusing on labor, delivery, breast-feeding, basic child care, and preparing the firstborn child to become a sibling was clearly the most common. Most of the mothers (73%) and some of the fathers (34%) reported that they read things to prepare themselves for the approaching birth event. More than 39 titles were mentioned by the parents, with the most common being *Parent Magazine* (published by Gruner + Jahr USA Publishing, New York); *Thank You, Dr. Lamaze*, by Marjorie Karmel (1983); *Your Second Child*, by Joan Solomon Weiss (1981); and *Baby and Child Care*, by Benjamin Spock and Michael Rothenberg (1985). Moreover, most of the mothers (56%) and fathers (66%) reported that they had read to their children two or more books dealing with birth and/or siblings. When asked precisely what they had read to their firstborn children, the parents listed 30 different titles. Those most commonly mentioned were *The Berenstein Bears' New Baby*, by Stan and Jan Berenstein (1974), and *Nobody Asked Me If I Wanted a Baby Sister* and *When That Baby Comes, I'm Moving Out*, both by Martha Alexander (1971, 1979). Other preparatory activities included things such as painting rooms in the house, getting baby furniture out of storage, or purchasing infant-care items.

PROCEDURES

Parents recruited to participate in this study were interviewed first via telephone to establish that they met basic sample requirements (e.g., that mothers were in or nearly in the third trimester of their second pregnancy, that only one firstborn child existed who was the offspring of these parents, and that they did not anticipate leaving the area for at least the next 15 months). The general purposes, objectives, and procedures of the study were described and, if the potential participants remained interested, a visit to the family's home by an undergraduate research assistant was scheduled. Nearly all the potential participants (95%) who met the basic requirements agreed to participate in the study. None of the families received any monetary remuneration in exchange for participation. Detailed summary letters describing the results of the project were promised and delivered, as were a number of informal oral presentations describing the project and its findings. Gifts were given to the children at the first postpartum visit as a goodwill gesture. Infants received items such as small squeeze toys, rattles, gripping toys or teething rings, and firstborn children received sets of bubbles and wands, toy cars, hand puppets, or books. Moreover, the firstborn children were sent greeting cards on their birthdays. All the families remained in the study until its completion.

So that the families would experience continuity in the interviewer/observer who came to their homes, five female undergraduate research assistants each were assigned six to eight families to follow over the full course of the study. Home visits were scheduled for 1 month prior to the birth of the second child, and for 1, 4, 8, and 12 months postpartum. The selection of these times was based upon juggling three sets of criteria: the developmental status of the second-born children, the various phases of the Family Adjustment and Adaptation Response process model, and the time with respect to the calendar year. Although these factors might appear to be independent, we did not want to risk confounding our data by having second births occur throughout the year. Our concern focused on the question of how the adjustment of the firstborn child might differ if the sibling arrived during the winter, when the mother and two children were more likely to be confined to the house, from if the birth occurred during the spring, when it was possible to get the firstborns outside. Moreover, in scheduling the future home visits we needed to consider things such as normative vacation times for our families (June and/or July) and traditional holidays (Thanksgiving and Christmas), when a home visit might be perceived as intrusive.

Subject recruitment began in January 1983, and, based on the approximate delivery dates provided by the mothers and their obstetricians, we assumed that most second-born children would be born somewhere between mid-March and late May. This window of time became the primary limitation for our pool of potential subject families. The 1-month prepartum and postpartum visits thus were conducted in March and April, and April and May, respectively. The two visits were conceptualized as providing pre- and postmeasures of the Adjustment Phase of the FAAR model. We had hoped that the next assessment would represent a time when the family had begun to reorganize its methods of functioning, but not consolidated this reorganization—that is, the early Restructuring subphase of the FAAR model. By operationalizing this time period as being 4 months postpartum, we were able to avoid the difficulty of scheduling home visits during the months of June and July. The 8-month postpartum assessment was selected to correspond to a period of important transitions for the newborn child (e.g., beginning to locomote, fear of strangers; see Kagan, Kearsley, & Zelazo, 1978), and thus provided an additional measure of this restructuring phase. By scheduling these visits in January and February we were able to avoid collecting data during the end-of-year holiday season. The last observation, scheduled for 12 months postpartum, was assumed to correspond to the second phase of family adaptation, the Consolidation subphase of the FAAR model, and to provide a benchmark of closure for the families.

Every home visit included the following assessments:

(1) The mother and the father were interviewed separately (in random order and out of hearing range of each other) using a structured interview composed of both open-ended and forced-choice items.

(2) While one of the parents was being interviewed, the other was asked to complete any of a number of standard instruments designed to assess perceived level of parental stress, perceived level of social support, and the temperamental style of family members.

(3) Firstborn children were interviewed (out of hearing range of the parents, if possible) using a structured interview of open-ended items.

(4) An observation of familial interaction in a semistructured situation was made by asking the family members to work together to build something out of wooden blocks or some other toy construction medium supplied by the interviewer/observer.

Since one of the assessment instruments (the Parenting Stress Index) was especially long, it was distributed to the parents two days prior to the scheduled home visit so that the parents could complete it and give it to the interviewer. Detailed descriptions of the assessment instruments are provided below.

INTERVIEWS

The primary focus of each of the five sets of interviews varied to reflect the principal concerns affecting the families at that time. The prenatal interview concentrated on obtaining a description of what the parents had done to prepare themselves and their firstborn child for the birth of a sibling, and on what the children understood about what was about to happen within their families. The first postpartum interview focused on obtaining an evaluation of these preparatory measures, an assessment of the newborn's temperament style, and an appraisal of the initial adjustments of both parents and firstborn children to having this infant in the family. The subsequent postpartum interviews then obtained assessments concerning various aspects of familial adjustment including sibling, parent-child, and marital relations, role adjustments and integration, and overall satisfaction with family life.

Research assistants were trained over a six-month period, during which they conducted trial interviews with volunteer mothers and fathers who were not part of the sample. These interviews were videotaped so that the performance of each interviewer could be analyzed and critiqued by the entire group of researchers. Once the interviewers reached an acceptable level of proficiency, some of the training sessions were "fixed" so that the researchers would have to adjust to difficult, sullen, or even verbally hostile subjects. For example, in some cases the volunteer mothers and fathers were being interviewed for the third or fourth time by the same researcher, and were complaining of growing tired and bored with our project. This training procedure initially was not well received by the group of interviewers, but they later acknowledged that the preparation was helpful when some of the parents in the formal sample became uncooperative or fatigued.

Parental Interviews

In most respects, the maternal and paternal interviews were identical. During the first postpartum interview many of the fathers had difficulty answering questions concerning the typical daily interactions of their children or the adjustments of their firstborn children without seeking confirmation for their responses or assistance from their wives. When informed that we wanted their own appraisals of the situations and not just confirmation of what their wives did (or would) tell us during their interview sessions, many of the fathers commented that it made no sense to them that we would be interested in their imperfect knowledge. Indeed, some of the fathers became so concerned about their abilities to provide accurate data that they simply refused to provide responses to items for which they felt unsure rather than risk providing misinformation. It is important to note that this refusal did not occur in a manner that was negative or suggestive of a lack of cooperation. The fathers appeared instead to be motivated by a genuine interest in the accuracy of the project. We therefore allowed the fathers to skip these questions and focus on those items describing their interactions and relationships with their wives and children.

In each interview, mothers were asked open-ended questions concerning their children's adjustments to the impending birth (prepartum), the introduction of the infant to the family (1-month postpartum), or the presence of a sibling (remaining three postpartum sessions). They were also asked to rate their children's overall adjustments at that point in time on a scale from 0 to 10 (0 = adjustment far less than expected/desired; 5 = adjustment about as expected/desired; 10 = adjustment far better than expected). After completing these ratings, the mothers were shown a list of 14 commonly reported behavior problems, with the explanation that these problems had been identified as areas of concern by other parents. The mothers were asked to indicate which, if any, had become problems with their firstborn children since the births of the infants (an additional "Other, please specify" category was included, but was rarely used by the mothers). We chose not to present this list at the prepartum visit because we did not want to risk sensitizing mothers to looking for particular types of responses or adjustment problems in their children. At the 1- and 4-month postpartum sessions, interviewers questioned each maternal report of a current problem to clarify that the problem had arisen since the birth of the infant and was not merely the continuation of an ongoing situation.

The list of the 14 problem areas was derived from the results of an emic analysis of parental interviews focusing on sibling relationships (Stewart, Van Tuyl, & Vala-Rossi, 1983). Harris (1968) defines *emic research* as focusing on "contrasts and discriminations significant, meaningful, real, accurate, or in some other fashion regarded as important by the actors themselves" (p. 571). A sample of 141 multiparous mothers, from the same socioeconomic status and geographic region as this sample, had been interviewed previously to obtain, among other things, examples of typical problems of adjustment displayed by firstborn children following the birth of a sibling. Items mentioned by at least 25% of these mothers were included in our list of 14 problem areas.

The decision to use a procedure based on our own emic data rather than adopt a preexisting instrument such as the Nadelman and Begun (1982) 26-item scale (or their derived 4-factor, 18-item scale) was based on two considerations: (a) our emic data provided a contemporary description of maternal concerns during the early postpartum period, and (b) the Nadelman and Begun factors were derived from items adapted from the posthospitalization questionnaire of Vernon, Foley, Sipowicz, and Schulman (1965), and utilizes prepartum rather than postpartum assessments of firstborn behaviors, thus complicating the question of their application for our needs. Nevertheless, our 14 items are quite similar to those described by Nadelman and Begun and may be conceptually grouped and statistically clustered into three primary sets of behaviors that bear a strong similarity to Nadelman and Begun's Immature Behavior, Proximity Maintenance, and Frustration/Aggression Factors. Specifically, our scales consist of (a) an Imitation group, including problems in toilet training, eating habits, methods of playing with toys, using baby talk, demanding a bottle/pacifier at bedtime and demanding a bottle/pacifier during the day; (b) an Anxiety group, including increased crying, increased clinging, increased use of security objects, and/or increased withdrawal; and (c) a Confrontation/Aggression group, including general confrontations and inappropriate physical acts (e.g., hitting, squeezing, slapping) directed at the baby, mother, father, or inanimate objects. The presence or absence of each of the 14 types of behavior was scored at each postpartum assessment.

The five parental interviews varied in content to reflect the principal issues facing the parents at that point in time. The prenatal interview focused on obtaining a description of the preparatory activities of the parents prior to the birth of their second child. The 1-month postpartum interview was designed to obtain an evaluation of these preparatory activities and a subjective description of family adjustment immediately surrounding the birth of the child. The 4-month postpartum interview explored issues of postpartum depression as well as descriptions of the time each parent spent with his or her spouse, firstborn child, and infant. At 8 months postpartum these questions were supplemented with others designed to provide more detail concerning the interaction of the two children. Finally, the 12-month postpartum interview included all these items plus a number of summation items asking parents to describe the past year's most significant changes in themselves and in their relationships with their spouse and children. The parents also were asked what advice, if any, they would offer to parents about to have their second child. Each of the five sets of parental interviews closed by asking the parent to describe the personal highlight of the previous week. This open-ended question quickly became a focal point of the interview for many of the parents, as they described personal or family events in vivid and elaborate detail.

Child Interviews

The interviews with the firstborn children, like those with their parents, varied in content over the course of the project. Every effort was made to interview the children in a setting where the parents would be physically close enough to make the children feel secure, yet not so close that the children's responses would be overheard by their parents. A few of the younger children requested and were permitted to sit on their mothers' laps during the initial interview, but all were interviewed alone at the next session. Many of the interviews took place as the research assistant and the child played together with some of the child's favorite toys.

The initial interview opened by asking the children if they knew that something special was going to happen soon in the family. If this introduction did not produce a discussion of the impending birth of a sibling, the interviewer directly asked, "Is your mom going to have a baby?" This question was followed by queries concerning the children's feelings about having a new baby, their thoughts about what sorts of things little babies did, and whether they would rather have a baby brother or sister. Subsequent interviews continued to explore the children's feelings about having a sibling by asking what they specifically liked and did not like about the baby, and whether they were happy that the baby was a brother/sister. The children were also asked whether they helped their mothers or fathers around the house, whether they helped in taking care of the baby, and, in each case, what specifically they liked and did not like to do in these endeavors. Questions concerning the interactions between the older children and their siblings were expanded in the 4-, 8-, and 12-month postpartum interviews by asking whether they played together, what sorts of things they played, and whether the older children attempted to teach the younger siblings. The closing questions of the last interview concerned whether the older child would like to have another baby brother or sister—if so, which and why; and if not, why not.

OBSERVATIONS OF
FAMILY INTERACTION

To observe familial interaction, interviewers asked family members to work together to build something out of wooden blocks or some other toy construction medium. Different play materials were used for each observation session, with the exception of the first and last sessions, in which the same materials were used. A random rotation of focal-individual time samples was obtained (see Altmann, 1974), with the behavior of each individual recorded for a 15-second period consisting of three 5-second units before the focus was shifted to another family member. If the focal individual was involved in some form of interpersonal interaction during a particular 5-second unit, then the behavior of each of the participants was recorded. A total of 15 minutes of interaction was recorded, resulting in 20 samples of 15 seconds' duration for each of mother, father, and child behaviors in the prepartum observation, and 15 such samples for each of the four family members in the postpartum sessions when the infant was also present. Obviously the newborns could not be expected to participate actively in these early postpartum sessions. The parents were, nonetheless, asked to have the infant in the room during these sessions if possible. The total number of behaviors per family member could exceed these figures if the person was involved in numerous interactions.

Observation Coding System

Behaviors recorded included the following:

(1) *talk:* verbal statements about the task or other family members in either neutral or positive manner

(2) *exploration:* verbal statements or suggestions concerning what might be done or what might be built (e.g., "What should we build?" or "Does that plane need anything else?")

(3) *declaration:* verbal statements to specify what will be done or what will be built (e.g., "Let's build a house.")

(4) *redirect:* verbalization or physical gesture functioning to keep another family member occupied with the building task or to return another's attention to the task

(5) *show:* a physical demonstration, in either neutral/positive or negative manner, of how to build a certain object or complete a phase of the construction

(6) *refusal:* verbal or physical indication of unwillingness to abide by another's declaration (e.g., "No, I don't want to build a house.")

(7) *prescriptive command:* statement or gesture functioning to maintain another's participation by indicating what the other is to do (e.g., "Do this" or "Hand me that block.")

(8) *proscriptive command:* statement or gesture functioning to maintain or restrict another's participation by indicating what the other is not to do (e.g., "Don't take that—it's mine.")

(9) *positive reinforcement:* reward of either verbal or physical mode

(10) *onlook:* when the focal subject watches the activity of the others

(11) *off task:* when the focal subject is not involved in the building task or is out of the room

Observer Training and Reliability

Observers were trained using a set of three pilot tapes created and coded under "ideal" conditions when the videotape could be stopped and replayed so as to provide the best possible means of obtaining an accurate and complete code. Training continued until all observers (coding under "real-life" conditions, i.e., the videotape could not be stopped) reached an 88% agreement criterion with each of the behavior categories. Agreement was assessed by computing a Pearson correlation coefficient for a set of 38 behaviors derived by expanding the list of behaviors described above to include specific behaviors directed by one particular family member to another. Tests were made to determine that slopes did not differ from unity and that intercepts did not differ from the origin to ensure further that similar code procedures were being employed across observers (cf. Stewart & Amaranth, 1983). Another set of three pilot tapes was similarly coded and then reserved to assess intraobserver agreement levels over the 15 months necessary to complete this study. These tapes were coded by the observers during the two weeks prior to the first home observation, and then were presented randomly without warning to the observers at eight points throughout the duration of the study. Agreement levels with the original code for each tape were assessed on a within-coder basis, and ranged between .83 and .98 throughout the duration of the study.

SCALES AND QUESTIONNAIRES

Considering both Gutmann's (1975) observations of gender differences in the response to the initial parental imperative and Kreppner, Paulsen, and Schuetze's (1982) descriptions of numerous patterns of familial adjustment at the second birth, we felt it necessary that instruments be selected to obtain broad multidimensional assessments of individual and couple adaptation to the birth of a second child. This selection process was further guided by the adoption of a social support model suggesting that the ease of transition at this point of family development would be determined largely by the nature and availability of a number of social supports, both internal and external to the family unit (cf. Cohen & Wills, 1985; Power & Parke, 1984). Specifically, we assumed parental stress to be the inverse of "ease of transition," and that the nature and magnitude of this stress would vary as a function of the levels of social support received from various sources, satisfaction with these support levels, and satisfaction with acquired parental role.

The following scales were completed at various points throughout the study:

(1) A version of Abidin's (1983) Parenting Stress Index, Form 5 (PSI) was completed separately by each parent within three days after the prepartum visit, and again just prior to (within three days of) the 4- and 12-month postpartum visits.

(2) A version of Cowan, Cowan, Coie, and Coie's (1978) Who Does What? Index was completed at the prepartum and 12-month postpartum visits.

(3) Crnic, Greenberg, Ragozin, Robinson, and Basham's (1983) Questionnaire on Social Support and Satisfaction with Parenting Scale were completed at each of the five interview sessions.

(4) The Rothbart (1981) Infant Behavior Questionnaire (IBQ) was completed by the mothers at 4 and 12 months postpartum.

(5) Lerner, Palermo, Spiro, and Nesselroade's (1982) Dimensions of Temperament Survey (DOTS) was completed by mothers and fathers; mothers and fathers provided self-evaluations at the prepartum and 12-month postpartum sessions, and mothers provided additional evaluations of the firstborn children at the prepartum and the 4- and 12-month postpartum sessions.

The PSI is rather large; the selection of this index as our principal assessment instrument demanded that the other indices be considerably shorter lest we risk overburdening our subjects.

The Parenting Stress Index

The Parenting Stress Index, developed by Abidin and his associates (Abidin, 1979, 1983; Burke & Abidin, 1980), was selected to provide assessments of the sources and levels of parental stress. It was thought that this index would provide a means of quantifying the parental perceptions of the transition event (the a and c, and aA and cC portions of the Double ABCX model) with respect to its degree of stressfulness. This instrument was developed to assist in the identification of parent-child systems under stress and at risk for the development of dysfunctional behaviors. Stress emanating from three domains—characteristics of the child, parent, and situational/demographic context—is assessed, and the use of 16 subdomain scores helps to identify specific sources of stress. Early research by Jenkins (1982) and Lafiosca (1981) indicates that the PSI is highly correlated with the State-Trait Anxiety Scale (.71 with state and .84 with trait subscales), a scale that is commonly employed in research on the initial transition to parenthood. Furthermore, the PSI appears to be sensitive to differences in the levels of support received by parents (Lawrence, 1982), and to be correlated significantly with marital adjustment (−.58 and −.44 for women and men, respectively) as assessed by the Locke-Wallace test (Awalt, 1981).

The PSI is a self-report instrument designed to identify parent and child systems that are subjectively perceived to be under stress. The instrument was designed to yield a total index score of stress in the parent-child system. It was anticipated that if this total score was found to be significantly different from the norms, then that score could be partitioned and analyzed as various domain and subscale scores, so that researchers and clinicians can focus on the various sources of stress. In designing the index a number of items were assigned to a priori domain scales (Child Characteristics, Mother Characteristics, and Situational/Demographic Characteristics) based on their face validity and the research domain represented. Nearly all of the items on the PSI are structured so that the parent is requested to indicate his or her level of agreement with a statement using a 5-point continuum ranging from 1 (strongly agree) to 5 (strongly disagree); a few items simply require that parents indicate whether a specific event has occurred in their family. Over 95% of the items on the PSI are directly related to specific research findings concerning the pressures and stresses present in raising children. The PSI was factor analyzed and a two-factor solution was developed accounting for 26% of the total variance. Although this figure might seem relatively low, it is in keeping with Abidin's (1983) position that stress is a multifaceted phenomenon affected by relatively discrete sources (Burke & Abidin, 1980). The first factor in order of magnitude (19.6% of the variance) contained items from the Mother Characteristics domain, and the second (6.6% of the variance) largely contained items from the Child Characteristics domain.

The Mother Characteristics domain has been renamed the Self or Parent domain for its use in this project to emphasize that both mothers and fathers may experience stress associated with raising children. The Self domain includes 71 items distributed among the following 8 subscales: depression (16 items); attachment (10 items); restriction of role (8 items); sense of competence (16 items); social isolation (7 items); realistic attitude about children (5 items); relationship with spouse (5 items); and health (4 items). The Child domain includes 54 items distributed among the following 6 subscales: child demandingness (13 items); child adaptability (12 items); child distractibility (9 items); moodiness (6 items); acceptability of child's behavior to parent (7 items); and child as a positive source of reinforcement (7 items). We reworded the items of the Child domain to produce a comparable set of items to assess parental stress associated with the second child. Specifically, we changed all references to "child" so that they would read "baby," we separated the domains within the scale by leaving the Child items at the beginning as they are in the original scale and placing Infant items at the end of the scale, and we specifically instructed the parents that "child" referred to the firstborn child and "baby" to the second-born. Finally, the Situational/Demographic domain was adopted in its original form, consisting of 12 items that compose the situational stress subscale and a 20-item life-events/demographic situation subscale.

A detailed summary of the psychometric qualities of the PSI, of its construct, discriminant, and factorial validity as ascertained from the results of numerous research projects, and of its normative stress scores is available in Abidin (1979, 1983) and Burke and Abidin (1980). Three-week test-retest reliability coefficients have been reported as .84, .70, .78, and .82 for the Child, Self, Situational/Demographic domains, and Total index, respectively, and alpha coefficients of internal consistency have been reported as .87, .91, .68, and .93 (Abidin, 1979, 1983). The standard instrument (157 questions) was used at the prepartum interview; subsequent postpartum assessments were made with an expanded version (211 questions) that included an Infant domain to complement, item for item, the Child domain. Brief descriptions of the subdomains within each of the four major domains, including the ranges of potential scores, are presented in Appendix A.

Loyd and Abidin (1985) have completed a revision of PSI, Form 5, and have recently presented Form 6 of the instrument. Although we certainly welcome advancements and improvements in the instruments of our discipline, it was a bit disconcerting to have this form released just as we were beginning our 8-month postpartum assessments. This revision was undertaken to derive a form of the index that would permit easier hand scoring and to reduce the overall length of the instrument. This reduction in the number of items was obtained primarily by omitting items with absolute loading values less than .50. This latest version was found to have even higher reliability than previous forms, thereby supporting its continued usefulness as a screening instrument. Moreover, the latest form has been found to possess even greater factorial validity. Specifically, the items of the Parent domain (Loyd and Abidin have also renamed this portion of the scale in Form 6) have been found to load into a seven-factor solution accounting for 44% of the variance, and the items of the Child domain produced a six-factor solution accounting for 41% of the variance.

Since we had already begun to collect data with Form 5 of the PSI before this newer version became available, we decided to finish the project with the same instrument. Still, it was quite interesting to note that the results of the more sophisticated analyses conducted by Loyd and Abidin (1985) provide strong support for the use of Form 5. For example, it is important to note that only 7 items were deleted from the original pool of 54 in the Child domain, and that these remaining 47 items formed factors that were identical to those identified a priori by Burke and Abidin (1980). Moreover, only 17 of the original 71 items of the Parent domain were deleted, and 7 of the original 8 a priori factors were identified. The single factor not found in the latest version of the index was realistic attitude about children. This subdomain was the smallest in Form 5, having only 5 items. Two of these were dropped in accordance with the new, more stringent .50 loading rule, and the other three items loaded on other related subdomains of the overall Parent domain, such as parent attachment and relationship with spouse.

The Who Does What? Index

This scale, developed by Cowan et al. (1978), was adopted to provide a detailed description of role differentiation within the family. This instrument further provides a multidimensional means of assessing role adjustment following the birth of a second child, as well as satisfaction with that adjustment, and thus provides a further assessment of the bB portion of the model. Moreover, the scale is very similar to those employed by Baruch and Barnett (1981, 1986) and Barnett and Baruch (1987) in their studies of fathers' participation in family work. Our modification of the Cowan et al. scale included 7 child-care tasks (giving the child a bath, responding to the cries of the child, choosing which toys to purchase for the child, playing with the child, and so on), 11 housekeeping tasks (cooking meals, making household repairs, cleaning, general yard work, providing income, and the like), and 10 infant-care tasks (determining the infant's sleep and feeding schedule, giving the infant a bath, responding to the infant's cries during the day and at night, playing with the infant, and so on). Parents were asked to indicate along a continuum for each of the 28 items which parent was responsible for "doing this task" in their actual family arrangement as well as under what they might perceive to be an ideal situation. It was assumed that the discrepancy between actual and ideal conditions might provide an inverse index of satisfaction with marital and parental roles to supplement Crnic et al.'s (1983) Parental Role Satisfaction index (cf. Barnett & Baruch, 1987; Baruch & Barnett, 1981, 1986; Cowan et al., 1978).

In our modification of the Cowan et al. (1978, 1985) Who Does What? questionnaire, each parent described the relative division of 7 child-care, 10 infant-care, and 13 household-maintenance tasks by noting who was responsible for performing each. The child-care tasks included the following: bathe or dress child, respond to cries, respond to cries during the night, choose or purchase toys for child, care for or arrange care for child when sick, play with child, put child to bed. The infant care items included the following: determine the daily schedule (feeding and sleeping) of infant; feed, diaper, bathe, or dress infant; respond to cries; respond to cries during the night; choose or purchase toys for infant; care for or arrange care for infant when sick; play with infant; and put infant to bed. The household tasks included arrange for sitters, plan or cook meals, clean up after meals, general household repairs, general household cleaning, shopping (especially for groceries), pay bills, wash clothes, make social arrangements, maintain correspondence with family or friends (primarily by making phone calls), supervise the repairs of automobile(s), provide the family income, and general yard work.

Parents were asked to rate each item on a 9-point scale, with 1 indicating that the mother had complete responsibility for performing the task, 9 that the father assumed this responsibility, and 5 that the task was performed equally by both parents. Assessments of the child-care and household responsibilities were made at both the prepartum and the 12-month postpartum sessions; the infant-care items were rated only at the postpartum session. On each occasion parents were asked to base their ratings on the way the family had functioned during the immediately preceding two-week period. Additionally, at the postpartum assessment parents were asked to indicate not only the actual division of responsibility on each item, but which rating would describe their notion of an "ideal" situation. Differences between these actual and ideal ratings have been conceptualized to represent an index of the parents' satisfaction with their familial pattern of role adjustment (with greater differences implying less satisfaction). This provides us with an additional assessment of family functioning during the Consolidation subphase of the adjustment and accommodation process (cf. Cowan et al., 1978; McCubbin & Patterson, 1982, 1983).

Assessments of Social Support and Role Satisfaction

The Satisfaction with Parenting Scale and the Questionnaire on Social Support developed by Crnic and his associates (Crnic et al., 1983; Ragozin, Basham, Crnic, Greenberg, & Robinson, 1982) were selected because each provides multidimensional assessments of parental satisfaction and support networks, and thus would represent the b and bB portions of the Double ABCX model. The Satisfaction with Parenting Scale includes two subscales, Parental Role Satisfaction and Degree of Pleasure in Child, to delineate the nature of the respondent's satisfaction with parenting. The Parental Role Satisfaction subscale addresses issues such as the availability of and satisfaction with various support services specifically oriented to child care and the parents' satisfaction with their current amount of child-care and household responsibilities, time for themselves, and social time away from the children. The Degree of Pleasure in Child subscale addresses issues such as the parents' degree of pleasure in various child-care chores, doubts about parental competence, irritation with the children, and overall feelings toward children. The Questionnaire on Social Support assesses support obtained from three ecologically distinct levels: community or neighborhood, friends or family, and intimate relationships. The items of the scale provide an index of the degree to which the parents have access to and are satisfied with various sources that may provide esteem support, informational support, social companionship, and/or instrumental support. As such, to use Cohen and Wills's (1985) terminology, the Questionnaire on Social Support may be described as providing a specific and functional index of the parents' social support network. Such an index is critical when one wishes to study the buffering effects of support networks in mitigating the effects of stressors.

Crnic et al. (1983) have found that maternal satisfaction scores can be predicted by levels of support and stress, the latter measured by the

Sarason, Johnson, and Siegel (1978) Life Experience Survey. Specifically, they found that mothers with greater stress were less positive in their attitudes and mothers with greater support were significantly more positive. They further report that intimate support had the most positive effect in lessening the impact of stress and in improving maternal attitudes concerning their role satisfaction and behavioral interaction with their infants. A similar effect was noted by Pedersen, Yarrow, Anderson, and Cain (1978), who found that husband's esteem for the wife as a mother was positively related to her skill in feeding the infant. Although their use of stress and support measures to predict maternal attitudes about parenting (i.e., satisfaction) certainly makes intuitive sense, one must be cautious in assuming that these factors necessarily relate to one another in only this simple linear, unidirectional manner. Indeed, one might just as well assume that the parent possessing high levels of social support or role satisfaction would be predicted to have a rather low level of perceived stress. This apparent paradox concerning the directionality of effect is easily resolved by recognizing that these realms of parental experience are better conceptualized as being causally related in a systemic or circular manner rather than in a simple linear fashion (cf. P. Minuchin, 1985).

The Questionnaire on Social Support, developed by Crnic et al. (1983), consists of a series of questions regarding the availability and/or satisfaction with sources of support at three ecological levels: intimate relationships, including spouse or other partner (5 items); friendships or family support (8 items); and neighborhood or community support (4 items). Questions concerning intimate relationships focus on the potential continuance and satisfaction with the relationship, the presence of someone with whom to share private feelings, and satisfaction with this arrangement. Questions dealing with friendship focus on the number of conversations and visits with friends, satisfaction with these events, the presence of someone with whom one can honestly share happiness or anger, and satisfaction with these arrangements. Questions about the community area focus on involvement in the neighborhood and with local organized groups, and satisfaction with these involvements. Crnic et al. (1983) have reported for these three domains of support internal consistencies (Cronbach's alphas) of .69, .65, and .50, respectively.

The Satisfaction with Parenting Scale is composed of two parts; one assesses parental role satisfaction and the other the degree of pleasure in infant/child. The Parental Role Satisfaction subscale includes 7 items that reflect parental satisfaction with amount of child-care responsibilities, household responsibilities, time for self, social time away from children, professional and nonprofessional advice about children, and people with whom to discuss any negative feelings about the children (internal consistency alpha = .61). The Degree of Pleasure in Child subscale includes 5 items that tap parental degree of pleasure in child-care chores, doubts about parental competence, irritation about the children, regrets about having children, and overall feelings about the children (internal consistency alpha = .48).

The relative brevity of this scale was part of its attraction as well as a basis for some initial concern. Assessments of the internal consistencies of the Parental Role Satisfaction and the Degree of Pleasure in Child subscales from the overall Satisfaction with Parenting Scale, and of the Intimate Support, Friend/Family Support, and the Community/Neighborhood Support subscales from the Questionnaire on Social Support were replicated using the data obtained from the prenatal assessments to bolster our confidence in this set of measures. Cronbach alphas of .65 and .75 were obtained for fathers and mothers, respectively, for the Parental Role Satisfaction subscale, and .72 and .73 for the Degree of Pleasure in Child subscale. Similar values were found with the mothers' social support data, with alphas of .73, .84, and .74 obtained for the Intimate, Friend/Family, and Community/Neighborhood subscales, respectively. The scales were slightly less internally consistent with the fathers, with values of .52, .66., and .75 being obtained for the three subscales. Overall, the scales appeared to be psychometrically sound despite the relatively few items included.

Assessments of Temperament

The mothers also were asked to complete the 89-item Dimensions of Temperament Survey (DOTS) developed by Lerner et al. (1982) to describe themselves as well as their firstborn children. These assessments were repeated 12 months after the birth of the second child, with an additional assessment of child temperament obtained 4 months after the birth. The mothers then were asked to describe their second-born children at the 4- and 12-month postpartum assessments using Rothbart's (1981) Infant Behavior Questionnaire. Fathers were asked to provide self-descriptions at the prepartum and 12-month postpartum assessments, but child and infant descriptions were not requested from the fathers.

Although both the DOTS and the IBQ have been derived to represent the original categories of temperament identified by Thomas and Chess (1977) in their New York Longitudinal Study and thus are quite similar, we chose to utilize the IBQ for infant assessments given its specificity for this age level. Moreover, we decided to employ the 89-item, 9-dimension version of the DOTS rather than the 42- or 34-item, 5-factor versions developed by Lerner et al., given the increased diversity of dimensional assessment provided by the former. Specifically, the DOTS provided us with assessments of parent and child temperament style defined in terms of activity level (12 items), rhythmicity (23 items), adaptability (10 items), threshold (10 items), intensity (8 items), mood (6 items), persistence of attention (6 items), distractibility (5 items), and approach/withdrawal (9 items). The IBQ, in turn, provides an assessment of infant temperament defined in terms of six rather than nine dimensions, including activity level (17 items), distress to limitation (19 items), distress and latency to approach sudden or novel stimuli (16 items), duration of orienting (11 items), smiling and laughter (15 items), and soothability (11 items). Since our primary focus was on intraindividual changes in perceived temperament rather than comparisons of mother-offspring or child-infant groups, the differences between the scales should not be important. Definitions of the dimensions of temperament assessed by each of these instruments are presented in Appendix B.

SUMMARY

This project utilized interviews, observations, and standardized questionnaires to assess the adjustments of all family members to the birth of a second child. All assessments and observations were made in the families' homes at set intervals prior to and after the birth. We attempted to limit the length of each of these measurement sessions to less than 90 minutes so as not to burden the family members unduly. To accomplish this end, we obtained some measures only at specific times, while we assessed other more variable factors at each session. Table 3.2 summarizes the timetable employed for the measures that have been described above.

Table 3.2 Timetable of Assessments

Measure	*Time Relative to Birth of Second Child (in months)*				
	−1	*+1*	*+4*	*+8*	*+12*
Observation of familial interaction	X	X	X	X	X
Quasi-structured interview					
mother	X	X	X	X	X
father	X	X	X	X	X
firstborn child	X	X	X	X	X
Questionnaires					
Parenting Stress Index	X		X		X
Who Does What?	X				X
Social Support	X	X	X	X	X
Satisfaction with Parenting	X	X	X	X	X
Temperament					
maternal self-report	X				X
paternal self-report	X				X
child self-report					X
firstborn by maternal report	X		X		X
infant by maternal report		X	X		X

PART III

The Findings

The results of this study are presented in a sequence of three chapters organized to address the primary objectives of this project. Each chapter includes commentary sections in which analyses are summarized and supplemental data from parental interviews are used to clarify further the implications of the particular findings. The integration of these commentaries is reserved for the concluding chapter.

Chapter 4 focuses on parental stress during the transition period, and is organized into four major sections. First, to address the question of differential parental responses to the stressors involved in the birth of a second child, the data obtained from the Parenting Stress Index for each of the primary domains of stress are summarized. Second, these analyses are supplemented by a shift in focus from mean levels of reported parental stress to categorically defined high levels of stress that are judged to place the family at risk. Third, a comparison is presented of maternal and paternal reports of levels of support for, and satisfaction with, their parental roles. Finally, to further our understanding of the effects of social support systems and individual satisfaction in mitigating parental and marital stress, the stress data, the sources of support measures, and the satisfaction with parental role data (all from the 12-month postpartum assessment) are related through canonical correlation procedures.

In Chapter 5 attention is focused on the general area of family organization and functioning, and on the process of reorganization following the birth of the second child. The analysis of the Who Does What? data is presented to describe the changes in parental responsibility for specific child-care and household tasks over time as well as the changes in the structure underlying the parents' division of labor strategy over the adjustment and accommodation phases. These analyses are extended by a presentation of the differences between the spouses' views of their actual as opposed to ideal divisions of task responsibilities.

The data describing the firstborn's adjustment during this transition period are presented in Chapter 6. This chapter begins with a description of maternal reports of so-called regressive behaviors. In light of the parental stress and role responsibility data presented above, one must be cautious when interpreting these reports and remember that the data are subjective parental perceptions rather than objective clinical accounts of the children's problems of adjustment. A summary of the information obtained from the maternal and child interviews follows to supplement these parental perceptions. The relation between the age of child and the type of behavioral problems is then considered. Next, maternal reports of self, child, and infant temperament are analyzed. Finally, a summary of the observation data obtained from the play sessions is presented to describe changes in parent-child play interactions over the course of the study. This last data set provides an alternative, and somewhat more objective, method of studying changes in parent-child relations.

Finally, in Chapter 7, we return to the FAAR process model of family adjustment and accommodation to summarize how these data illustrate the pileup of demands, the family's initial coping responses, their subsequent self-reorganization efforts, and their gradual integration of these changes in establishing a revised family system. The results of various analyses from Chapters 4 through 6 are integrated to reflect the systemic principles of circular causality and interdependence. For example, the discussion of the increased strain associated with the initial adjustment phase includes an examination of how the strain experienced by the mothers might be circularly related to difficulties experienced by the firstborn children in adjusting to the presence of a sibling. Differences in husbands' and wives' respective "parental imperatives" or their concepts of equity and equality are discussed to illustrate how these factors might influence the roles assumed by husbands and wives during the reorganization process. This discussion focuses on the paradoxical situation of the husband/father's being thought of as a "helper" to his wife or a "baby-sitter" for his own children, while the activities of the wife/mother would not be described in this manner. Finally, the larger arena of changing roles of mothers and fathers in a changing society is briefly considered, and attention is focused on "stuck-at-home" mothers and newly active fathers. The material in this chapter, and that of the preceding chapters, was presented to the study parents, who participated in a series of public forum sessions. Reactions of these parents to our analyses and interpretations have been included here to supplement our overall results.

4

Parental Stress and Its Mediation Through Support Networks

A number of analyses were conducted to assess parental perceptions of the sources of stress affecting their lives during the transition associated with the birth of a second child. The first set of analyses addressed the issues of parental differences in perceptions of stress, as assessed by the Parenting Stress Index, and changes in the assumed sources of stress over time. These analyses were followed by a focus on those parents reporting levels of stress deemed clinically high. The third set of analyses focused on parental support networks and satisfaction with parenting as assessed by the Questionnaire on Social Support and the Satisfaction with Parenting Scale. A series of canonical correlation procedures were then used to investigate the extent to which social support and/or parental satisfaction might serve as a buffer to stress. The following specific questions are addressed by these analyses:

(1) Do mothers and fathers experience different stressors?
(2) How much of this stress is actually "high" stress?
(3) Do parents differ in their degree of satisfaction with parenting?
(4) Do the social support networks of mothers and fathers differ?
(5) How do parents utilize support networks or role satisfaction to mitigate stress?

DIFFERENCES IN PARENTAL
PERCEPTIONS OF STRESSORS

Do mothers and fathers experience different stressors?

To examine this issue, data concerning parental stress derived from the PSI were analyzed separately for each of the four primary domains of stress—Self, Child, Infant, and Situational/Demographic. The BMD-P series statistical package was used for all analyses reported in this section (Dixon et al., 1983). The within-subject factors were parent (mother versus father) and time (prepartum, 4-, and 12-month postpartum for all except the Infant domain, where, obviously, no prepartum assessment could be made).[1] Child gender was treated as a between-groups factor in all preliminary analyses, but was excluded from the final set of analyses due to its insignificance as either a main effect or an interaction component. The age of the firstborn child also was treated as a between-groups factor in a preliminary set of analyses, but also was excluded from the final set of analyses due to its relatively meager contribution in accounting for the observed variance.[2] The means, standard deviations, and pertinent MANOVA and ANOVA statistics for these data are presented in Table 4.1. The parents' Total stress scores and each of their four domain scores were treated as dependent variables in separate ANOVA procedures, and a MANOVA procedure was conducted using the total scores of the Self, Child, and Situation domains (BMD-P4V). The Infant domain data were excluded from this analysis simply to avoid the undue complexity of an incomplete design necessitated by the absence of these data at the prepartum assessment; the Total index scores were excluded due to their linear relation to the other domain scores.

Significant multivariate effects for parent, $F(3, 38) = 4.12, p < .0125$; time, $F(6, 35) = 5.48, p < .0004$; and the interaction of parent and time, $F(6, 35) = 2.74, p < .0272$, were detected. Univariate effects for parent were detected only for the Self domain and the Total stress scores, with the means of each indicating that mothers reported higher levels of stress than did fathers. Significant univariate effects for time were detected for the Total stress scores, as well as for the Child, Self, and Infant domains. Tukey HSD post hoc procedures (using the .05 level of significance) were conducted with the means for Total score and those of the Child and Self domains. The results of these procedures revealed an increase in level of stress from the prepartum to the 4-month postpartum assessments, and then an increase only at the 12-month assessment; those for the Infant domain revealed an increase in stress level from 4 to 12 months. No significant interactions of the factors of parent and of time of measure were detected at the univariate level. A series of MANOVA and ANOVA procedures were then employed to analyze the subscales within each of the four major domains.

Self domain. Considering first the eight subscales of the Self domain, significant multivariate effects were detected for both parent, $F(8, 33) = 7.40$, $p < .0001$, and time, $F(16, 25) = 3.72$, $p < .0016$. Further analyses of the parent effect indicated that wives reported higher levels of stress than did their husbands on each of the following four subscales: depression, restriction of role, relationship with spouse, and personal health. Supplemental information obtained through interviews of the parents proved useful in interpreting these effects. Of the 17 mothers who had held part- or full-time employment positions outside the home prior to the births of the second children, only 8 had returned to work by the 4-month postpartum interview. Comparisons of these 8 "back-to-work" mothers with the 9 "still-at-home" mothers revealed that the latter experienced significantly greater social isolation, $t(15) = 2.303$, $p < .036$; greater depression, $t(15) = 2.450$, $p < .031$; and greater difficulties with their spouses, $t(15) = 2.983$, $p < .012$. The still-at-home subgroup did not differ from mothers who had not held positions of outside employment prior to the birth of the second child (i.e., the self-described "homemakers," $N = 24$) on any of these variables (all t values were less than 1.00). Conversely, the means of the back-to-work subgroup were significantly lower, indicative of less stress, than those of the homemakers.

Further analyses of the time effect utilizing univariate analysis of variance followed by Tukey HSD procedures (again, using the .05 level) indicated the following significant effects: The overall level of depression was highest at the first postpartum assessment; the overall sense of role restriction and the overall difficulty with the spouse was initially low, but then increased at 4 months postpartum and remained high at 12 months; and overall health scores declined (i.e., with time, health issues became less of a source of stress). The interaction of parent × time was not significant at the MANOVA level; it also was not significant at the ANOVA level for any variable except self health, where it indicated that the improvement in health was experienced only by the wives, $F(2, 39) = 6.43$, $p < .0039$.

Child domain. Only a significant multivariate effect for time, $F(12, 29) = 4.02$, $p < .0011$, was detected in the Child domain. Follow-up analyses indicated four distinct patterns of differences at the univariate level. First,

Table 4.1 Summary of Parenting Stress Index Data

| | Mother | | | | | | Father | | | | | | MANOVA and ANOVA Statistics | | |
| | -1 Month | | +4 Months | | +12 Months | | -1 Month | | +4 Months | | +12 Months | | Parent | Time | Parent × Time |
	M	SD	M	SD	M	SD	M	SD	M	SD	M	SD	F(1, 40)	F(2, 39)[a]	F(2, 39)
Child															
demandingness	27.9	5.5	29.9	5.6	30.9	6.3	28.5	5.2	28.0	6.1	29.9	5.7	1.54	5.74**	2.84
adaptability	25.0	4.4	26.8	5.0	27.0	4.6	26.4	4.8	26.8	4.4	27.2	5.0	.63	3.30*	1.02
distractibility	26.0	3.8	26.5	3.4	25.3	3.7	25.6	3.8	26.3	3.9	25.3	3.4	.13	4.21*	.20
moodiness	11.5	2.8	12.2	3.1	12.8	3.7	11.5	2.8	12.2	4.0	13.2	3.3	.09	9.34***	.17
acceptability	12.7	3.2	14.4	3.0	13.9	3.4	12.7	3.0	13.5	3.3	13.5	3.4	1.39	6.68**	.72
reinforcement	11.2	2.8	12.6	3.1	12.7	3.4	11.1	2.7	11.6	2.9	11.8	3.2	2.89	5.78**	1.66
Multivariate F ratios													F(6, 35) 1.35	F(12, 29) 4.02***	F(12, 29) .78
Self															
depression	36.2	7.9	38.9	8.2	37.6	8.4	31.6	7.2	34.0	8.4	34.7	7.3	10.84**	7.51***	1.32
attachment	20.5	3.6	21.2	3.3	20.7	3.5	20.5	3.5	20.6	3.8	21.2	3.9	.02	1.06	.84
role restriction	22.3	4.6	24.4	4.6	24.4	4.7	18.7	4.0	21.0	4.6	21.2	4.1	19.17****	15.06****	.14
sense of competence	37.2	6.4	37.1	6.8	38.4	7.8	34.9	6.7	35.9	7.3	36.5	7.5	2.64	2.63	.34
social isolation	16.1	5.6	16.7	4.1	16.7	3.8	15.8	4.4	16.7	4.4	17.4	4.6	.02	2.93	.47
realistic attitude	12.7	2.4	13.1	2.4	12.6	3.8	12.8	2.7	13.0	2.9	12.9	2.6	.07	.58	.12
spousal relationship	13.0	4.2	14.7	4.1	14.2	3.7	11.7	3.2	13.1	3.7	13.0	3.5	7.63**	7.23***	.14
health	12.2	2.4	11.0	2.6	10.4	2.7	9.2	2.2	9.7	2.1	9.3	2.2	19.42****	4.67*	6.43**
Multivariate F ratios													F(8, 33) 7.40****	F(16, 25) 3.72**	F(16, 25) 1.09
Situational/Demographic															
situations	23.6	4.0	25.3	4.2	25.8	4.3	23.6	4.0	24.4	4.9	24.6	3.8	2.77	9.78****	2.17
life events	8.8	5.6	7.8	4.3	5.6	6.3	9.0	4.9	7.7	3.5	5.0	5.7	.14	5.60***	.22
Multivariate F ratios													F(2, 39) 1.45	F(4, 37) 7.82****	F(4, 37) 1.17

(Continued)

Table 4.1 (Continued)

| | Mother | | | | | | Father | | | | | | MANOVA and ANOVA Statistics | | |
| | −1 Month | | +4 Months | | +12 Months | | −1 Month | | +4 Months | | +12 Months | | Parent | Time | Parent × Time |
	M	SD	M	SD	M	SD	M	SD	M	SD	M	SD	$F_{(1, 40)}$	$F_{(2, 39)}$[a]	$F_{(2, 39)}$
Infant															
demandingness	—	—	24.2	6.7	27.2	5.2	—	—	25.3	6.3	26.5	6.0	.04	6.33*	1.84
adaptability	—	—	28.1	6.4	29.1	5.5	—	—	28.3	6.2	27.8	5.1	.41	.07	3.01
distractibility	—	—	23.8	3.7	25.3	4.3	—	—	24.1	3.4	24.7	3.1	.09	3.78	1.16
moodiness	—	—	10.9	3.4	11.8	2.4	—	—	11.2	3.2	11.7	2.6	.02	2.88	.75
acceptance	—	—	12.8	3.1	13.6	3.3	—	—	12.8	2.9	13.3	3.8	.05	2.42	.19
reinforcement	—	—	11.2	2.6	12.5	2.5	—	—	11.5	6.0	12.2	3.3	.00	14.71***	.63
Multivariate F ratios													$F_{(6, 35)}$ .23	$F_{(6, 35)}$ 3.67**	$F_{(6, 35)}$ .94
Totals															
Total	316.3	41.5	334.0	43.1	329.8	46.3	304.0	43.9	313.0	53.7	315.8	48.0	6.13*	11.78****	.82
Child	114.3	17.0	124.1	18.6	122.7	19.7	116.3	17.2	118.5	19.6	120.2	19.2	.88	8.73***	2.21
Self	169.6	26.4	176.9	26.2	175.8	27.8	155.2	25.2	163.7	29.7	165.8	27.9	8.43**	9.48***	.58
Situational	32.4	6.9	33.1	6.3	31.4	8.4	32.5	7.2	32.1	6.3	29.6	7.1	2.01	2.14	1.13
Infant	—	—	111.3	21.0	118.8	17.6	—	—	113.5	19.5	116.1	18.1	—	—	—
Multivariate F ratios—three levels of time (Infant scores excluded)													$F_{(3, 38)}$ 4.12**	$F_{(6, 35)}$ 5.48***	$F_{(6, 35)}$ 2.74*

NOTE: All contrasts involving the time factor are reported with Greenhouse-Geisser adjusted degrees of freedom and probability levels.

a. Univariate degrees of freedom for time and parent × time with Infant subdomain variables are 1, 40.

*$p < .05$; **$p < .01$; ***$p < .001$; ****$p < .0001$.

parental reports of problems with their children's degree of moodiness and their inability to adjust to changes in the physical or social environment increased gradually over the three times of assessment. None of the contiguous points of measure showed a significant increase in stress, but an overall increase was found when the prepartum and 12-month measures were compared. Second, parental reports of the overall acceptability of their children's physical, intellectual, or emotional characteristics and their sense of the children as sources of positive reinforcement revealed changes, indicating that these areas became greater sources of stress by the 4-month assessment, and that this elevated level remained high through the 12-month session. Third, parental reports of their children's levels of overactivity, restlessness, or general distractibility were highest at the 4-month postpartum period, with both the earlier and later assessments being equally lower, that is, showing an inverted U curve. Fourth, parental reports of the degree of demandingness they experienced from their children did not differ significantly from the prepartum to the 4-month postpartum assessments, but showed a significant increase at 12 months.

Situational/Demographic domain. For the two variables of the Situational/Demographic domain only a time effect was noted, $F(4, 37) = 7.82$, $p < .0001$, with the families' situational stress factors showing an increase and their life-events index showing a decline in stress over time. (Note that these effects canceled each other out when we considered the total score for this domain.) These differences emerged only when comparing the prepartum to the 12-month postpartum scores, a period when the increase in situational stress was associated primarily with an increase in the size of the household and a decrease in family income. The decrease in life-event stress was due largely to a combination of the omission of the no-longer-applicable stresses associated with pregnancy, and an increased stability in employment-related situations that had been obtained by most families by the time of the final assessment. Specifically, those women who held employment positions outside the home either had returned to them or had decided not to return to them, but they were no longer categorized as having recently left a position of employment.

Infant domain. Stress associated with the Infant domain was assessed at the 4- and 12-month postpartum visits. Only a significant time effect was found for the six items of this domain, $F(6, 35) = 3.67$, $p < .0063$. Follow-up analyses revealed that three variables accounted for this overall effect, with each showing an increase in stress level over time. These variables included parental reports of the demandingness of the infants, their sense of the infants as a source of positive reinforcement, and a trend ($p < .0588$) for an increase in parental reports of the general distractibility of the infants.

Comparison of Child and Infant domains. An analysis was conducted to compare parental reports of stress associated with the Child and Infant domains. To accomplish this, the factor offspring (child versus infant) was added to the other within-family factors (i.e., mother versus father, time of assessment), and the time factor was limited to the two postpartum assessments. Significant overall effects due to time, $F(6, 35) = 3.06, p < .0165$; offspring, $F(6, 35) = 9.68, p < .0001$; and the interaction of time and offspring, $F(6, 35) = 2.58, p < .0354$, were detected. Neither the parent effect nor any interaction involving this factor was found to be significant at the multivariate level. Univariate analyses revealed significant time effects for the variables demandingness/degree of bother, moodiness, and reinforces parent, with the means of each indicating a higher level of stress at the 12-month assessment. The offspring effect was detected at the univariate level for demandingness/degree of bother, distractibility, moodiness, and acceptability, with the means of each indicating that the firstborn child was perceived as the greater source of stress. A trend ($p < .0675$) also was detected for the infant to be perceived as a greater source of stress associated with the adaptability subscale. The time × offspring interaction was detected at the univariate level for the subscales of distractibility and reinforcement, and as a trend ($p < .1030$) for acceptability. Post hoc analyses of the means for these subscales indicated that the stress associated with the infant increased over time, while that associated with the firstborn child decreased.

Individual stability in level of stress. All of the data presented up to this point have dealt with group means rather than the scores of individual parents. A question might be raised concerning the stability over time of the parents' perceptions of feeling stressed. To address this issue, Pearson product-moment and Spearman rho correlation coefficients were calculated separately for the mothers' and fathers' scores on each domain and subdomain across the three times of assessment. The results of the Pearson procedures are presented in Table 4.2; the results of the Spearman calculations were nearly identical to their interval-scaled counterparts, and, in the interest of brevity, are not presented.

The statistics in Table 4.2 indicate that the parents' individual perceptions of feeling stressed were quite stable over time. Indeed, for both mothers and fathers, more than 93% of the coefficients calculated exceeded the magnitude required for the .05 significance level. It should be

Table 4.2 Stability Coefficients for the Parenting Stress Index over Time

| | *Mothers* | | | *Fathers* | | |
	−1 and 4	4 and 12	−1 and 12	−1 and 4	4 and 12	−1 and 12
Total score	.71	.80	.83	.86	.83	.82
Child domain total	.43	.52	.74	.75	.75	.67
demandingness	.57	.57	.53	.76	.72	.64
adaptability	.47	.47	.57	.49	.54	.47
distractibility	.61	.39	.50	.64	.68	.61
moodiness	.71	.73	.55	.69	.48	.50
acceptability	.50	.70	.55	.39	.58	.30
reinforcement	.45	.43	.66	.51	.56	.41
Self domain total	.74	.86	.74	.80	.78	.82
depression	.71	.82	.78	.68	.70	.67
attachment	.59	.59	.66	.57	.58	.78
role restriction	.54	.64	.57	.62	.59	.61
sense of competence	.66	.69	.67	.65	.78	.66
social isolation	.31	.64	.24	.72	.64	.83
realistic attitude	.58	.51	.45	.50	.51	.54
spousal relationship	.39	.60	.60	.67	.60	.77
health	.56	.43	.54	.44	.38	.23
Situational/Demographic total	.69	.46	.30	.70	.45	.40
situations	.70	.65	.70	.76	.59	.60
life events	.52	.22	.03	.39	.18	.11
Infant domain total	—	.40	—	—	.63	—
demandingness	—	.31	—	—	.45	—
adaptability	—	.56	—	—	.44	—
distractibility	—	.22	—	—	.24	—
moodiness	—	.50	—	—	.45	—
acceptability	—	.14	—	—	.60	—
reinforcement	—	.39	—	—	.68	—

NOTE: Pearson product-moment correlations; critical value (df = 39) at .05 level is 31. Times of assessment: −1 = prenatal, 4 = 4 months postpartum, 12 = 12 months postpartum.

noted, however, that finding a correlation coefficient to be significantly different from zero is not the same as finding evidence of individual stability. To establish stability one must look instead for coefficients that exceed some conceptually meaningful criterion. For example, one might define individual stability as being indicated by coefficients that are equal to or exceed .70 (roughly equivalent to having 50% of the variance accounted for by the individual). If this definition of stability is adopted, we find conceptually significant Total score and Self domain score stability across the three times of assessment for both mothers and fathers, suggesting that the ordinal position of the parents with respect to these scores remained relatively stable over the course of the study. That is, those parents who initially perceived themselves as experiencing higher levels of stress continued to do so, and, similarly, those who initially reported lower levels of stress remained at the lower end of the distribution.

In addition to stability of these scores, the data in Table 4.2 reveal that maternal reports of depression were quite stable over time and that paternal reports in this subdomain were only slightly less consistent. Paternal stress associated with the fathers' perceptions of being socially isolated was far more consistent than that reported by the mothers. Fathers were somewhat more stable than mothers in their reports of stress in the Child domain, and, in particular, in the Child demandingness subdomain. Maternal reports of Child moodiness or of having stress associated with the acceptability of the child's behavior were more consistent than were paternal reports. Interestingly, both parents were less consistent in their reports of stress within the Infant domain; perhaps the rapid developmental changes in the infant render stressors in this domain less stable.

Comments on Parental Differences in Perceived Stressors

Our analyses of the Parenting Stress Index data indicate that although the birth of a second child reflects a remarkable commonality of experience for both parents, adjustment to this event also involves a different set of factors for mothers and for fathers. The statistical analyses presented above and in Table 4.1 clearly indicate that although mothers experienced both higher levels of stress and a wider range of stressors than their spouses did, the fathers also experienced the birth of the second child as a stressful event. The statistics presented in Table 4.2 supplement these results by revealing a rather high level of consistency over time in both maternal and paternal perceptions of stress. For both mothers and fathers, lack of objectivity in thinking about or interacting with their children was the most common source of stress: At the 12-month assessment over 50% of the parents scored in the high range (i.e., greater than the 85th percentile) on the realistic attitude about children subscale. Items on this subscale include "Sometimes my child does things that bother me just to be mean," "When my child misbehaves or fusses too much, I feel responsible, as if I didn't do something right," and "I feel that every time my child does something wrong it is really my fault." According to Abidin (1979), high scores on this subscale suggest that the parent lacks objectivity when he or she thinks about or interacts with the child. Parents who obtain high scores may be overly invested in or too close to the child to see the child as a separate person; moreover, they may engage in a relationship that is overprotective yet rejecting, with discipline being applied at times in an inappropriate manner and/or degree. The fact that both parents found the firstborn child to be a source of stress at 4 months postpartum—especially in terms of their perceptions of the child's moodiness, acceptability of behavior, and the potential to serve as a reinforcer—is interesting in light of other data on this sample. In a report focusing on the adjustment patterns of these firstborn children, Stewart, Mobley, Van Tuyl, and Salvador (1987) found that this same period was especially characterized by increased anxiety and withdrawal on the part of the firstborns.

By 12 months postpartum, the demandingness of the firstborn also was perceived as a major source of stress by many of the parents. One would do well to consider the role that the second-born infants may play in this increased demandingness on the part of the child. Stewart et al. (1987) found that at the 12-month session, most of the firstborns reported that their infant siblings had become quite intrusive and bothersome. However, when mothers were queried at the 8- and 12-month sessions about the most significant change in each child's behavior, and in their interaction, most stressed that the two children were sharing and playing together well. Nevertheless, at these same sessions, the firstborns complained that the younger siblings kept getting into the firstborns' things, breaking their toys, and interrupting their play. Very different perspectives on "playing together" are clearly revealed by these reports, and the parents' sense of the greater demandingness of their firstborn child may in part stem from a failure to consider the demands that having to share or play with a younger sibling place on the older child. Thus an insufficiently realistic attitude about children may have contributed to their perceptions of the firstborn as having become too demanding.

The stressful effects that the older child's behavior had on fathers appeared to lag behind the effects reported by the mothers. Much of the increase in the fathers' stress may be related to their having assumed a more active role in child-care responsibilities and thus becoming more aware of the difficulties of this endeavor. Alternatively, it might stem from having heard their wives' reports of the moodiness, restlessness, or unacceptable behavior of the firstborns (cf. Russell, 1982). It is interesting in this context that fathers, more so than mothers, reported during their interviews that they were experiencing difficulties with not feeling emotionally close enough to their firstborn children. These difficulties were not apparent in the fathers' scores on the parental attachment subscale of the PSI, for on this subdomain the fathers' scores did not differ significantly from those of the mothers. Given the stress caused by such feelings, together with that of finding neither the firstborn child nor the second-born infant to be a source of positive reinforcement, it could be inferred that the fathers were somewhat anxious concerning their performance in their new role. Maternal stress appeared to derive both from the difficulties of caring for the firstborn child and from a constellation of factors related to the relationship with the spouse, the mother's employment situation, or both. Recalling Hoffman's (1977) observation concerning the impact that paternal participation in child-care activities has on mothers who do not work outside the home, it is especially interesting that the highest levels of stress associated with such factors as depression, social isolation, and marital difficulties were experienced either by traditional homemakers or by formerly employed women who had not yet returned to their jobs by the 4-month postpartum session.

A common aspect of stress experienced by mothers and fathers is reflected by their scores on the social isolation subscale, which indicates this to be a shared source of stress in their lives. Perceived stress in this subdomain was especially stable for the fathers over the course of the transition period. Further examination of the experiences that are common to mothers and fathers can be facilitated by transforming the PSI data from their original interval scales to categorical assessments indicative of scores that can be considered to represent meaningfully high levels of stress, and then investigating the concordance or discordance of parental reports of high stress within the family.

How much of this stress is actually "high" stress?

The analyses reported in the above section address mean differences between husbands and wives and the changing levels of stress they experienced over the 13 months of the study, but they do not tell us anything in terms of a clinical assessment of high stress. Even though differences between the parents and changes in their levels of stress over time were found, many of these levels of stress were within what might be considered normative ranges. Abidin and his associates (Abidin, 1979,

1983; Burke & Abidin, 1980) have provided clinical interpretations of the results of the PSI, including cutoff points to indicate high or at-risk levels of stress, that were based on a sample of more than 500 mothers. Abidin suggests that parents scoring above the 85th percentile on the Total scale score be offered referral for professional consultation, and that subdomain and subscale scores exceeding the 85th percentile be used as guides by the consultant. Applying this criterion to the data in this study, it becomes readily apparent that parental reports of high levels of stress varied widely across the different subdomains. The frequencies of our 41 mothers and fathers, as well as of both parents within a single family, reporting such high levels of stress over the duration of this study are shown in Table 4.3.

The frequencies of high-stress data were analyzed using log linear analysis procedures (BMD-P4F) for multidimensional contingency tables (see Bishop, Fienberg, & Holland, 1975), which permit describing the relations among several categorical variables simultaneously. The technique is based on fitting a hierarchical equation (i.e., a linear model) to a table of cell frequencies, such that the logarithms of the cell frequencies are written as an additive function of main effects, and the interactions in a manner similar to the way cell means are dealt with in analysis of variance. The log linear and ANOVA procedures differ in that with the latter models one seeks to assess the effects of independent factors on a dependent variable and to partition overall variability, whereas with the former one seeks to describe the structural relations among the variables corresponding to the dimensions of the contingency table.

Fienberg (1977) makes a distinction between *response* variables, which are free to vary in controlled conditions, and *explanatory* variables, which are regarded as fixed, either by experimental design or because rational consideration suggests they may play a causal role in the situation under study. The distinction between response and explanatory variables need not be firm in a given situation and, especially in exploratory analyses such as this one, one may choose different sets of response variables from the same data. In the case of the data presented in Table 4.3, our choices of primary explanatory variables were time of assessment and parental identity, with the various domains of stressors being conceptualized as response variables. To facilitate interpretation of these analyses we first chose to fit a log linear model to the total frequencies of all three domains (i.e., Self, Child, and Situational/Demographic) assessed at each of the three times, and then to fit models for each of the sets of subscales of the four major domains of stressors. Due to their low frequency, analyses were not conducted in instances of both parents reporting clinically high levels of stress, or of stress reported to be associated with the subscales of the Situational/Demographic domain by either parent.

Total domain scores. For the 2 (parent) × 3 (time) × 3 (type of stressor; i.e., total scores for Child, Self, and Situational/Demographic domains) table of frequencies, a simple model including two main effects—time and type of stressor—was found to be sufficient in approximating the observed frequencies. The main effect for time indicated that the number of parents classified as reporting high levels of stress increased significantly between the prepartum and postpartum assessments, LR χ^2 (2, N = 115) = 5.96, p < .0501. The main effect for type of stressor indicated that more parents reported high levels of stress associated with the Child domain than with any of the other three domains, and that the Situational/Demographic domain seemed to be a less common source of high stress, LR χ^2 (2, N = 115) = 37.97, p < .0001. The model incorporating these two terms fit the observed frequencies very well, GF χ^2 (13, N = 115) = 10.43, p < .6587.

Self domain. The analysis of the 2 (parent) × 3 (time) × 8 (subscale type of stressor) table of frequencies of high stress within the Self domain indicated that a model including 2 two-way interaction terms was necessary to approximate the observed values. The first of these terms was the interaction of parent and type of stressor. The analysis of this effect indicated that, overall, mothers reported higher-than-expected frequencies associated with role restriction and health problems but lower-than-expected frequencies of social isolation, whereas fathers reported higher-than-expected frequencies associated with social isolation and problems of realistic attitudes concerning children but lower-than-expected frequencies of role restriction, LR χ^2 (7, N = 416) = 20.59, p < .0044. The other term involved the interaction of time and type of stressor, which indicated a nearly significant change in the frequency for particular stressors over time, LR χ^2 (14, N = 416) = 20.17, p < .1248. This change was largely accounted for in that health become a less frequently reported cause of high stress, and an unrealistic attitude about children was more frequently reported over time. Together these terms produced a model that approximated the observed frequencies extremely well, GF χ^2 (16, N = 416) = 10.81, p < .8208.

Child domain. The analysis of the 2 (parent) × 3 (time of assessment) × 6 (subscale type of stressor) table of frequencies of high stress within the Child domain revealed that a simple model involving only two main effects—time and type of stressor—was sufficient to produce a good fit to

Table 4.3 Frequencies of Clinically High Levels of Stress

	Mothers			Fathers			Both		
	−1 Month	+4 Months	+12 Months	−1 Month	+4 Months	+12 Months	−1 Month	+4 Months	+12 Months
Child									
demandingness	9	10	15	8	12	12	4	3	7
adaptability	1	6	9	6	4	7	0	0	2
distractibility	12	13	8	11	8	6	1	3	0
moodiness	10	12	18	13	9	17	4	9	11
acceptability	7	18	15	13	4	12	1	8	7
reinforcement	10	16	17	11	7	14	2	6	10
Self									
depression	8	11	10	7	2	6	1	4	1
attachment	4	9	7	4	6	10	0	1	0
role restriction	4	10	8	3	0	2	0	1	0
sense of competence	7	8	12	6	5	8	1	1	3
social isolation	7	10	10	9	9	15	2	2	3
realistic attitude	10	10	24	13	11	21	2	6	15
spousal relationship	8	15	9	7	2	6	1	2	3
health	24	11	11	7	4	6	3	3	3
Situation									
situations	0	0	0	0	0	0	0	0	0
life events	6	5	5	4	7	3	3	1	2

(Continued)

Table 4.3 (Continued)

	Mothers			Fathers			Both		
	−1 Month	+4 Months	+12 Months	−1 Month	+4 Months	+12 Months	−1 Month	+4 Months	+12 Months
Infant									
demandingness	—	4	5	2	—	5	—	1	1
adaptability	—	12	15	13	—	8	—	8	5
distractibility	—	5	5	2	—	4	—	0	1
moodiness	—	7	3	12	—	7	—	7	0
acceptability	—	5	11	9	—	11	—	2	3
reinforcement	—	6	14	9	—	14	—	3	7
Totals									
Total	6	11	11	7	2	7	0	3	2
Child	6	12	13	11	7	12	1	5	5
Self	9	11	10	7	1	6	0	4	1
Situational	1	1	3	1	2	2	0	1	1
Infant	—	8	7	7	—	8	—	3	3

the original matrix. The main effect for time indicated that the frequency of parents reporting high levels of stress increased steadily from the prepartum to the 12-month postpartum assessment, LR χ^2 (2, N = 380) = 14.04, $p < .0009$. The main effect for type of stressor indicated that more parents experienced stress due to their children's moodiness and inability to provide adequate positive reinforcements, as well as that few parents found their children's ability to adapt to be a cause for high levels of stress, LR χ^2 (5, N = 380) = 23.06, $p < .0003$. The nonsignificant goodness-of-fit chi-square statistic indicates that the fitted values derived by using this simple, two-main-effect model approximates the observed data quite well, GF χ^2 (28, N =380) = 22.87, $p < .7394$. The absence of a main effect for parent, or of any interaction effect including the parent factor, suggests a commonality of experience for mothers and fathers.

Infant domain. The analysis of the 2 (parent) × 2 (time; note that prepartum assessments of Infant stress were impossible) × 6 (subscale type of stressor) table of frequencies of high stress in the Infant domain indicated that a very simple model including only a main effect of type of stressor was sufficient to approximate the observed frequencies. This effect indicated that, overall, a larger-than-expected number of parents reported high levels of stress associated with the infants' inability to adapt to their environments and to provide adequate positive reinforcements, and that a smaller-than-expected number reported high stress associated with their infants' demandingness and distractibility, LR χ^2 (5, N = 188) = 28.65, $p < .0001$. The model with this single term approximated the observed frequencies rather well, GF χ^2 (18, N = 188) = 17.70, $p < .4758$. As with the data of the Child domain, the lack of significance of the parent factor as either a main or interaction effect again suggests a commonality of experience for the parents.

Comments Concerning
"High" Stress Levels

The absence of overall parent effects or interaction effects including the parent factor in all analyses except that of the Self domain data suggests that mothers and fathers share a common experience in terms of what is perceived to be stressful during this transition period. The parental differences in the Self domain certainly make intuitive sense—mothers who have just delivered babies might be expected to experience more health-related problems and to have a greater sense of role restriction, and their husbands might be expected to report greater problems associated with social isolation and unrealistic attitudes about children but less role restriction given their new increased involvement in child-care activities. (See results and discussion in Chapter 5 concerning changes in family role definitions.) The fact that, overall, more mothers than fathers were found to have higher levels of stress associated with the Self domain may also be interpreted by suggesting that the role strain they experience at the second birth may be qualitatively different from that experienced by fathers.

Both W. Stewart (1977) and Grossman, Eichler, and Winickoff (1980) have reported that multiparous mothers appear to be more interested in extrafamilial roles and to exhibit less positive affect and less optimal behavior toward infants than do primiparous mothers, even when the age of the mother is controlled. Since all the mothers of our sample must be multiparous, it is logical to assume that they may, after the birth of their second children, find child care tedious and the potential social isolation and role restrictions inherent in having very young children especially stressful. Indeed, the data indicate that mothers did experience higher levels of stress associated with a sense of role restriction than did their husbands, and the frequency of mothers reporting clinically high levels of stress in this subdomain was greater than expected. Mothers who did not return to their careers outside the home by the fourth month postpartum experienced higher levels of social isolation than did the other mothers. Furthermore, since most (71% at the 12-month session) of the mothers indicated that the second child would also be their last baby, one could argue that their perceptions of the stressors associated with the birth of a child might be biased in a positive direction. Specifically, it is logical that these mothers might report very low levels of infant-related stress as they delight in this final experience with an infant and strive to obtain the greatest possible pleasure from this soon-to-end phase of life. The same stressors may be present in a quantitative sense, but the perceptions of these stressors may be qualitatively different due to the distinctive characteristics of the situation.

The data further suggest a shift in the role definitions of fathers that complements the reports of W. Stewart (1977) and Grossman et al. (1980) for mothers, in that as the fathers became more interested or involved in intrafamilial roles after the second birth, they became aware of sources of stress already known to the mothers. The frequency of fathers reporting high levels of stress in the Child domain or the realistic attitude subdomain at the first assessment is similar to that of the mothers. Furthermore, these frequencies increased over time, as did the numbers of fathers reporting high stress in other subdomains, such that the collective groups of mothers and fathers did not differ significantly at the 12-month assessment. The increases noted in the "both" columns of these stressors over time further suggest, first, that the mothers and fathers within a given family share a common experience and, second, that focusing exclusively on the differences between mothers and fathers could be misleading.

Another point needs to be made before concluding this commentary on high stress—although many of the parents did experience significant levels of stress while adjusting to the birth of a second child, the process of adjustment need not be conceptualized in a strictly negative manner. One might look at the frequencies reported in Table 4.3 and conclude that an alarmingly large number of parents were experiencing levels of stress high enough to warrant possible intervention. Indeed, nearly 27% of the mothers ($N = 11$) and 17% of the fathers ($N = 7$) scored high enough at the postpartum sessions so as to be offered referrals for consultation. (Two families accepted the offer and obtained consultation.) Most of this high stress was associated with perceived moodiness in the firstborn child, parental sense of incompetence, social isolation, and problems of unrealistic attitudes concerning children. On the other hand, one must bear in mind that these data were obtained during a process of family transition and role adjustment, a time when one would expect a certain degree of moodiness in the child to be present and parental doubts concerning role behavior to arise. McCubbin and Patterson (1982, 1983) have pointed out that the differences in parental perception and appraisal of the transition demands and the inherent meaning of the transition event (i.e., the cC factor) may vary from the positive notion of an opportunity for growth to the negative assumption of the imminent demise of the family. One father summarized the positive attitude of viewing the transition as a period for potential growth by saying that "it took only one child to make my wife a mother, but two to make me a father."

Finally, these stress data might be supplemented by considering one further issue involving parental expectations and family composition. Parents were interviewed separately at each of the times of assessment to obtain additional information describing their adjustments following the birth of the second child. Prior to this birth, parents were asked to indicate their preference for the gender of the second-born child. Most preferred that the second-born child be of the opposite gender of the firstborn, χ^2 (1) = 27.99, $p < .001$, $\phi = .73$. At the 1-month postpartum interview, parents were asked to recall their immediate reactions to learning the gender of the second-born children and to rate their recalled feelings on a scale, with 1 indicating strong disappointment and 10 indicating extreme pleasure. Mothers who had stated preferences for daughters and fathers who had stated preferences for sons and who had then failed to obtain these children reported scores indicating greater disappointment when compared to the grand mean for this measure, t (12) = 2.83, p < .05 for mothers, and t (9) = 2.81, p < .05 for fathers. (Note that unequal cell sizes prohibited contrast to anything other than the grand mean.) Of the 13 mothers who did not obtain preferred daughters, 5 failed to recall ever having stated such a preference, and even denied having done so. More important, 11 of these 13 mothers and 3 of the 10 fathers scored within the "high" range on the depression subdomain of the PSI at the 4-month postpartum session. The 12-month postpartum interview included a query as to whether the parents anticipated having a third child. A total of 9 of the 12 mothers and 8 of the 12 fathers responding affirmatively were of the original group of parents who failed to obtain their gender preference at the second birth.

PARENTAL SATISFACTION
AND SOCIAL SUPPORT FACTORS

Do parents differ in their degree of satisfaction with parenting?
Do the social support networks of mothers and fathers differ?

Parental responses on the Parental Role Satisfaction and Degree of Pleasure in Child subscales of the Satisfaction with Parenting Scale, and those on the Questionnaire on Social Support, with its three distinct ecological levels of support—Community/Neighborhood, Family/Friends, and Intimate Relationships—were analyzed using both the MANOVA and ANOVA procedures with parent (mother versus father) and time of assessment (prepartum and each of the four postpartum assessments) treated as within-subject factors and the individual family conceptualized as the unit of analysis. The means, standard deviations, and pertinent multivariate and univariate analysis of variance statistics are presented in Table 4.4. Significant multivariate main effects were detected for parent, $F(5, 36) = 34.29$, $p < .0001$, and time, $F(20, 21) = 424.53$, $p < .0001$, and the interaction of parent and time also was found to be significant, $F(20, 21) = 280.27$, $p < .0001$. Univariate tests of this overall interaction effect were conducted with the five dependent variables, and a significant effect was found with each. To facilitate the

Table 4.4 Summary of Role Satisfaction and Support Data

	−1 Month M	SD	1 Month M	SD	4 Months M	SD	8 Months M	SD	12 Months M	SD	Parent F(1, 40)	Time F(4, 37)	Parent × Time F(4, 37)
Parental Role Satisfaction													
mother	17.1	4.0	17.9	4.5	19.1	3.2	15.8	4.3	20.7	3.1	0.53	236.21****	77.72****
father	16.1	4.4	15.8	4.4	17.7	2.2	18.2	3.5	20.7	3.0			
Degree of Pleasure in Children													
mother	15.0	2.9	14.7	3.2	15.9	3.2	11.6	2.3	15.7	2.3	0.05	33.14****	41.85****
father	12.0	2.7	14.2	2.9	15.1	3.2	15.3	3.0	15.6	2.3			
Community/Neighborhood support													
mother	9.1	2.2	8.8	1.9	9.8	2.0	10.3	2.0	9.3	2.2	18.30****	27.81****	19.85****
father	6.2	1.7	7.1	2.0	8.7	2.0	9.1	1.9	9.3	1.6			
Friend/Family support													
mother	22.1	4.5	27.7	3.2	28.4	3.2	24.1	4.0	23.6	4.5	115.98****	77.47****	56.77****
father	11.6	2.7	16.9	3.8	18.9	4.0	19.5	4.1	20.9	3.8			
Intimate support													
mother	20.3	2.5	21.3	2.4	20.8	2.9	20.7	3.1	15.9	2.6	0.94	95.32****	9.49***
father	19.8	2.7	19.1	2.2	21.1	1.8	18.0	2.4	15.9	2.6			
Multivariate F ratios											$F(5, 36)$ 34.29****	$F(20, 21)$ 424.53****	$F(20, 21)$ 280.27****

NOTE: All contrasts involving the time factor are reported with Greenhouse-Geisser adjusted degrees of freedom and probability levels.
$*p < .05$; $**p < .01$; $***p < .001$; $****p < .0001$.

interpretation of these interaction effects, MANOVA and ANOVA analyses of the time factor were conducted separately for each parent. Significant multivariate effects for time were detected for both mothers, $F(20, 21) = 241.86$, $p < .0001$, and fathers, $F(20, 21) = 558.57$, $p < .0001$, and all univariate tests revealed significant time effects.

Further analyses of these interaction effects utilized Tukey HSD procedures to consider first changes over time within each parent, and then differences between parents at the same points in time. The Parental Role Satisfaction means for the mothers did not differ significantly between the prepartum and 1-month postpartum sessions, but then an increase in satisfaction was noted at the 4-month assessment. A significant drop in maternal role satisfaction was observed at the 8-month session, before a final rebound at the 12-month assessment. The means for the fathers showed a gradual, steplike increase over time, with the means of the prepartum and 1-month postpartum sessions showing no difference, those of the 4- and 8-month sessions being significantly higher but not different from each other, and that of the 12-month session still higher. Comparisons of mothers and fathers at each time of assessment indicated no difference between the parents at either the prepartum or the 12-month sessions, that mothers were significantly more satisfied than fathers at the 1- and 4-month sessions, and that fathers were more satisfied than mothers at the 8-month session, when maternal scores fell to their lowest level.

The means of the mothers on the Degree of Pleasure in Child measure revealed no differences across the prepartum and 1-, 4-, and 12-month postpartum sessions, but a significant decline in pleasure was noted at the 8-month session. The means for the fathers increased significantly from the prepartum to the postpartum sessions, with none of the postpartum sessions differing significantly. Comparisons of the parents at each time of assessment revealed significant differences at the prepartum session (mothers reporting greater pleasure) and at the 8-month postpartum session (mothers reporting less pleasure).

Maternal scores on the Community/Neighborhood index of social support did not differ across the times of assessment except for an increase at the 8-month postpartum session. On the other hand, the means for the fathers revealed a steady increase from each session to the next. Significant differences between the parents (i.e., mothers consistently scoring higher) existed at each time of measurement with the exception of the final assessment. Maternal scores on the Family/Friends index were higher at the 1- and 4-month postpartum sessions, with the scores of the other three sessions not differing significantly. Paternal scores on this index revealed a marked increase from the prepartum to the 1- and 4-month postpartum sessions, and then a further increase at the 8- and 12-month sessions. At each time of assessment the mothers' means on the Family/Friends support measure were significantly higher than those of the fathers.

Finally, on the index of Intimate support, the means of the mothers did not differ across the prepartum, 1-, 4-, and 8-month postpartum sessions, but dropped significantly at 12-month sessions. Paternal scores on the Intimate support index did not differ across the prepartum and 1-month postpartum sessions, but fathers showed a significant increase at the 4-month session before they paralleled the maternal drop in these scores at both the 8- and 12-month sessions. Maternal and paternal scores on Intimate support did not differ from one another at any of the times of assessment except for the 1-month postpartum session, where the mothers reported higher levels of support than did the fathers.

Comments on Role Satisfaction and Social Support

The most striking feature of these data is that a major transition appears to take place for fathers between the prepartum and postpartum assessments, while for mothers the period between the 4- and 8-month sessions appears to be a more critical time of adjustment. Maternal scores on both the subdomains of the Satisfaction with Parenting Scale were relatively stable throughout the duration of this project, except for a major decline at the 8-month session. The increase in the maternal score on the Community/Neighbor support index suggests that the mothers may have been seeking assistance from those sources to cope with the events that were having such a negative impact on their satisfaction scores. The developmental transition occurring in the infants between 7 and 9 months of age (see Emde, 1977; Kagan, Kearsley, & Zelazo, 1978) certainly must be considered in accounting for these changes in maternal role satisfaction and pleasure in children. That fathers might be less sensitive to these changes would make intuitive sense given the fact that care of the infants appeared to be primarily the mothers' responsibility.

Indeed, the paternal data at the 8-month session suggest that this period was merely one point in the midst of the fathers' progression toward greater satisfaction with their roles as parents, greater pleasure being derived from their children, and greater senses of support from their Community/Neighbors and Family/Friends. These increases occurred between the prepartum and 1-month postpartum sessions for Degree of Pleasure in Child and the two support measures, and between the 1- and 4-month sessions for Parental Role Satisfaction. This suggests that the fathers might have been coping with the stress of this period of family transition by seeking support from these sources, by becoming somewhat more active in child care (see Chapter 5 for results and commentary concerning changes in role definition), and by discovering that these activities could serve as significant sources of reinforcement. The paternal increase in Intimate support at the 4-month session might be interpreted as an indication that the mothers valued the increased paternal participation and therefore become more supportive of the efforts of their husbands, or that the fathers became more aware of the support already being offered by their wives.

The satisfaction with parenting and the sources of support data continue to present a picture of both commonality and gender differences in parental adjustments to the second birth. Initially, mothers and fathers differed on all satisfaction and support measures except for Intimate support, with mothers consistently showing both greater satisfaction and greater support. Although different patterns of change over time were observed, it is interesting to note that by the 12-month postpartum session the mothers and fathers did not differ appreciably in their reported levels of satisfaction or support in any dimension except the network of Family/Friends, and even here fathers had increased their scores dramatically such that the difference between the parents was cut in half.

The Questionnaire on Social Support appears on the surface to be generic in that it addresses the availability of support in dealing with "problems." However, when this index is combined with a Satisfaction with Parenting Scale and used in a longitudinal study of familial adjustment, it would appear logical to assume that the parents would probably limit the range of "problems" to those involving their children, parental responsibilities, or spousal relationships. That mothers would be more involved with and would receive more support for problems of a familial nature from their close friends than would fathers is to be expected with a sample such as ours. Indeed, most of the fathers indicated that their friends tended to be business associates and that they rarely discussed family matters with such associates. When one considers the findings, reported in Chapter 5, concerning role definition, in particular the observation that the wives were primarily responsible for maintaining social arrangements and for making calls to friends and extended family members, then it

Table 4.5 Simple Correlations Between Satisfaction and Support Measures and Child Domain Stressors

	1	2	3	4	5	6	7	8	9	10	11
1 Parental Role Satisfaction		.44	.39	.48	.43	-.32	-.44	-.42	-.33	-.51	-.46
2 Degree of Pleasure in Child	.30		.06	.43	.61	-.37	-.22	-.41	-.41	-.45	-.43
3 Community support	.29	-.22		.22	.07	-.07	-.24	-.06	-.18	-.22	-.07
4 Family/Friend support	.49	.19	.42		.58	-.34	-.24	-.38	-.46	-.38	-.40
5 Intimate support	.43	.36	-.12	.16		-.08	-.23	-.34	-.36	-.50	-.48
6 Demandingness	-.44	-.51	.15	-.15	-.02		.61	.55	.69	.58	.31
7 Adaptability	-.43	-.44	.14	-.16	-.12	.66		.58	.60	.77	.46
8 Distractibility	-.34	-.05	-.25	-.27	.01	.41	.41		.47	.51	.58
9 Moodiness	-.33	-.54	.35	-.06	-.26	.70	.68	.25		.62	.52
10 Acceptability	-.44	-.54	.16	-.20	-.28	.54	.53	.28	.75		.54
11 Reinforcement	-.52	-.43	.11	-.34	-.25	.49	.46	.26	.63	.68	

NOTE: Correlations for mothers are below main diagonal; those for fathers are above. Critical value of r with df = 39 at the $p < .05$ level is .31; at the $p < .01$ level, .41.

makes sense that these potential sources of support would serve them more than they would the fathers.

SOCIAL SUPPORT AND PARENTAL SATISFACTION AS BUFFERS TO STRESS

How do parents utilize support networks or role satisfaction to mitigate stress?

A series of canonical correlation procedures was conducted to investigate the extent to which various constellations of social support or parental satisfaction measures might be predictive of specific levels of parenting stress. Separate analyses were conducted for mothers and fathers for the sources of stress associated with the Child, Infant, and Self domains, with all data being drawn from the 12-month postpartum assessment. The simple correlation coefficients for the items of these three spheres of parental adjustment are presented in Tables 4.5, 4.6, and 4.7, for Child, Infant, and Self domain stressors, respectively. Since canonical

Table 4.6 Simple Correlations Between Satisfaction and Support Measures and Infant Domain Stressors

	1	2	3	4	5	6	7	8	9	10	11
1 Parental Role Satisfaction		.44	.39	.48	.43	-.34	-.43	-.26	-.38	-.53	-.47
2 Degree of Pleasure in Child	.30		.06	.43	.61	-.32	-.30	-.44	-.44	-.44	-.45
3 Community support	.29	-.22		.22	.07	-.27	-.47	-.09	-.14	-.38	-.19
4 Family/Friend support	.49	.19	.42		.58	-.12	-.35	-.04	-.38	-.35	-.43
5 Intimate support	.43	.36	-.12	.16		-.30	-.25	-.28	-.35	-.45	-.53
6 Demandingness	-.14	-.24	-.01	-.08	-.05		.51	.31	.46	.74	.37
7 Adaptability	-.05	-.13	-.02	-.09	-.04	.62		.23	.49	.49	.42
8 Distractibility	-.28	-.53	.06	-.20	-.15	.55	.40		.28	.50	.42
9 Moodiness	-.02	-.25	-.04	-.06	.07	.74	.71	.52		.68	.64
10 Acceptability	-.16	-.27	-.03	.05	-.09	.57	.49	.41	.65		.73
11 Reinforcement	-.22	-.37	-.04	-.14	-.12	.46	.52	.46	.66	.72	

NOTE: Correlations for mothers are below main diagonal; those for fathers are above. Critical value of r with df = 39 at the $p < .05$ level is .31; at the $p < .01$ level, .41.

correlation procedures require two rather than three vectors of scores, and since we know of no statistical procedure that would allow us to describe the relationships between three such vectors, our first decision regarding this series of analyses concerned whether the data of any of the three domains could be grouped such that only two vectors of scores remained. Even though doing so would greatly reduce the number of canonical procedures necessary to complete this analysis, such grouping decisions must be made carefully if one is to ensure the interpretability of results.

The correlations presented in Tables 4.5, 4.6, and 4.7 did not provide any clear empirical basis for the decision. The items of the satisfaction and support measures, with the exception of Degree of Pleasure in Child and Community support, tended to be positively correlated with one another (from .19 to .61). On the other hand, the items of each of these spheres tended to be negatively correlated with the stress items. While the sign of these correlations may be simply an artifact of the wording of the items in the respective scales, it makes intuitive sense that inverse relationships would exist between the stress and both the support and the

Table 4.7 Simple Correlations Between Satisfaction and Support Measures and Self Domain Stressors

		1	2	3	4	5	6	7	8	9	10	11	12	13
1	Parental Role Satisfaction		.44	.39	.48	.43	-.59	-.46	-.36	-.55	-.41	-.19	-.51	.09
2	Degree of Pleasure in Child	.30		.06	.43	.61	-.58	-.52	-.50	-.55	-.54	-.30	-.59	.12
3	Community support	.29	-.22		.22	.07	-.12	-.08	-.06	-.01	-.03	-.08	-.02	-.03
4	Family/Friend support	.49	.19	.42		.58	-.62	-.26	-.38	-.50	-.72	-.13	-.46	-.01
5	Intimate support	.43	.36	-.12	.16		-.60	-.39	-.41	-.62	-.60	-.20	-.60	-.14
6	Depression	-.49	-.52	.04	-.32	-.29		.58	.63	.73	.80	.43	.80	.18
7	Attachment	-.47	-.32	-.04	-.44	-.20	.51		.29	.61	.42	.57	.50	.09
8	Role restriction	-.44	-.31	-.28	-.48	-.16	.42	.35		.59	.63	.22	.79	.29
9	Sense of competence	-.60	-.58	.02	-.29	-.23	.76	.65	.49		.72	.36	.69	.09
10	Social isolation	-.54	-.37	-.29	-.76	-.29	.67	.54	.56	.51		.30	.76	.23
11	Realistic attitude	-.24	-.22	.09	-.34	-.08	.56	.22	.23	.35	.41		.32	.27
12	Spousal relationship	-.53	-.17	-.20	-.40	-.52	.39	.22	.41	.32	.47	.22		.27
13	Health	-.20	-.56	.12	-.23	-.24	.49	.39	.53	.39	.40	.34	.10	

NOTE: Correlations for mothers are below main diagonal; those for fathers are above. Critical value of r with df = 39 at the $p < .05$ level is .31; at the $p < .01$ level, .41.

satisfaction measures. Moreover, since Crnic, Greenberg, Ragozin, Robinson, and Basham's (1983) Parental Role Satisfaction subscale includes items addressing the availability of professionals and others with whom one can discuss problems concerning the children, the concepts of support and satisfaction may be confounded to some degree.

We may theorize that support acts either as a second-order factor leading to satisfaction or as a buffer to mitigate the effects of stressful situations, but to do so would demand imposing an unnecessarily restrictive assumption regarding the direction of causality. Even if such a position is taken, it need not suggest that a person could not be satisfied with her or his role as a parent unless an adequate support network existed. Certainly numerous paths toward either role satisfaction or reduced stress may be hypothesized, and a diverse array of potential supporters may be available. On the other hand, one could just as well conceptualize these measures of role satisfaction and degree of pleasure in children as being supports of an internal nature rather than from members' external networks, such that the parent might be seen as possessing two sources of potential buffers to mitigate stressful situations. Thus the parent who lacks a strong external support network but who possesses positive attitudes concerning his or her role as a parent and/or who derives pleasure from activities as a parent could still be seen to have a buffer against stress. Indeed, the parent who possesses both positive parental role satisfaction and a high degree of pleasure in children may have little need for establishing or maintaining social support networks. In the interest of clarity and brevity, we decided to consider the satisfaction and the support items as a single set, but we did so with reservation, because we would prefer to consider simultaneously all three spheres as being governed by a systemic and circular rather than linear form of causality (see P. Minuchin, 1985).[3]

Since these analyses were conducted with a sample of only 41 families (insufficient for path analysis), the results presented below are best considered to be descriptive rather than of a hypothesis-testing nature. On the other hand, despite the smallness of the sample relative to the total number of variables, the normality, linearity, and lack of multicollinearity of the variables used in these analyses have been found to be acceptable. (See Marascuilo & Levin, 1983, or Tabachnick & Fidell, 1983, for detailed discussions of the assumptions underlying canonical correlation analysis.) The tables presenting these analyses include the following statistics: Bartlett's (1947) test for the significance of the k smallest eigenvalues; the eigenvalues themselves, which indicate the percentage

Table 4.8 Canonical Correlations Between Parental Support/Satisfaction Variables and Child Stress Subdomains

| | *Mothers* | | *Fathers* | |
	Loading	*Standard Coefficient*	*Loading*	*Standard Coefficient*
Support/satisfaction				
Parental Role Satisfaction	.689*	.794	.699*	.291
Degree of Pleasure in Child	.755*	.572	.787*	.271
Community/Neighborhood support	−.223	−.391	.185	−.014
Friend/Family support	.299	.032	.696*	.127
Intimate support	.178	−.422	.909*	.546
percentage variance	.243		.490	
redundancy	.155		.252	
Child subdomains				
demandingness	−.875*	−.656	−.395	.264
adaptability	−.750*	−.303	−.476	.569
distractibility	−.262	.299 ·	−.642*	−.359
moodiness	−.745*	.313	−.642*	−.299
acceptability	−.759*	−.322	−.817	−.888
reinforcement	−.753	−.330	−.789*	−.288
percentage variance	.516		.416	
redundancy	.329		.214	
Canonical correlation	.799		.717	
Eigenvalue	.638		.514	
χ^2 (Bartlett's)	53.67		47.90	
df = 30	p < .005		p < .020	

*The squared multiple correlation of this variable with all variables in the other set is sufficiently large such that its associated F ratio is greater than unity at the $p < .05$ level.

of variance overlap between the pairs of variates; the canonical variable loadings derived from the correlations of the canonical variables with the original variables to assist in interpreting variate patterns (Darlington, Weinberg, & Walberg, 1973); the percentages of variance extracted by each canonical variate from its own set of variables; and the redundancy indices for each variate to assess the reduction in uncertainty in predicting the level of one set of variables gained by knowing the values of the other (Stewart & Love, 1968). These statistics were obtained through the use of the BMD-P6M program (Dixon et al., 1983).

The pertinent statistics for the mother and father solutions when one considers the areas of stress in the Child domain are presented in Table 4.8. For both parents a single canonical variate was significant—the specified linear combinations of support/satisfaction variables overlapped, with 64% and 51% of the total variation in the combination of Child domain stressors for mothers and fathers, respectively. The variate loadings for the mothers suggest that those mothers with low levels of degree of pleasure in the child (.755) and low parental role satisfaction (.689) also tended to have higher levels of stress associated with the following subdomains: child demandingness (−.875), acceptability of the child's behavior (−.759), the failure to perceive the child as a source of positive reinforcement (−.753), the child's inability to adapt to changes in the environment (−.750), and general moodiness in the child (−.745).

For fathers, the pattern of loadings was quite different: Those fathers who experienced low levels of support from their wives (.909), low degree of pleasure in the child (.787), low parental role satisfaction (.699), and low levels of support from family and friends (.696) also tended to have higher levels of stress associated with the acceptability of the child's behavior (−.817), a failure to find the child to be a source of positive reinforcement (−.789), or a perception that the child was too easily distracted (−.642), too moody (−.642), and too demanding (−.395). A greater reduction in uncertainty was found for the mothers' data by using the stress data to predict a lack of support/satisfaction (.329 versus .155), while for fathers only a slightly greater reduction in uncertainty was found in predicting stress from the lack of support/satisfaction rather than the reverse (.252 versus .214). It should be noted further that, although intimate support (i.e., from the spouse) and support from friends and family had predictive power only in accounting for stress experienced by fathers, these data should not be interpreted to suggest that the lack of predictive power with mothers necessarily implies that these mothers failed to receive support from their husbands, families, or friends.

The analyses with the variables associated with the Infant domain are presented in Table 4.9. The first eigenvalue in the solution for the mothers was of insufficient magnitude to warrant further analysis. Very low reported levels of maternal stress in the Infant domain, and hence a relative lack of variability, appear to be part of the cause for this limitation. With fathers, however, a single-variate solution was obtained that accounted for approximately 51% of the variability in the fathers' reported Infant domain stress. This linear combination suggests that fathers who experienced low levels of parental role satisfaction (.807), low support from their communities or neighbors (.752), and a low degree of pleasure in the infant (.524) also experienced higher levels of stress due to not finding the behavior of the infant acceptable (−.857), perceiving the infant as lacking sufficient ability in adapting to changes in the

Table 4.9 Canonical Correlations Between Parental Support/Satisfaction Variables and Infant Stress Subdomains

| | Mothers | | Fathers | |
	Loading	Standard Coefficient	Loading	Standard Coefficient
Support/satisfaction				
Parental Role Satisfaction	.581	.346	.807*	.373
Degree of Pleasure in Child	.943*	.861	.524*	.131
Community/Neighborhood support	−.076	−.035	−.752*	.550
Friend/Family support	.374	.076	.627	.145
Intimate support	.345	−.128	.580	.216
percentage variance	.298		.444	
redundancy	.108		.228	
Infant subdomains				
demandingness	−.419	−.046	−.559	.377
adaptability	−.221	.214	−.788*	−.606
distractibility	−.909*	−.890	−.379	.101
moodiness	−.389	.304	−.574*	.264
acceptability	−.450	.026	−.857*	−1.027
reinforcement	−.642	−.545	−.716*	−.059
percentage variance	.303		.442	
redundancy	.110		.227	
Canonical correlation	.603		.717	
Eigenvalue	.363		.514	
χ^2 (Bartlett's)	23.43		45.89	
$df = 30$	$p < .797$		$p < .032$	

*The squared multiple correlation of this variable with all variables in the other set is sufficiently large such that its associated F ratio is greater than unity at the $p < .05$ level.

environment (−.788), not feeling the infant was a source of positive reinforcement (−.716), and seeing the infant as too moody (−.574). The reductions in uncertainty did not differ appreciably with direction of the prediction (.228 versus .227).

The analyses using the variables associated with the Self domain are presented in Table 4.10. The solution for the mothers produced two significant eigenvalues, and thus two pairs of canonical variates. The first variate represents a 73% overlap in the variances of the support/satisfaction measures and those of Self domain stress, and the second a 59% overlap. The first pair of variates implies that mothers with lower levels of support from family or friends (.908) and with lower parental role satisfaction (.736) tended to experience a greater sense of social isolation (−.937) and role restriction (−.642), less attachment to their children

Table 4.10 Canonical Correlations Between Parental Support/Satisfaction Variables and Self Stress Subdomains

	Mothers First Variate		Second Variate		Fathers First Variate	
	Loading	Standard Coefficient	Loading	Standard Coefficient	Loading	Standard Coefficient
Support/satisfaction						
Parental Role Satisfaction	.736*	.260	.277	.487	.717*	.370
Degree of Pleasure in Child	.477	.229	.766*	.769	.807*	.408
Community support	.334	.027	-.441	-.154	.058	-.212
Friend/Family support	.908*	.706	-.371	-.665	.790*	.416
Intimate support	.421	.117	.229	-.167	.751*	.118
percentage variance	.377		.210		.471	
redundancy	.274		.123		.339	
Self subdomains						
depression	-.592*	.469	-.501	-.268	-.894*	-.306
attachment	-.623*	-.089	-.188	.401	-.618*	-.166
role restriction	-.642*	.002	-.083	.384	-.627*	.002
sense of competence	-.609	-.315	-.674*	-1.025	-.837*	-.153
social isolation	-.937*	-.832	.064*	.478	-.874*	-.402
realistic attitude	-.420	-.124	-.076	.268	-.297	.087
spousal relationship	-.616*	-.250	.004	-.039	-.816*	-.181
health	-.430	-.108	-.470*	-.579	.081	.280
percentage variance	.392		.122		.475	
redundancy	.286		.071		.341	
Canonical correlation	.854		.765		.848	
Eigenvalue	.729		.585		.719	
χ^2 (Bartlett's)	95.45		52.40		76.08	
	$p < .0001$		$p < .003$		$p < .005$	
	$df = 40$		$df = 28$		$df = 40$	

*The squared multiple correlation of this variable with all variables in the other set is sufficiently large such that its associated F ratio is greater than unity at the $p < .05$ level.

(–.623), greater difficulties with their spouses (–.616), and greater depression (–.592). The second pair of variates adds that those mothers who failed to obtain an acceptable degree of pleasure in their children (.766) also lacked a sense of competence in their lives (–.672) and may have been in poorer health (–.470). In this two-variate solution, a slightly greater reduction in uncertainty was obtained by using maternal support/satisfaction data to predict levels of stress (total of .397 versus .357). For fathers the single significant pair of variates (72% of variance overlapped) suggested that those who failed to obtain an acceptable degree of pleasure in their children (.807), lacked support from both family and friends (.790) and from their wives (.751), and failed to obtain satisfaction from their roles as parents (.717) tended to experience a wide array of stressors associated with the Self domain. In particular, these fathers experienced greater depression (–.894) and social isolation (–.874), lacked a sense of competence (–.837), had more difficulties with their wives (–.816), felt restricted in their life roles (–.627), and felt less attached to their children (–.618). Once again, uncertainty indices associated with paternal data do not differ appreciably with direction (.339 versus .341).

Comments Concerning the Mitigation of Stress Through Support Networks

The series of canonical analyses revealed considerable differences between mothers and fathers concerning the manner in which satisfaction, support, and stress variables were related. Although we cannot empirically contrast the maternal and paternal canonical variates derived above, we may ascertain at the descriptive level (using the standardized coefficients and the squared multiple correlations of each item in one set of variates with the items of the other) that the structures relating support/satisfaction scores with those of stress differ for mothers and fathers. More important, the inconsistency of the direction for optimal prediction, as suggested by the redundancy indices, supports the suggestion that researchers abandon simple linear models when attempting to explain the relationships among parental stress, satisfaction, and support networks. Maternal stress associated with the child appeared to be a better predictor of maternal lack of satisfaction with parenting than the inverse, but for fathers the opposite was true. Maternal stress in the Self domain was best predicted by various support measures, while for fathers the direction of prediction appeared insignificant. Research employing path analysis techniques with multidimensional concurrent and sequential assessments of parental stressors, satisfaction, and sources of support is needed to further our understanding of the systemic interdependence of these factors.

The importance of support from their spouses in helping fathers to mitigate the stress related to the Child domain appears to be a logical extension of the reports from Crnic et al. (1983) and Pedersen, Yarrow, Anderson, and Cain (1978) concerning the role of intimate support from the husband in enhancing the wife's performance as a mother. Specifically, the wives may be seen as behaving reciprocally to provide the support necessary for their husbands to develop effective parenting skills. These data support Belsky's (1979) position that wives may serve to interest their husbands in, and enhance their understanding of, child and infant development. We suggest that the wives were instrumental in guiding their husbands through this difficult role transition through their support and encouragement of paternal involvement in caregiving. That this involvement does not appear to a large degree following the first birth is probably due to both the fact that society traditionally has not viewed men as "significant others" in the realm of child care and the fact that the mothers may not have needed the fathers' assistance when they had only one child. The importance to fathers, but not mothers, of community support (i.e., neighbors or local support and educational groups) in lessening infant-related stress supplements this interpretation; these groups may offer fathers further reassurance while the fathers enter their new roles (cf. Russell, 1978). Mothers, on the other hand, appear to rely very little on support from their spouses, communities, or families and friends, and seem to draw their strength primarily from their satisfaction with their parenting role or their degree of pleasure derived from their children, suggesting that their overall satisfaction with their parenting role may serve as an internalized source of support.

NOTES

1. Greenhouse-Geisser adjusted degrees of freedom and probability levels were used with all analysis of variance procedures involving the factor time as either a main effect or part of an interaction effect. All of the epsilon values, a measure of the degree of violation of the sphericity assumption, associated with each significant univariate test of time or time-related interaction effect were greater than .80, thus meeting Hertzog and Rovine's (1985) heuristic for adopting MANOVA procedures with mixed models.

2. MANOVA and ANOVA procedures were conducted separately with the Child, Infant, and Self domain variables, with child age treated as a three-level between-groups factor

(2-, 3-, and 4-year-olds), and parent and time treated as within-groups factors. No multivariate or univariate effects for child age or interaction effects including the factor child age were detected with the Child and Infant domain stressors. Multivariate effects for age, $F(16, 62) = 1.84$, $p < .0459$, and for the interaction of age and parent, $F(16, 62) = 2.56$, $p < .0043$, were detected with the Self domain. At the univariate level, the main effect for age was detected only with depression, $F(2, 38) = 3.05$, $p < .0591$, where greater stress was found among parents of 3- and 4-year-olds than among parents of younger firstborns. Univariate interaction effects were detected with each of the following subdomains: attachment, $F(2, 38) = 4.34$, $p < .0201$; role restriction, $F(2, 38) = 6.05$, $p < .0052$; social isolation, $F(2, 38) = 5.51$, $p < .0079$; and relationship with spouse, $F(2, 38) = 3.75$, $p < .0325$. With each variable, the age of the firstborn child had no effect on the levels of stress reported by the mothers. On the other hand, fathers of 4-year-olds reported greater role restriction, social isolation, and troubles with their spouses than their counterparts with 2- or 3-year-olds; fathers with 2-year-olds reported less stress associated with attachment than did the other fathers.

3. Additional canonical correlation procedures were conducted with the stress scores of each of the three domains and with the satisfaction and sources of support scores each used as separate vectors. We conducted these analyses to ascertain whether the combination of the satisfaction and support measures into a single vector had either produced results that would not be found in separate analyses or hidden relationships that would be apparent only in separate analyses. These procedures provided a pattern of item loadings that, in essence, replicated the results reported here. For example, if one compared the composite of the item-loading patterns derived from the separate canonical analyses of support measures and satisfaction measures each with the Child domain stressors with the single pattern obtained from the analysis employing a single satisfaction/support vector, it was obvious both that nothing was gained by conducting separate procedures and that nothing was lost by combining the satisfaction and support measures into a single vector. Specifically, if one constructed templates of the results of the satisfaction with stress and the support with stress analyses, and placed these templates on top of each other, the patterns of loadings (i.e., the signs and the relative magnitudes of both the variable loadings and the associated standardized coefficients) and the patterns of the squared multiple correlations of variables with the items in the other vector would be virtually identical to those reported here.

5

Parental Redefinition of Roles: The Who Does What? Index

Three analyses were conducted to assess potential between-parent differences and changes in the parental ratings of responsibility for the infant, child, and household tasks included in the Who Does What? Index. The first analysis addressed the issue of changes in ratings of actual task responsibility over time. The second analysis focused on identifying the relationships among the child-care and housekeeping tasks such that a structure of family task definition might emerge and changes in this assumed structure over time—that is, family adjustment and accommodation—could be described. The final analysis focused on the differences between maternal and paternal perceptions of "actual" and "ideal" with respect to the family division of responsibilities. The following specific questions are addressed by these analyses:

(1) Does the assignment of task responsibility change over time?
(2) Is there a pattern of role responsibility across families?
(3) Do parents agree on what the role division is, or on what it should be?
(4) Is the perception of a discrepancy between "actual" and "ideal" role divisions associated with greater stress?

MOTHERS' AND FATHERS' PERCEPTIONS OF TASK RESPONSIBILITIES

Does the assignment of task responsibility change over time?

Parent effects. MANOVA and ANOVA procedures were conducted for each of the sets of 7 child-care and 13 household tasks, with parent (mother versus father) and time (prepartum versus 12-month postpartum) as within-family factors. The means, standard deviations, and MANOVA and ANOVA statistics pertinent to these analyses are presented in Table 5.1. Overall parent effects were detected for both the child-care tasks, $F(7, 34) = 2.56$, $p < .05$, and the household tasks, $F(13, 28) = 9.38$, $p < .0001$. Within the child-care set, univariate parent effects were detected for the following four tasks: respond to the child's cry, respond to the child's cry at night, choose toys for the child, and care for the child when the child is sick. One might describe the apparent differences by suggesting that the mothers' ratings were biased toward the 1 or "Mother" end of the scale, whereas the fathers' were biased toward the 9 or "Father" end. The consequence of these biasing effects was that mothers underestimated their husbands' contributions and overestimated their own contributions, that the husbands overestimated their own contributions and underestimated the contributions of their wives, or both. Within the household tasks, univariate parent effects were detected for the following nine items: arranging for sitters, washing dishes, making repairs around the house, general household cleaning, shopping (especially for groceries), making social arrangements, telephoning family, supervising automobile repairs, and general yard work. As with the child-care items, the comparison of mean values indicates that mothers and fathers maintained the overestimation of their own relative contributions or, alternatively, the underestimation of that of their spouses.

Time effects. Significant time effects also were detected for each of these sets of items: $F(7, 34) = 6.26$, $p < .0001$, for child care, and $F(13, 28) = 11.00$, $p < .0001$, for household tasks. Considering the child-care tasks, increased involvement on the parts of the fathers was found on each of the items except bathing or dressing the child and putting the child to bed at night; this latter item was reported as one equally shared by the parents. Similarly, significant increases in the fathers' involvement in household tasks were noted for every item except making repairs around the home, shopping, washing clothes, doing yard work, and contributing to the household income. Over time, a significant increase in the wives' relative contributions to household income also was noted.

Interaction effects. The multivariate interaction of parent and time was significant for both the child-care items, $F(7, 34) = 5.74$, $p < .0002$, and the household task items, $F(13, 28) = 6.24$, $p < .0001$. Significant interaction effects at the univariate level were detected for the following child-care items: bathing or dressing the child, responding to crying at night, caring for the sick child, and putting the child to bed. In each case, post hoc contrasts (Tukey HSD procedures computed at the .05 level of significance) indicated that fathers reported an increase in their own relative contributions toward these activities, and that mothers did not report the fathers' increases. Significant interaction effects were noted with the following household task items: arranging for sitters, washing dishes, shopping, paying bills, and supervising auto repairs. Post hoc contrasts with these variables indicated that fathers reported increases in their contributions toward arranging for sitters and washing dishes that were not noted by their wives, that they reported increases in their shopping and bill-paying activities whereas mothers reported decreased contributions on the parts of their spouses, and that mothers reported increases in their own responsibilities for auto repairs whereas fathers reported no such changes.

Comments on Parental Differences
and Changes in Ratings

The means shown in Table 5.1 clearly indicate that, prior to the birth of the second child, the mothers were principally responsible for nearly all child-care and household tasks. The fathers' responsibilities were limited to providing income, doing yard work, and seeing that automobile repairs were made, and to sharing in the tasks of playing with the child and putting the child to bed. As indexed by the differences between the prepartum and the 12-month ratings, 68% of the fathers indicated that they had increased their child-care activities at the latter period so that they now shared responsibilities with their spouses on all items except caring for a sick child; a similar shift was also reported by 51% of the mothers. Although most of the mothers and fathers (83% in each case) indicated that the fathers had increased their involvement in household tasks over the year, the overall pattern of primary responsibility remained as stereotypically defined as it had been in the earlier assessment. Specifically, fathers were responsible for such tasks as providing income, making repairs, and doing yard work, while mothers did the laundry, cooked meals, and did the shopping. Care of the second-born infant at this time appeared to be primarily a maternal responsibility, with the possible exception of playing with and putting the infant to bed, for which the parents shared responsibility (see Table 5.1). This overall change in task division appears similar to two of the patterns described by Kreppner, Paulsen, and Schuetze (1982)—the father looks after the firstborn child somewhat more regularly, thus allowing the mother to be

Table 5.1 Summary of Who Does What? Data

	Mother						Father						MANOVA and ANOVA Statistics					
	−1 actual		+12 actual		+12 ideal		−1 actual		+12 actual		+12 ideal		Time Effects on "Actual" Data			Contrast of "Actual and Ideal" Data		
													Parent	Time	Parent × Time	Parent	Type	Parent × Time
	M	SD	M	SD	M	SD	M	SD	M	SD	M	SD	$F_{(1,40)}$	$F_{(1,40)}$	$F_{(1,40)}$	$F_{(1,40)}$	$F_{(1,40)}$	$F_{(1,40)}$
Child care																		
bathe	3.29	1.35	3.05	1.73	4.24	1.34	3.12	1.55	3.66	1.61	4.07	1.27	0.84	1.99	18.84****	1.34	19.88****	5.23
cry	3.24	0.99	3.59	1.56	4.68	0.82	3.56	1.25	4.32	1.60	4.56	1.07	5.37*	16.52***	2.10	1.71	25.18****	8.24**
cry night	2.29	1.08	3.17	2.11	4.54	1.61	2.80	1.50	4.56	2.35	4.68	1.66	11.79**	42.54****	7.33**	6.26*	10.42**	11.15**
toys	3.39	1.20	3.68	1.49	4.93	0.79	3.68	1.21	4.39	1.43	4.83	1.02	5.36*	16.73***	3.92	2.24	29.99****	9.45**
sickness	1.88	1.31	1.95	1.41	4.00	1.55	2.20	1.05	2.83	1.75	3.73	1.69	7.22**	5.05*	8.31**	1.33	78.53****	11.16**
play	4.42	1.12	4.54	1.05	4.98	0.72	4.42	1.00	4.71	1.31	5.07	0.85	.20	6.72*	1.50	.65	8.40**	.12
bed	4.68	1.71	4.17	1.74	4.68	1.29	4.66	1.56	4.88	1.74	5.22	1.31	1.40	1.46	15.13***	7.39**	6.19*	.25
Multivariate F ratios (all with $df = 7, 34$)													2.56*	6.26**	5.74***	1.63	16.02****	3.10*
Housework																		
sitters	1.51	0.95	1.66	1.53	3.39	1.67	1.76	0.86	2.22	1.60	2.54	1.52	4.65*	8.50**	4.73*	.49	26.90****	11.02**
cooking	1.83	1.45	2.02	1.75	3.68	2.09	2.12	1.05	2.63	1.71	2.88	1.65	2.86	12.72***	3.37	.13	16.15****	8.87**
dishes	2.32	1.37	2.73	1.64	4.80	1.83	3.02	1.65	4.00	1.99	4.00	1.87	14.72***	72.44****	13.55***	.68	24.93****	26.82****
repairs	7.44	1.55	7.10	1.84	7.17	1.66	8.00	1.58	8.00	1.58	7.90	1.32	6.57*	3.89	3.89	10.64**	.00	.20
cleaning	2.27	1.24	2.42	1.32	4.29	1.81	3.22	1.11	3.46	1.43	3.76	1.41	23.10****	11.48**	.39	1.10	36.14****	22.41****
shopping	2.42	1.61	2.29	1.65	3.73	1.95	3.24	1.83	3.66	2.56	3.76	2.05	11.82**	1.70	7.59**	4.54*	14.23***	6.21*
pay bills	4.02	3.18	3.61	3.11	4.15	2.44	3.15	1.84	4.56	3.29	4.54	2.78	.01	10.51**	44.33****	4.94*	1.23	2.03
washing	1.76	1.16	1.71	1.15	2.98	1.84	1.93	1.40	2.05	1.73	2.34	1.68	1.03	.52	3.02	.44	16.64****	5.26*
social	2.85	1.33	3.12	1.60	4.27	1.16	4.07	1.25	4.24	1.39	4.54	1.16	23.34****	10.50**	.61	11.41**	18.05****	11.59**

(Continued)

Table 5.1 (Continued)

	Mother −1 actual M	SD	+12 actual M	SD	−1 ideal M	SD	+12 ideal M	SD	Father −1 actual M	SD	+12 actual M	SD	−1 ideal M	SD	+12 ideal M	SD	Actual Data: Parent $F(1,40)$	Time $F(1,40)$	Parent×Time $F(1,40)$	Contrast: Parent $F(1,40)$	Type $F(1,40)$	Parent×Time $F(1,40)$
Housework (continued)																						
calls	2.83	1.36	2.98	1.60	—	—	4.83	0.95	4.05	1.02	4.27	1.22	—	—	4.27	1.05	22.39****	4.62*	.20	3.46	35.41****	25.72****
car	7.05	2.20	7.42	1.94	—	—	7.27	1.61	8.00	1.74	8.10	1.64	—	—	7.88	1.36	7.45*	12.49****	8.40**	7.44**	.82	.05
income	8.29	1.19	8.15	1.42	—	—	6.54	1.63	8.34	1.11	8.20	1.50	—	—	7.32	1.47	.05	7.60**	.00	3.81	32.30****	4.26*
yard	6.58	1.87	6.63	1.78	—	—	6.37	1.87	7.66	1.35	7.51	1.58	—	—	6.90	1.50	12.34***	.61	2.55	8.06**	3.53	1.76
Multivariate F ratios (all with $df = 13, 28$)																	9.38****	11.00****	6.24****	3.33**	10.40****	4.23****
Infant																						
schedule	—		1.81	1.35	—		2.49	1.58	—		2.20	1.74	—		2.37	1.67	—	—	—	.32	5.13**	3.37
feeding	—		2.95	1.38	—		4.12	1.08	—		3.29	1.33	—		3.76	1.11	—	—	—	.00	34.35****	4.99**
diapering	—		3.32	1.33	—		4.51	1.19	—		3.37	1.34	—		3.61	1.18	—	—	—	4.96*	21.48****	8.53**
bathe	—		2.56	1.78	—		4.24	1.24	—		2.85	1.78	—		3.49	1.63	—	—	—	1.41	47.12****	8.93**
cry	—		3.05	1.55	—		4.32	1.42	—		4.10	1.39	—		4.32	1.10	—	—	—	5.22*	17.77****	9.12**
cry night	—		2.29	1.75	—		4.05	1.90	—		3.07	2.15	—		3.44	1.96	—	—	—	.10	20.49****	8.96**
toys	—		3.24	1.64	—		4.68	1.01	—		3.42	1.34	—		4.44	1.10	—	—	—	.03	50.73****	2.39
sickness	—		1.83	1.38	—		3.71	1.71	—		2.61	1.95	—		3.78	1.74	—	—	—	2.22	53.73****	4.10
play	—		4.34	0.91	—		4.88	0.33	—		4.37	1.30	—		4.76	0.62	—	—	—	.10	21.75****	.37
bed	—		3.58	1.73	—		4.49	1.45	—		4.29	1.98	—		4.68	1.39	—	—	—	4.43*	12.78***	2.34
Multivariate F ratios (all with $df = 10, 31$)																	—	—	—	3.42**	22.70****	1.87

MANOVA and ANOVA Statistics — Time Effects on "Actual" Data; Contrast of "Actual and Ideal" Data

NOTE: All contrasts involving the time factor are reported with Greenhouse-Geisser adjusted degrees of freedom and probability levels.

*$p < .05$; **$p < .01$; ***$p < .001$; ****$p < .0001$.

more intimate with the newborn, and he takes greater responsibility for household tasks, thus permitting the mother either greater time with both children or more time free of familial responsibilities. The third pattern described by Kreppner et al., in which the parents appear interchangeable, was not evident in our data, even at the level of individual families.[1]

These data also reveal a consistent, systematic, between-parent difference whereby each parent is seen to underestimate the spouse's relative contributions and/or overestimate his or her own for all categories. DeVault's (1985) concept of "invisible work" suggests a means of interpreting this finding. DeVault describes as *invisible* any work that is unrecognized, unacknowledged, or undefined as work, and suggests that the internal work of housework—that is, the planning, scheduling, monitoring, and arranging—often is overlooked in sociological and economic analyses of housework. The parents in this study were asked to provide ratings that would indicate who was "responsible for doing these tasks." If one is willing to assume that mothers are likely to have the greater responsibility for the invisible aspects of housework, and that fathers may well be unaware that these invisible aspects even exist, then a probable basis for the observed bias in ratings becomes obvious. "Responsible for doing" would imply to mothers both the planning/monitoring of the task as well as its actual performance, whereas for fathers this phrase would be limited to only the issue of task performance. If this is indeed the case, then the ratings of mothers would be biased toward the wife end of the continuum, whereas those of fathers would show a shift toward the other pole. This consistent bias is particularly notable given the large number of mothers who reported high levels of stress associated with their relationship with their spouses.

Despite the significant parent effect in the distributions of household task responsibilities, levels of agreement displayed both within and across families were high when these tasks were grouped categorically—that is, when one trichotomized the 9-point scale to create a simpler 3-point index representing mother's, shared, and father's tasks. Spouses agreed well with respect to which tasks categorically were the mother's (procuring nearly all infant-care items, cooking, washing, making all types of social arrangements, and so on), the father's (providing income, doing yard work and making repairs, and the like), or shared responsibilities (playing with and putting the child to bed). These data also indicated a shift toward a somewhat more egalitarian arrangement as the fathers became more active in household tasks and child care.

FAMILIAL STRUCTURE OF PARENTAL DIVISION OF RESPONSIBILITY

Is there a pattern of role responsibility across families?

Interest in the overall patterns of the familial division of parental and household duties led to the following questions, and to a series of smallest space analyses. Lingoes (1966, 1979) describes a pattern as a collection, or complex, of variables possessing some "organizing principle" not deducible from its constituent elements. Smallest space analysis is a general nonmetric method of dimensional simplification concerned with the concept of relative distance (Guttman, 1968; Lingoes, 1973). The objective in smallest space analysis is to decrease the dimensionality of the data matrix, such as a set of Pearson product-moment correlations, while maintaining the monotonicity condition; that is, it seeks to identify the form or pattern existing among the elements of a correlation matrix. A normalized stress coefficient (Kruskal, 1964) is used as a measure of the ability of a solution of k dimensions to represent adequately the ordinal relations within the data. Resulting dimensional loadings (coordinates) for each subject or variable are used to locate that item in the k-dimensional space close to other items scored similarly on the original scale of measure. Smallest space analysis offers a representation of the relative distances among a set of subjects or variables using as few coordinates as possible to portray the entire configuration faithfully (see Guttman, 1968; Lingoes, 1966, 1973).

Jones (1960) has described the difference between smallest space analysis and factor analysis by noting that the researcher using the structural, inductive approach of factor analysis rests content after finding and naming the factors, whereas the researcher using the pattern, deductive approach of smallest space analysis looks for some organizing principle that not only accounts for the pattern of intercorrelations but also can relate the factors to one another through concepts such as complexity and similarity. Jones further notes that the researcher using smallest space analysis is not looking for a structural hypothesis: Structure is already assumed, and the purpose of this technique "is to provide best-fitting values for the assumed structural parameters" (p. 12). Furthermore, it is generally the case that smallest space analysis will result in a more parsimonious solution, since regions rather than points and the relationships among them serve as the units of analysis (Lingoes, 1979).

Given these distinctions, smallest space analysis appears to be the technique of choice in our systems analysis of familial adjustment. In planning to conduct a molar analysis of the Who Does What? data, we assumed the existence of an underlying structure. Intuition suggests that at least two dimensions would be necessary to describe the pattern of parental role responsibility. The primary dimension was expected to be one that would separate tasks on the basis of gender of the parents; indeed, no matter how egalitarian a couple attempts to be, they often resort to defining certain tasks as being the chief responsibility of either the wife or the husband. It was assumed that the second dimension would represent whether the task was more or less a pleasurable family activity, such as playing with the child, or an individual chore, such as paying bills or arranging for sitters.

Prepartum and Postpartum Role Structures

A 20 × 20 matrix of correlation coefficients (composed of the 7 child-care tasks and 13 household tasks) was constructed from parental ratings of their reported responsibilities at the prepartum and the 12-month postpartum assessments. (The ratings for infant-care tasks were not included in these analyses due to the infants' absence at the prepartum assessment.) Separate matrices initially were constructed for maternal and paternal ratings, but the absence of significant differences between comparable elements of these matrices—that is, between pairs of analogous correlation coefficients from the maternal and paternal matrices—led us to combine maternal and paternal scores within the family to form overall matrices of parental scores. In solving for the eigenvalues of these matrices, it was found that a smallest space solution involving two dimensions would be sufficient. A "scree" plot of the eigenvalues of each of these matrices further supported the decision to compute two-dimensional solutions (Cattell, 1966). These solutions represented the relations among the variables rather well (Kruskal stress indices = .241 and .204 for prepartum and postpartum matrices, respectively).

Graphic representations of these prepartum and postpartum solutions are presented in Figures 5.1 and 5.2, respectively. Coordinates for the tasks have been standardized so that the four-quadrant space depicted by this two-dimensional solution extends 100 units in each direction. As expected, the first and major dimension (depicted horizontally), that is, the dimension associated with the larger, first eigenvalue in each solution, can be described as separating the 20 tasks according to whether they were

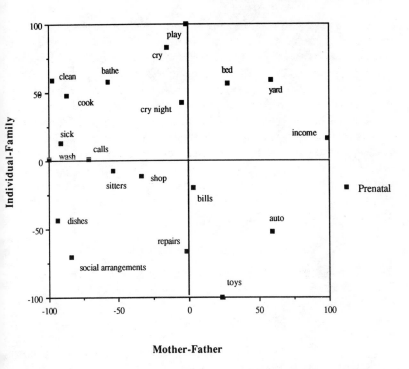

Figure 5.1. Two-Dimensional Display of Prenatal Household and Child-Care Task Coordinates

predominantly maternal responsibilities (far left), paternal responsibilities (far right), or shared (center). Note that at both periods the primarily maternal tasks include washing laundry, washing dishes, and caring for a sick child; that the primarily paternal tasks include providing for the family income, caring for the yard, and seeing to automobile repairs; and that the shared tasks include playing with the child, paying bills, and choosing toys for the child.

The second dimension in each solution can be conceived as separating the 20 tasks according to whether they were interpersonal familial activities such as playing with the child or responding to the child's cry (located at the top of the vertical axis), or activities that did not involve the interaction of family members, such as choosing toys for the child, making repairs around the house, or making social arrangements. The organization of tasks along this dimension was not as clear-cut as in the

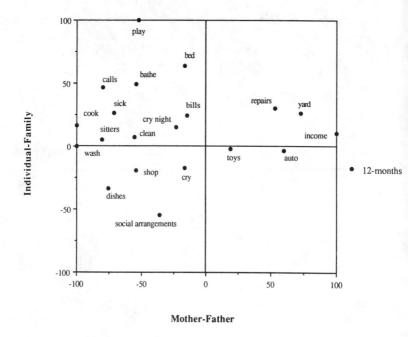

Figure 5.2. Two-Dimensional Display of 12-Month Postpartum Household and Child-Care Task Coordinates

first dimension. Initially, we anticipated that the second dimension would represent a continuum from enjoyable (e.g., play) to isolated, chore-type (e.g., paying bills) activities. The proximity of the item "respond to the child's cry" to "play with child" forced us to reject this assumption: It would be difficult to maintain that responding to a child's cry constitutes a pleasurable experience. As it emerged from the data, the second dimension is better conceived as a continuum ranging from activities that involve more than one family member (i.e., those above the midrange of the dimension) to activities performed in isolation (i.e., those below the midrange). Although no independent evidence exists to support the idea that some tasks are more "social" and others more "isolated," this interpretation was readily accepted by the parents involved in the project when they heard our presentation at the public forums held at the completion of the study. (A discussion of these forums and parental reactions to the data is presented in Chapter 7.)

A notable difference in the solutions depicted in the two figures is that whereas the variability along the first dimension remains constant, the second dimension decreases dramatically from the prepartum to the postpartum periods, a decrease due largely to a movement of items away from the noninteractive or isolated pole. This shift represents the primary component in describing the change in pattern over the course of familial adjustment to the birth of the second child.

Changes in Structure over Time

The change in position of each task within the two-dimensional space is represented in Figure 5.3; the plots shown in Figures 5.1 and 5.2 have been superimposed and the isomorphic points connected with a straight line to represent the change in terms of Euclidean distance. These distances were normalized to facilitate the description of the tasks showing the greatest and least amount of overall change in position. Euclidean distance (i.e., distance measured as a straight line between two points in two-dimensional space) offers an index of the greatest overall change for a given task with respect to its position within the entire set of tasks; city-block distance (i.e., distance measured along each of the two perpendicular axes) provides a description of its changes with respect to each dimension. The largest Euclidean changes (Z scores greater than 1.00) were noted for the following four tasks: making household repairs, responding to the child's cry, choosing toys for the child, and cleaning the house. Two of these, making repairs and housecleaning, were also noted to involve significant city-block shifts along the first dimension, reflecting greater involvement on the part of the fathers. Significant city-block shifts toward the family/interactive pole of the second dimension were noted for making repairs and for choosing toys, while shifts toward the isolation pole of this dimension were noted for responding to the child's cry and cleaning the house. The smallest amount of Euclidean change (Z scores less than −1.00) was noted for washing clothes, providing for family income, and washing dishes.

Considering the changes in terms of city-block rather than Euclidean distances, the greatest shifts along the first dimension were noted for increases in paternal responsibility in making repairs, making social arrangements, and cleaning the house; the greatest shifts for increases in maternal responsibility were in playing with the child, putting the child to bed, and arranging for sitters. Along the second dimension, shifts

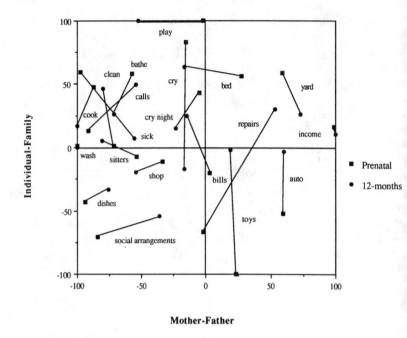

Figure 5.3. Overlay of Prenatal and Postpartum Household and Child-Care Task Coordinates to Reveal Changes in Task Responsibility over Time

indicating greater family interaction occurred in making household repairs, choosing toys, and making calls to extended family members; shifts indicating a decline in familial interaction were noted with responding to the child's cry, responding to the cry at night, and cleaning the house. The least amount of city-block change along the mother-father dimension was seen in washing clothes, overseeing auto repairs, providing family income, and choosing toys for the child; the least amount of change along the interaction-isolation dimension was noted for playing with the child, shopping, providing family income, and washing clothes.

Comments Concerning the Changes in Structure

The findings indicate that the parents assigned responsibilities for parental and household tasks along stereotypical gender-role distinctions. Concurrently, the pattern of change suggests that the fathers assume (or are forced to assume) a greater responsibility for housekeeping tasks after the birth of a second child, primarily for tasks such as making repairs, making social arrangements, and cleaning the house. In view of the MANOVA and ANOVA results presented earlier, one might have assumed that shifts toward greater paternal responsibility might have been found for more of the child-care tasks. Instead, results of the smallest space analysis indicate that such tasks as playing with the child or putting the child to bed shifted toward maternal responsibility, and that the greatest shift in paternal responsibility was in the area of making household repairs, a task that failed to show a mean increase in the previous analysis. When attempting to reconcile this apparent contradiction, it is critical to recall that the MANOVA and ANOVA analyses dealt with mean scores rather than the correlations among the tasks. Analyses of means indicate that in terms of absolute involvement, fathers become more active in child-care and other household tasks. Results of the smallest space analysis further suggest that the topology of parental task responsibility changed from the prepartum to the postpartum assessments. If the horizontal dimension is conceptualized as three regions representing mother's, shared, and father's work, it is apparent that most of the tasks remained within the same region over the course of the study. Indeed, the only tasks that moved from one region to another were making repairs (which moved from shared to the father), playing with the child and shopping (which moved from shared to the mother), and making social arrangements (which moved from mother to shared). In short, the overall division of task responsibility remained relatively stereotypical, with most of the care of the firstborn child and most household tasks remaining maternal activity.

The reduction in variance in the second dimension from the prepartum to the postpartum assessments instead becomes the primary change in structure for these families. If this dimension is partitioned into three sections, one can see that six tasks migrated from the "family" pole toward the midrange (yard work, responding to child's cry, responding to child's cry at night, bathing child, cooking meals, and cleaning house) and three tasks moved from the "isolated" pole toward the midrange (choosing the child's toys, arranging for automobile repairs). On the other hand, only two tasks moved out from the midrange toward the family pole (caring for the child when sick and making calls to friends), and none moved toward greater isolation. We may speculate that the shift of making repairs toward the father and the interactive poles is in part due to the fathers' inclusion of their firstborns in these tasks in the role of "Dad's little helper." It is important to note that the restriction of variability along the second dimension is due primarily to a migration of some tasks away from the isolation pole. Tasks such as playing with the child or putting the child to bed maintained their initially high scores, thereby indicating continued interaction.

PARENTAL AGREEMENT ON ACTUAL VERSUS IDEAL RESPONSIBILITIES

Do parents agree on what the role division is, or on what it should be?

Parent effects. Using the 12-month data, a set of MANOVA procedures was then conducted on each of the three sets of tasks with parent (mother versus father) and type of rating (actual versus ideal) treated as within-family factors. Significant overall parent effects were detected for household tasks, $F(13, 28) = 3.33$, $p < .0037$, and for infant care, $F(10, 31) = 3.42$, $p < .0041$, but not for child care, $F(7, 34) = 1.63$, $p < .1613$. At the univariate level, significant parent effects were detected for 6 of the 13 household tasks—making repairs around the house, shopping, paying bills, making social arrangements, supervising auto repairs, and yard work. Within the infant-care set, parent effects were noted for diapering the infant and responding to the infant's cry. Even though the multivariate analysis was not significant, two items of the child-care set—responding to the child's cry at night and putting the child to bed—did reveal significant differences due to the parent. In all but one of these cases, the difference between the fathers' and mothers' ratings was again a matter of each parent overestimating his or her own contributions and/or underestimating those of the spouse. The single exception was for diapering the infant, where fathers claimed even less responsibility than their wives attributed to them.

Type of rating effects. Significant multivariate effects for type of rating were detected for child care, $F(7, 34) = 16.02$, $p < .0001$; household tasks, $F(13, 28) = 10.40$, $p < .0001$; and infant care, $F(10, 31) = 22.70$, $p < .0001$. Moreover, at the univariate level, significant differences between actual and ideal assessments were detected for every item of the child- and infant-care activities, and for every household task except making repairs around the house, paying bills, supervising auto repairs, and yard work. For each of the items showing a significant type of rating effect, the direction of the difference was the same—the ideal situation was one of greater involvement of the fathers.

Interaction effects. Significant, or near significant, parent-by-type-of-ating interactions also were found in each of the three analyses: child care, $F(7, 34) = 3.10$, $p < .0123$; household tasks, $F(13, 28) = 4.23$, $p < .0007$; infant care, $F(10, 31) = 1.87$, $p < .0897$. Hotelling T-square procedures were used to assess differences in the mothers' and fathers' descriptions of actual and ideal, and to compare the actual and ideal descriptions within each parent group. On the infant-care tasks, mothers' actual and ideal scores differed significantly overall, $F(10, 31) = 13.11$, $p < .0001$, as well as at each univariate level. The direction of the difference was uniform—in the ideal situation, the fathers would assume a greater responsibility for the care of the infant than they did in reality. Fathers' ratings also showed a significant overall difference, $F(10, 31) = 5.86$, $p < .0058$, in the direction that ideally they would do more in caring for the infant. At the univariate level, however, this desire to be more involved in infant care specifically did not apply to 5 of the 10 items—determining the infant's schedule, diapering the infant, responding to crying either day or night, or putting the infant to bed. Although no overall differences had been found in the mothers' and fathers' descriptions of their actual division of infant-care responsibilities, their descriptions of the ideal situation did differ somewhat, $F(10, 31) = 1.98$, $p < .048$, with mothers indicating that fathers should assume more responsibility for diapering and dressing infants.

No differences were found between the mothers' and fathers' ratings in either the actual or the ideal allotment of child-care responsibilities, but large actual versus ideal differences were found for each parent. For mothers there was a large overall difference, $F(7, 34) = 13.80$, $p < .0001$, as well as significant differences on each of the seven tasks. Once again the differences were in a uniform direction, indicating that in the ideal situation, the fathers would assume greater responsibility for each of the child-care tasks. The fathers likewise revealed significant differences between their actual and ideal scores, $F(7, 34) = 3.34$, $p < .008$, but these differences were limited to only two of the seven tasks—choosing the child's toys and arranging for the child's care when sick. In each case, fathers indicated that in the ideal situation they would contribute more.

A greater range of differences was found concerning the household tasks. First, mothers' and fathers' descriptions of their actual division of the tasks differed, $F(13, 28) = 3.85$, $p < .0001$, with fathers claiming greater responsibility than acknowledged by their wives for cleaning up after meals, making household repairs, general housecleaning, shopping, making social arrangements and calling friends, and caring for the yard. The spouses also differed in their assessment of the ideal situation, $F(13, 28) = 2.21$, $p < .028$, with wives indicating that they would like their husbands to be more involved in arranging for sitters, fixing and cleaning up after meals, and making calls to family and friends. Husbands, on the other hand, indicated that their wives should assume greater responsibilities in making repairs around the house, seeing that the automobile was repaired, and providing income for the family. The comparison of the mothers' descriptions of actual and ideal divisions of labor again revealed significant differences, $F(13, 28) = 9.15$, $p < .0001$, once again indicating the wives' desire that their husbands assume a greater responsibility for nearly all the tasks. Wives appeared to agree somewhat with their husbands by indicating that the ideal situation would include assuming a greater responsibility for providing family income. No overall differences were detected between the fathers' descriptions of their actual and ideal conditions.

Is the perception of a discrepancy between "actual" and "ideal" role divisions associated with greater stress?

The Who Does What? data provide another means to explore the nature of stress experienced by parents adjusting to the birth of a second child. Specifically, one may conceptualize the perception of differences between the actual and ideal division of task responsibility within a family as a measure of individual dissatisfaction, and then assess the strength of this measure to predict the level of stress experienced by the parent. Rather than consider each of the 30 child-care, infant-care, and household tasks as separate items that would provide unique dissatisfaction scores, we wanted to reduce the number of variables to a single dissatisfaction score. One must use care in selecting difference scores as an index of dissatisfaction across a diverse set of items, because it is possible for dissatisfaction to exist on some but not other tasks, and even for the nature of the dissatisfaction to vary across tasks. Considering that difference scores are obtained by subtracting actual from ideal ratings, it is possible that the wife might want very much for her husband to be more active in one task, thereby producing a positive dissatisfaction value, while wanting herself to be equally more active on another, thereby producing a negative value. A simple sum of differences across items thus would have positive and negative values canceling each other out and may suggest that the woman is not dissatisfied overall. A sum of absolute dissatisfaction measures would provide a means of avoiding this situation, but absolute scores would confound the perception that the husband is not doing his share and the woman is being unfairly burdened with that of the wife either feeling guilty for not doing her own fair share or feeling good about escaping a task she may not have wanted to do in the first place—in short, the sum of absolute differences ultimately would be uninterpretable.

Composite discrepancy scores. One solution to this dilemma of computing a single summary dissatisfaction measure would be to compute two such measures instead of one—the first measure would be the sum of the positive differences, representing the desire that the husband assume a greater responsibility for the tasks, and the other, the absolute sum of the negatively signed differences, representing the desire that the wife assume greater responsibility. These pairs of dissatisfaction indices were calculated separately for mothers and fathers for each of the three areas of child-care, infant-care, and household tasks. A three-way ANOVA was conducted with these data, treating Parent (mother versus father), Task (child-care versus household versus infant-care), and Direction (father do more versus mother do more) as within-family factors. Significant main effects for Task, $F(2, 80) = 126.17$, $p < .0001$, and for Direction, $F(1, 40) = 176.10$, $p < .0001$, were detected. The main effect for Task indicates that, overall, the parents perceived the greatest degree of discrepancy from ideal to be associated with household tasks, while the least discrepancy from ideal was found with infant-care tasks. (As before, Tukey HSD post hoc contrasts were made at the .05 level.) The main effect for Direction indicated that mothers and fathers agreed that the ideal situation would not be obtained unless the fathers became more active in all types of tasks. The presence of a number of significant interaction effects requires that these main effects be qualified. In particular, significant Parent × Task, $F(2, 80) = 4.15$, $p < .019$; Parent × Direction, $F(2, 80) = 10.04$, $p < .003$; and Parent × Task × Direction, $F(2, 80) = 8.12$, $p < .0006$, interaction effects were detected. The means, standard deviations, and t-test comparisons necessary to decompose this three-way interaction are presented in Table 5.2.

The t ratios presented in the right-hand column of Table 5.2 contrast maternal and paternal responses of each type of task and direction of desired change. Note that mothers and fathers did not differ significantly in their perceptions of the magnitude of the changes desired for child-care tasks or for increases in maternal responsibility with infant care, but that the differences between parental desires were significant for each type of

Table 5.2 Comparison of Overall Parental Satisfaction with Role Division

| Domain | Mother | | Father | | t ratio |
	M	SD	M	SD	(df = 39)
Child care					
father do more	14.71	4.90	15.32	5.11	0.77
mother do more	5.24	3.64	5.73	3.88	0.80
t ratio	8.37***		7.66***		
Infant care					
father do more	13.51	7.75	8.00	5.21	3.42**
mother do more	1.07	2.70	1.90	5.62	.85
t ratio	9.22***		5.16***		
Household					
father do more	21.12	6.54	17.51	5.93	2.63*
mother do more	7.80	4.95	11.05	6.09	2.60*
t ratio	10.17***		4.39**		

*$p < .05$; **$p < .01$; ***$p < .001$.

directional change in the household tasks and in the desire for greater paternal responsibility in infant care. The *t* ratios presented within the columns of mother and father means contrast the values for "father do more" and "mother do more" within each type of task. In all six of these contrasts, the significant difference is in the direction that both mothers and fathers perceive that greater paternal rather than maternal responsibility is necessary for ideal role division. The three-way Parent × Task × Direction interaction might now be understood by noting that although both mothers and fathers agree that the fathers need to become more active in family tasks, in the cases of infant-care and household tasks, the mothers sense a greater discrepancy from ideal than do the fathers.

Discrepancies in child care. These composite dissatisfaction measures appear to provide an adequate summary of the distinctions between actual and ideal divisions of responsibility presented above. The issue to be explored now is whether these dissatisfaction measures can be used to predict higher levels of stress. Correlation coefficients were computed for mothers and fathers to determine the association between each of these six measures of dissatisfaction (maternal and paternal dissatisfactions in child-care, infant-care, and household task responsibility) and the parental stress, support, and satisfaction measures presented in Chapter 4. Only those coefficients exceeding the .05 significance level will be presented.

For the mothers, the perception that the fathers ought to assume greater responsibility for child-care tasks was independent of the support and satisfaction measures, and of all overall parental stress domain scores; it was positively associated with stress that was within the personal health ($r = .40$) and the child demandingness ($r = .35$) subdomains. Mothers who themselves wanted to be more involved in child-care tasks tended to have less stress associated with child moodiness ($r = -.34$) and the acceptability of the child's behavior ($r = -.38$). The fathers' perception that they ought to assume greater responsibility for child care was independent of all paternal support, satisfaction, and stress measures, but it was positively associated with maternal Total stress ($r = .31$), maternal Self domain stress ($r = .32$), maternal stress associated with not finding the child positively reinforcing ($r = .33$), and with maternal sense of isolation ($r = .32$). These findings suggest that the fathers might feel that they should become more involved in child care as a way of easing the burden they sense their wives are experiencing.

The mothers' perception that they ought to do more in the area of child care was independent of all support, satisfaction, and stress domain scores; it was negatively associated with the child moodiness ($r = -.34$) and child as a positive reinforcement ($r = -.38$) subdomains, suggesting either that mothers who experienced less stress in these areas tended to be those who wanted to assume greater responsibility for child care or that those who experienced greater stress in these areas did not want greater responsibility. For fathers, the perception that their wives ought to be more responsible for child care was independent of all support, satisfaction, and stress measures.

In the area of infant-care tasks, the mothers' perception that their husbands ought to assume greater responsibility was negatively associated with their Parental Role Satisfaction ($r = -.32$) and positively associated with stress associated with the acceptability of the child's behavior ($r = .31$), the child as a source of positive reinforcement ($r = .31$), and problems in the relationship with the spouse ($r = .35$); it was independent of all Infant stress subdomains. The mothers' perception that they ought to be more active in infant care was positively associated with overall stress in the Infant domain ($r = .37$), and with problems associated with infant moodiness ($r = .45$) and not finding the infant to be a source of positive reinforcement ($r = .33$). For fathers, the perception that they ought to be more involved in infant care was independent of all support, satisfaction, and stress measures. On the other hand, the fathers' perception that their wives ought to be more involved in this domain was positively associated with their own Total stress ($r = .31$), their Self domain ($r = .38$), and their Infant domain scores ($r = .36$). Subdomains of stress associated with paternal perceptions that their wives ought to be more involved with infant care included relationship with the spouse ($r = .34$), sense of isolation ($r = .35$), infant moodiness ($r = .32$), and problems of not finding the infant to be a source of positive reinforcement ($r = .34$). When these results are considered simultaneously with those concerning the fathers' perceptions of their increased involvement in child-care tasks, an interesting pattern is suggested: It appears that the fathers want to escape from infant-care responsibilities and the stress associated with these tasks by having their wives assume a greater responsibility in this domain; the fathers' apparent willingness to be more involved in child-care tasks might be conceptualized as the price they are willing to pay to avoid responsibility for these infant-care tasks.

Discrepancies in household tasks. Turning finally to the household tasks, maternal perception that wives ought to be more involved in this area were independent of all support, satisfaction, and stress measures. On the other hand, maternal perception that the husbands ought to be more active in this area was negatively associated with a wide array of stressors, including Total stress ($r = -.41$), overall Child domain stress ($r = -.39$), child demandingness ($r = -.32$), child moodiness ($r = -.39$), acceptability of the child's behavior ($r = -.42$), total Self domain stress ($r = -.38$), maternal depression ($r = -.32$), sense of attachment ($r = -.31$), sense of competence ($r = -.37$), and sense of social isolation ($r = -.40$). Collectively, these statistics suggest that the mothers who want to assume even greater responsibility for household tasks are psychologically healthy and content with their roles as homemakers. The fathers' perceptions that they themselves ought to be more responsible for household tasks and that their wives ought to be more responsible were independent of all measures of support, satisfaction, and stress.

Comments Concerning
Parental Perceptions of Role Divisions

Cowan and Cowan (1983) have proposed that differences between parental ratings of ideal and actual distributions provide an index of satisfaction with role differentiations. If this is so, then our data certainly suggest that mothers were significantly less satisfied with familial role arrangements than were fathers. However, one must be cautious to temper any statement based on the statistically significant differences that were reported by stressing the lack of categorical disagreement. Indeed, the magnitude of the large majority (80%) of the mean differences in maternal actual and ideal scores was less than 2.0 on the 9-point scale, and it was less than 1.0 in 33% of the instances. This lack of discrepancy between maternal perceptions of actual and ideal role divisions suggests that the mothers were saying, "This is the way it is, and I'd like my husband to do more" rather than "I do this, and I wish he would do it instead."

The concept of invisible work (DeVault, 1985) again may be invoked to explain why the mothers sensed a significant difference between the actual and ideal divisions of household and child-care tasks and the fathers did not: They alone were aware of and performing the invisible aspects of housekeeping. An observation made independently by all interviewers—which suggests that some of the mothers may not have been interpreting the form in the same manner as their husbands—supports this interpretation. Recall that we obtained these data by asking each parent who actually performed each of the tasks listed. The interviewers reported that some mothers qualified their statements with comments such as "Well, he actually does it all the time, but not unless I tell him when to do it, and how to do it, and then remind him to do it a few more times." Such sentiments may have contributed to creating an overall bias whereby mothers attributed less credit to their husbands for performing the tasks than the husbands gave themselves. Such comments also may be interpreted as indicating some maternal dissatisfaction with their role differentiations, hence the high maternal scores on the relationship with spouse subdomain of the PSI. Alternatively, the husbands' overestimations of their contributions may be due in part to their thinking of the sheer frequency with which they performed various tasks without realizing how often their wives may do the same things on a daily basis. Researchers employing the Who Does What? Index in the future may be well advised to include instructions requesting that spouses describe their responsibilities in terms of who *does* the task and who *sees that it gets done*.

Data that were obtained through the parental interviews provide additional evidence of a shift in parental and individual role definition over the course of this study. At the conclusion of each interview each parent was asked to indicate what had been the "highlight" of his or her previous week. Responses were categorized as related to (a) activities with the spouse, (b) activities involving the entire family, (c) independent activities involving the spouse with their own same-sex friends, (d) job- or profession-related events, and (e) personal events. The highlights reported by the wives were largely and consistently (between 50% and 68% of all responses) within either the spouse alone or family categories. In contrast, husbands displayed a marked shift, from describing at the prepartum session job-related or personal events as highlights (51% of responses) to indicating family events by the 8- and 12-month postpartum interviews (63% of responses at each time). Furthermore, the frequency with which husband and wife independently reported the same event as the highlight of their week increased more than fourfold from the prepartum to the postpartum sessions (from 7% to a range of 26% to 34%).

In short, even though differences exist between the mothers' and fathers' perceptions of ideal and actual divisions of household and child-care tasks, these data indicate the fathers are beginning to become more cognizant of their role in family interaction and the day-to-day functioning of the family. They appear to be shifting their interests, or at least the highlights reported to the interviewers, from personal (e.g., "I shot a hole-in-one on the course," or "I beat Jim 6-2, 6-4 in tennis") or career (e.g., "I got a raise," or "My boss recognized my good work") events to parental activities (e.g., "I went on a long bike ride with Jason," or "Our daughter Megan had a big birthday party last Saturday."). Paternal involvement in such family interactions will be the focus of the latter sections of Chapter 6.

NOTE

1. Maternal reports of fathers' increased involvement in child-care activities were used to partition the sample for a between-groups assessment of the effect this factor might have on the levels of stress or satisfaction with parenting. Separate MANOVA and ANOVA procedures were conducted with the sets of Child, Infant, and Self domain stressors, and the Satisfaction with Parenting Role data. No main effects or interactions were detected that would indicate that the presence or absence of a shift toward greater paternal involvement contributed to differences in any of these variables. Moreover, no associations were found between the fathers' shifting toward a more active involvement in child care and the age or gender of their firstborn children.

6

Firstborn Adjustment and Parent-Child Relations During the Transition Period

In the previous chapters the focus has been primarily on parental stress factors, and on how the parents altered their respective role definitions during this transition period. This chapter shifts the attention from the parents to the firstborn children, and examines their reactions and adjustments to becoming older brothers and sisters. Some of these data have been reported previously in Stewart, Mobley, Van Tuyl, and Salvador (1987). Interviews were conducted with the firstborns at each of the five assessments to obtain information concerning their interactions with their newborn siblings, their feelings about having siblings, and their perceptions of changes in their relationships and interactions with their parents. We anticipated that some of the children, especially the 2-year-olds, might be too inhibited during interviews to provide useful information. Therefore, we planned to use these data primarily to supplement parental reports and ratings of firstborns' adjustments. The following specific questions are addressed by these analyses:

(1) What types of adjustment problems do mothers report?
(2) How do mothers rate firstborns' overall adjustment?
(3) What do the firstborns say about their own adjustment?
(4) Does the age of the firstborn have any effect?
(5) Does the perceived temperament of any family member change over the transition period?
(6) Do family interactions change over the transition period?

FIRSTBORN ADJUSTMENT
TO THE BIRTH OF A SIBLING

What types of adjustment problems do mothers report?

The relations among the factors of (a) gender of firstborn child, (b) gender of sibling, (c) time of assessment (the four postpartum interviews), (d) presence or absence of problematic situations, and (e) type of problem (the 14 items described in Chapter 3) were examined using a log linear analysis procedure (BMD-P4F) for multidimensional contingency tables (see Bishop, Fienberg, & Holland, 1975). The 14 behaviors were divided into an Imitation group (including problems in toilet training, eating habits, methods of playing with toys, using baby talk, demanding a bottle/pacifier at bedtime, and demanding a bottle/pacifier during the day), an Anxiety group (including increased crying, increased clinging, and increased use of security objects and/or increased withdrawal), and a Confrontation/Aggression group (including general confrontations and inappropriate physical acts, such as hitting, squeezing, or slapping, directed at the baby, mother, father, or inanimate objects).

During each of the postpartum parental interviews, the mothers and fathers were queried concerning the presence or absence of each of the 14 behavior problems. Considerable agreements were detected among mothers and fathers concerning the presence or absence of each of the 14 types of problems, with phi coefficients ranging from .86 to .98. Nearly all disagreements between mothers and fathers involved situations where the father failed to report the presence of a problem that had been indicated by the mother. In the interest of simplicity and generalizability to other research, we have chosen to analyze only maternal reports of problem occurrences.

As discussed in Chapter 4, log linear procedures are employed to describe simultaneously the relations among several categorical variables. The technique is based on fitting a hierarchical linear model to a table of cell frequencies, so that the logarithm of the cell frequency is written as an additive function of main effects and interactions in a manner similar to the way in which cell means are dealt with in analysis of variance. Again, critically important to understanding the objective of this analytic procedure is Fienberg's (1977) distinction between *response* variables, which are free to vary in controlled conditions, and *explanatory* variables, which are regarded as fixed. Specifically, the "presence or absence of problem" may be conceptualized as either a response variable, if one collapses the "type of problem" category so as to consider the presence of any type of problem, or an explanatory variable, when "type of problem" becomes the focus of study and one considers whether specific types of problems may or may not be observed at particular times. As was the case in the log linear analysis presented earlier, it should be understood that the terms *effect* and *interaction* are used descriptively rather than inferentially. It should further be noted that a potential lack of independence between these observations may exist given our decision to treat "time of assessment" as a categorical, explanatory factor when it might more accurately be described as a repeated measures factor. Thus the assumption of independent observations, which is basic to chi-square procedures, has been violated. Given the exploratory nature of this study, we do not view the violation as a vital threat, so long as the analyses are considered to be primarily descriptive.

The log linear analysis revealed that two interaction terms made a significant contribution to the overall chi-square value of the full (i.e., saturated) model. These terms included the four-way interaction among gender of firstborn child, gender of sibling, time of assessment, and overall presence of problems, labeled TRIC (for time, regressive behavior, infant gender, and child gender), LR χ^2 (3, N = 2,296) = 10.87, p < .01, and a three-way interaction among time of assessment, overall presence of problems, and type of problem displayed, labeled PTR (for problem type, time, and regressive behavior), LR χ^2 (39, N = 2,296) = 60.28, p < .02. These two terms then were used in a hierarchical model in an attempt to fit the observed frequencies. The nonsignificant goodness-of-fit chi-square statistic indicates that our fitted values approximate the observed frequencies quite well, GF χ^2 (312, N = 2,296) = 97.47, p < .99.

Changes in Problem Type over Time

The PTR effect is shown in Table 6.1 by indicating the number of children reported to display problematic behavior of each of the 14 types over the four times of assessment; here "type of problem" is the response variable, whereas "time" and "regressive behavior" are treated as explanatory. The PTR effect might be explained by noting (a) that more so-called regressive behaviors were reported at the 1-month post-partum interview than at any other time, and (b) that the types of behavior problems reported varied with the time of the interview, with early (1-month postpartum interview) reports being characterized by high rates of display of each category of response (especially general

Table 6.1 Frequency of Reported "Regressive" Behavior Problems Partitioned by Type of Behavior and Time of Measurement (PTR Effect)

Type of Problem	Time Since Birth of Sibling			
	1 month	4 months	8 months	12 months
Imitative				
toilet	16	8	6	6
eat	14	7	10	6
play	13	7	7	8
talk	16	6	7	12
bottle/day	11	3	3	2
bottle/night	8	1	1	2
Anxiety				
security object	16	14	5	7
crying	28	21	16	14
clinging	26	16	13	12
Confrontation				
general argument	30	15	29	28
hit baby	15	4	18	14
hit mom	19	1	14	7
hit dad	16	6	10	3
hit object	17	16	12	7

SOURCE: From R. B. Stewart, L. A. Mobley, S. S. Van Tuyl, and M. A. Salvador, "The Firstborn's Adjustment to the Birth of a Sibling: A Longitudinal Assessment," *Child Development, 58,* 341-355. Copyright 1987 by the Society for Research in Child Development. Reprinted by permission.

confrontations, crying, and clinging), those at the 4-month interview by high rates of crying and use of security objects but with much less imitation or confrontation with family members, those at the 8-month interview by a renewed high level of confrontation but little imitation and less anxiety, and those at the 12-month interview by confrontation primarily with the baby, but with an increase in imitation in the form of baby talk.

The PTR effect collapses the gender of child and infant factors, and thus describes a pattern of response over time for the average sample child. To assess how well this normative pattern applied at the individual level, the maternal reports were studied by two researchers working independently to determine how many of the 41 children displayed this particular pattern. Both researchers found that 21 of the children (51%) showed this pattern of initially high problems in all areas, followed by continued high anxiety at the 4-month interview, confrontations at the 8-month interview, and confrontations focused on the sibling at the 12-month interview. The only other discernible pattern involved 5 children (12%) who initially displayed problems in all areas but then remained high only in confrontations throughout the remainder of the study. The rest of the children were found to show other unique patterns over time ($N = 11$, or 27%) or to have few problems after the initial assessment ($N = 4$, or 10%).

Effect of Sibling
Gender Combinations

The interpretation of the TRIC effect requires caution. This effect collapses the "type of problem" factor to consider the presence of any problem as the response variable. At a cursory level, the TRIC effect indicates that a greater frequency of "regressive" problems was reported for same-gender dyads, especially at the 1- and 8-month sessions. One must be cautious with this interpretation, however, because our sample did not include equal numbers of dyads in each of the four child/infant gender groups. Indeed, because our sample consisted of more all-male ($N = 15$) and all-female ($N = 11$) sibling dyads than of older males with sisters ($N = 10$) or older females with brothers ($N = 5$), one would expect these cells to contain a greater overall frequency of problematic behaviors. When the "type of problem" factor was collapsed, we obtained a frequency per child of the number of regressive behavior problems reported at each time of assessment. These scores, ranging conceptually from 0 to 14, were found to be normally distributed. Therefore, we conducted a subsequent analysis of the TRIC effect via an analysis of variance with repeated measures procedure (BMD-P2V) using the number of regressive behavior problems reported per child as the dependent variable; these data are presented in Table 6.2.

This analysis revealed significant interaction of the time, child gender, and infant gender factors, $F(3, 111) = 3.28$, $p < .04$. As in previously reported analyses, Greenhouse-Geisser adjusted degrees of freedom and probability levels were used with all analyses of variance procedures involving the factor time either as a main effect or as part of an interaction effect. Separate analyses were conducted to determine first the significance of the child gender × infant gender interaction at each time of measurement, and then the significance of the time effect independently for each of the four groups. Significant gender interaction effects were found only at the 1- and 8-month sessions. In each case, Scheffé

Table 6.2 Mean Frequency per Child of Regressive Behavior Problems
Partitioned by Child and Infant Gender and Time of Measurement
with Results of Significance Tests (TRIC Effect)

| | Time After Birth of Sibling | | | | ANOVA: Time Effect | | |
	1 month	4 months	8 months	12 months	F	df	p
Male child							
male infant	6.67	3.20	4.73	3.93	6.15[a]	3,56	.007
female infant	5.00	3.20	2.30	2.00	4.08[b]	3,27	.046
Female child							
male infant	2.40	2.60	1.80	3.00	.22	3,22	.693
female infant	7.54	3.27	4.36	3.09	8.93[a]	3,30	.005
ANOVA: child gender × infant gender interaction							
$F(1, 34)$.	6.71[c]	.18	12.43[d]	2.04			
p	.014	.677	.001	.234			

SOURCE: From R. B. Stewart, L. A. Mobley, S. S. Van Tuyl, and M. A. Salvador, "The Firstborn's Adjustment to the Birth of a Sibling: A Longitudinal Assessment," *Child Development, 58*, 341-355. Copyright 1987 by the Society for Research in Child Development. Reprinted by permission.
NOTES: a. Higher at 1- and 8-month sessions.
   b. Decline from 1- to 4-month session and from 4- to 8-month session.
   c. Female child-male infant significantly lower than other dyads.
   d. Same-gender dyads significantly higher than mixed-gender dyads.

procedures indicated that the same-gender dyad groups did not differ from one another in their respective mean frequencies, but did have more reported problems than the mixed-gender groups, which also did not differ from one another. No significant main effects were found in any of these analyses. In analyses conducted for the four groups of sibling gender composition, significant time effects were detected for all groups except those composed of older sisters with younger brothers. For each of the same-gender groups, the significant time effect indicated that the number of problems was highest at the 1-month interview and lowest at the 4- and 12-month interviews, with the number at the 8-month session falling somewhere in between; the time effect for the group of older boys with younger sisters was one of a steady decline in the frequency of reported problems.

How do mothers rate firstborns' overall adjustment?

The maternal responses to the open-ended question and the overall rating of their children's adjustments present a slightly different picture. At all sessions, the responses to the open-ended question were rather sketchy and brief, consisting of statements such as "Oh, things are pretty good" or "I have no complaints." The overall ratings of adjustment tended to support this generally positive outlook, with group mean ratings of 7.73, 7.59, 7.00, 6.63, and 6.53 being obtained for the five times of assessment, respectively. An analysis of variance for repeated measures procedure (BMD-P2V) revealed a significant time of assessment effect, $F(4, 148) = 2.76$, $p < .03$. Post hoc Scheffé comparisons of these means indicated no significant difference between the prepartum and 1-month postpartum means, and no differences among the 4-, 8-, and 12-month means, but a significant decline in mean rating from the two earlier to the latter three assessments. Neither child gender nor infant gender, nor interactions including these factors, was found to be significant. When queried concerning their evaluations of the procedures employed to prepare their children for the birth of a sibling, most mothers (95%) felt that their preparations had been adequate, but only 62% of those attending organized sibling preparation classes indicated that these programs had been especially beneficial.

What do the firstborns say about their own adjustment?

A number of questions on child interviews were written to provide supplemental information concerning the firstborn's adjustment to the birth of a sibling. At the prebirth interview, 82% of the firstborns indicated either very positive or positive feelings about becoming a "big brother or sister," and only 11% expressed any negative feelings. This figure remained remarkably stable through the postpartum assessment, when 80% of the children still indicated positive to very positive feelings about having a sibling. At the conclusion of the 12-month postpartum interview, we asked the children if they would now want to have another brother or sister, and 63% responded affirmatively; only 29% of the mothers and the fathers indicated that they wanted to have additional children. Those children who wanted additional siblings expressed a clear preference that the gender of the next sibling be the opposite of the current sibling, so that the firstborn could have "one of each," χ^2 $(1, N = 26) = 6.13$, $p < .02$.

Firstborn children were asked to indicate what they did to help their mothers with the babies, what they liked about their new siblings, and what they did not like about them (the first two responses to each question were recorded). All the children indicated that they helped their mothers care for the younger siblings, and 95% of the mothers confirmed that this was true. Such help included getting diapers for the mother when she was changing the infant (90%), soothing the infant when he or she was upset (88%), and occupying the infant when the mother was busy elsewhere (83%). When asked what they liked about their siblings, the modal reply was liking to cuddle or smile at the younger siblings; between 52% and 68% of the children gave this response over each of the four postpartum interviews. The second most frequent response at all postpartum interviews concerned liking to play with the new sibling.

The most common response to "What is it that you do not like?" was some indication that the infant cried too much; the percentage of children making this response dropped steadily from an initial high of 74% to a final low of 29% at the 12-month interview. Initially, only 2 children (5%) indicated that they did not like the baby because he or she was intrusive with respect to their possessions or their ability to play freely, or was aggressive (pulling child's hair). This figure increased steadily to 15% at the 4-month session, 50% by the 8-month, and 85% by the 12-month interview. The children reporting such intrusion/aggression tended to be from the same-gender dyads, χ^2 $(1, N = 35) = 4.10$, $p < .05$. Maternal responses to the query "What is the most significant change in your child's behavior, your infant's behavior, and their interaction?" supplemented these findings. By the 8- and 12-month sessions, mothers commonly stated that their infants had become more independent and their firstborns more cooperative, and that the children were now able to play together and share their toys. Indeed, 75% of the mothers' reports at the 12-month session included references to cooperation and/or sharing, whereas only 12% included any mention of infant intrusion or aggression.

Does the age of the firstborn have any effect?

The relation between the age of the firstborn child (recorded to the nearest half month at the time of the sibling's birth) and the type of regressive behavior was explored by computing biserial correlation coefficients (BMD-P7D). At the 1-month postpartum session, there was a significant correlation with presence of baby talk, with older children more likely to display this behavior, $r = .30$, $p < .05$. There were also trends ($p < .10$) detected indicating that younger children were more likely to display problems associated with using a security object ($r = -.26$), demanding a bottle at night ($r = -.26$, $p < .10$), and toilet training ($r = -.28$); the last trend reached statistical significance at the 8-month session ($r = -.36$, $p < .05$). This effect might be presented another way by noting that at the 1-month session 46% of the 2-year-olds and 53% of the 3-year-olds, but only 15% of the 4-year-olds, were reported to have toilet-training problems, whereas by the 8-month session such reports applied to 38% of the 2-year-olds, but to none of the 3- or 4-year-olds. Reports of problematic clinging behavior at the 8-month session appeared to be somewhat curvilinear with respect to the age of the child, with 46% of 2-year-olds, 82% of 3-year-olds, and 60% of 4-year-olds being so indicated. No other age effects or trends were noted.

A subsequent analysis was conducted using child gender and age as between-groups factors, and treating the sum of all problem types at each time of assessment as the dependent variable in a repeated measures ANOVA (BMD-P2V). Only a significant time effect was detected, $F(3, 68) = 11.73$, $p < .0001$, once again indicating that a greater frequency of behavioral problems was reported at the 1- and 8-month postpartum sessions. This analysis was followed by a MANOVA procedure employing the same between-group factors and repeated measures design, but considering the totals for the imitation, anxiety, and confrontation groups of items to be the dependent variables (BMD-P4V). Once again, the only significant effects detected were those for overall time, $F(9, 27) = 3.02$, $p < .0125$, and univariate effects of time for imitation, $F(1.68, 58.65) = 10.36$, $p < .0003$; for anxiety, $F(2.44, 85.47) = 9.65$, $p < .0001$; and for confrontation, $F(2.60, 91.03) = 5.86$, $p < .0018$. Post hoc contrasts of means indicated that frequencies of imitation and anxiety declined steadily over the four sessions, whereas confrontations were reported at high rates at the 1- and 8-month sessions.

Comments Concerning
Firstborn Adjustment

The parental report data of this study are consistent with those of previous studies in that more problems with toilet habits, demands for bottles, clinginess and other anxiety displays, and increased confrontations and aggression were reported following the sibling's birth (Dunn, Kendrick, & MacNamee, 1981; Field & Reite, 1984). Our data further indicate that the reaction of the firstborn child varies with respect to the child's gender as well as the gender of the sibling, but that the age of the child at the time of the sibling's birth does not appear to play as important a role. Due to the absence of a control group of children having no siblings, caution should be used in interpreting these results. Indeed,

Nadelman (personal communication, December 1985) has found that some of the behaviors attributed to the presence of a sibling have also been noted in the repeated maternal reports of matched nonsibling children.

It is also worth considering that our decision not to obtain prepartum assessments of firstborn behavior problems directly, but to ask what had become problems since the birth, may have inadvertently sensitized parents to the fact that problems could arise after siblings were born. Based on the information derived from our emic analysis of familial postpartum adjustment (Stewart, Van Tuyl, & Valla-Rossi, 1983), we felt it was safer to assume that most parents already expected behavior problems on the part of the firstborn soon after the birth of a sibling than to risk sensitizing parents to look for particular types of problems. Indeed, many of the mothers of this previous sample described their children in terms of "regression" in a psychoanalytic sense. One may therefore question the extent to which the increased behavior problems among the matched nonsibling children studied by Nadelman may be attributable to their mothers' having been interviewed previously. Moreover, our procedure required retrospection on the part of the parents, a task for which accuracy may be an issue. This problem was alleviated, in part, by having the interviewers question each parental report of a problem to assure that it was newly arisen, as well as probe for additional problem behaviors. The design issues affecting this or any longitudinal study are complex; although we fully agree with Nadelman's concern and encourage future researchers in this area to employ control groups, we remain unclear concerning the relative costs and benefits of employing a true pre-post design.

Given the similarity in both methods and subjects, a detailed comparison of our results with those of Nadelman and Begun (1982) appears beneficial. The latter reported that maternal responses to open-ended queries were more negative (as rated by a coder) at the postpartum session, with 64% of the mothers reporting negative changes in their children's behavior. Our maternal ratings of the overall adjustments of the children similarly revealed a negative shift, but one that did not reach statistical significance until the 4-month postpartum session. Perhaps the sibling preparation classes attended by our families, but not by those of the Nadelman and Begun sample, had been successful in at least delaying negative evaluations. Our informal assessment of these programs suggests that they focus primarily on the firstborn's preparation for separation from the mother at labor and delivery and on the initial adjustments that are made when the mother and infant return to the home. If this is the case, then negative evaluations might not be expected to appear until the families have progressed beyond the time frame of the classes.

Nadelman and Begun also report being struck by the number of items and children that showed either improved mean scores or no change at all after the birth of the sibling. However, of the 26 items they measured, only 4 revealed significant differences between the pre- and postbirth assessments; when the sample was partitioned by gender, three significant differences were noted for boys and five for girls. Specifically, boys were described as spending more time sitting or lying around doing nothing, and as not being easy to talk with, but as not following the mother around as much. Girls were described as having increased their use of a pacifier or bottle, fussing more about going to bed, playing well with other children less frequently, enjoying hearing about babies less, but decreasing their own baby talk. Nadelman and Begun do point out that one should be careful using words like *positive* or *improved*, and note, for example, that although not following the mother around may seem positive in and of itself, it may be viewed as a sign of withdrawal when considered in the context of the other changes.

Nadelman and Begun interpret the lack of significant changes between the pre- and postpartum assessments as evidence that the late pregnancy period may be as stressful as the immediate postpartum period. Because they provide no analysis of the statistical power of their procedures, it is more conservative to conclude that they simply may have failed to detect changes such as those reported in this study. Not only was their time frame limited to one month postpartum, but they reported having a severely restricted range of ratings, with only three items achieving means as large as 3 ("sometimes") on their 5-point scales. It may be that their mothers were hesitant to indicate that something was "often" or "almost always" (the 5 on their scale) a problem with their children, whereas our mothers, presented with a 2-point scale ("Is this or is this not a problem with your child?"), may have been more willing to indicate that a problem existed without having to define its severity or frequency. On the other hand, the Nadelman and Begun mothers were described as giving long, detailed, written responses that were more negative than their immediately following ratings of specific behaviors, whereas our mothers gave very brief, sketchy, generally positive responses. In short, the differences between our results and those of Nadelman and Begun may well be attributed to distinctions in the rating scales employed.

Our data support Dunn and Kendrick's (1982) argument that the apparently regressive behaviors often displayed by firstborns soon after the birth of a sibling might better be considered a form of imitation or mimicry rather than a reversion to a less mature stage of development. Moreover, Nadelman and Begun's (1982) position that one must consider the mode of the firstborn's response rather than merely its frequency is supported. Indeed, the shift in the children's modes of response from the 1- to the 12-month sessions suggests that they are altering their strategies to regain or maintain parental involvement lost within the changing family conditions. As such, the process of adjusting to the birth of a sibling may be conceptualized as an extended period of parent-offspring conflict in the manner suggested by Trivers (1974). Of course, these data might also be interpreted as support for the psychoanalytic theory of "regression" and/or "displacement" following the birth of a sibling; indeed, we did not attempt to devise a critical test to disprove these notions, but only to gather empirical evidence to describe the process consonant with Trivers's conceptualization.

From such a perspective, one might interpret what we have labeled the PTR effect as the child's ongoing attempt to find a strategy for reobtaining the lost interaction with, or attention from, the mother. Initial responses included high frequencies of behaviors categorized as confrontations with the mother and the infant, increased displays of anxiety, and an increased use of babylike imitative behaviors. Interestingly, older children chose to act like babies through the use of "baby talk" rather than through an abandonment of acceptable toilet or feeding habits. It may be that the 4-year-olds of this sample had been sufficiently socialized to view such transgressions as unacceptable; on the other hand, the toileting and feeding problems of the 2- or 3-year-olds may not be intentional but merely products of a heightened sense of anxiety. By the 4-month post-partum assessment, reports of imitative behaviors were greatly reduced, as were those of confrontations with the mother and infant. It is reasonable to assume that children of all age groups had learned by then that neither confrontations with the mother and/or infant nor imitation of the infant was likely to produce a desirable form of attention or interaction, and they therefore quickly abandoned these strategies. It also appears reasonable that displays of anxiety would remain high at this time (the 4-month postpartum session) because the children had learned merely what not to do, rather than what to do, in order to resolve their dilemma.

The associations between increased confrontations with infants at the 8- and 12-month assessments and interview reports of infant intrusiveness suggest that the children were again modifying their strategies in accordance with changes within their environments. Note that the children reported the infants' intrusions into their play activities in response to the query: "What is it you dislike about your brother/sister?" The mothers, in contrast, noted the same phenomenon in stating the most significant changes in the children's and infants' behaviors, describing it in a much more positive light as increased independence on the part of the infant and an increased willingness of the child to share with his/her younger sibling. Of course, the mothers may be aware of the firstborn's feelings yet still report that the siblings interact more and more socially. This difference in perspective supports Dunn and Kendrick's (1980) report of a decrease in maternal attention, and sensitivity, to the interests of the firstborn child following the birth of a sibling. The associations between infant behavior and confrontations with the firstborn may also help to explain why children with siblings of the same gender are reported to experience greater adjustment difficulties. If one is willing to assume that siblings of the same gender may be in greater competition for the same sorts of reinforcements, or even the same sorts of playthings, then it is logical to assume that these siblings would experience a greater sense of rivalry.

CHANGES IN TEMPERAMENT OVER THE TRANSITION PERIOD

Does the perceived temperament of any family member change over the transition period?

It was not possible, given the limited amount of time we had during home visits, to complete objective assessments of the temperament characteristics of the children. Rather than completely ignore this potentially important aspect of family functioning, we decided to include two short scales so that we might at least obtain parental reports of their own and their children's temperament characteristics. We use the term *temperament* to refer to individual differences in reactivity and self-regulation that are assumed to have a constitutional basis (see Rothbart & Derry-berry, 1981). Furthermore, we assume a developmental position, and, rather than assuming life-span stability for temperament, expect that an individual's previous temperamental characteristics might act to constrain the changes in reactivity and self-regulation observed after a major maturational shift or transition. These descriptions of temperament are not necessarily meant to be interpreted as valid assessments of temperaments, but instead are presented as subjective parental perceptions of their children' characteristics.

The stability of each dimension of temperament was assessed individually for each group of family members. These coefficients, presented in Table 6.3, were calculated via both Pearson product-moment and Spearman rank-order procedures so as to assess stability in terms of dimension scores as well as the ordinal position of subjects across the sample. You may recall from the discussion of stability in parental reports of sources of stress (Table 4.2 in Chapter 4) that we defined individual stability as being indicated by coefficients that were equal to or exceeded .70. If this definition is again adopted, then the statistics presented in Table 6.3 indicate the relative absence of individual stability with respect to temperament dimensions. Indeed, with the exception of child and paternal rhythmicity, none of the temperament dimensions appears to be very stable for any of the family members.

Repeated measures MANOVA and ANOVA procedures were conducted with each set of temperament dimensions, and revealed significant changes in the scores of the children, $F(18, 23) = 4.92$, $p < .0002$; the fathers, $F(9, 32) = 2.22$, $p < .0475$; and the infants, $F(6, 35) = 62.00$, $p < .0001$; but no such change over time was detected with the scores of the mothers' temperament ratings, $F(9, 32) = 0.53$, $p < .8436$. The statistics for these data are presented in Table 6.4. The changes over time were explored further via Tukey HSD procedures at the .05 significance level. Changes in children's temperament scores were found with the following dimensions: activity level showing an inverted U function, a steady increase in the intensity of response, a decreased range of mood expression, and an increased tendency to approach rather than withdraw from new stimuli from the pre- to the postpartum sessions. Changes over time in infant temperament scores were detected for each of the six dimensions, though only as a trend ($p < .077$) in the case of smiling and laughter. The direction of the changes detected was of increased activity level, slightly

Table 6.3 Stability Coefficients for Temperament Scales[a]

	−1 and 4 months		4 and 12 months		−1 and 12 months	
Child—DOTS						
activity level	.48	(.43)	.36	(.31)	.14	(.14)
rhythmicity	.73	(.65)	.65	(.60)	.72	(.67)
adaptability	.48	(.57)	.58	(.61)	.52	(.53)
threshold	.30	(.30)	.47	(.48)	.43	(.47)
intensity	.54	(.56)	.36	(.38)	.15	(.18)
mood	.05	(.09)	.33	(.31)	.23	(.21)
attention span	.53	(.51)	.42	(.41)	.43	(.42)
distractibility	.34	(.33)	.32	(.44)	.26	(.26)
approach/withdrawal	.62	(.66)	.52	(.60)	.48	(.62)
Mother—DOTS						
activity level					.47	(.48)
rhythmicity					.41	(.42)
adaptability					.57	(.62)
threshold					.52	(.48)
intensity					.47	(.51)
mood					.50	(.45)
attention span					.19	(.23)
distractibility					.39	(.43)
approach/withdrawal					.53	(.55)
Father—DOTS						
activity level					.43	(.38)
rhythmicity					.79	(.80)
adaptability					.47	(.50)
threshold					.62	(.66)
intensity					.56	(.57)
mood					.57	(.56)
attention span					.35	(.34)
distractibility					.29	(.25)
approach/withdrawal					.62	(.68)
Infant—IBQ						
activity level			.39	(.39)		
smiling and laughter			.44	(.35)		
soothability			.41	(.23)		
distress to limitations			.28	(.08)		
duration of orienting			.29	(.34)		
distress and latency to approach stimuli			.10	(.42)		

NOTE: Critical value of r with df = 39 at the $p < .05$ level is .31; at the $p < .01$ level, .41.

Table 6.4 Means and Tests of Time Effects for Temperament Scales

	-1 month		4 months		12 months		Time
	Mean	SD	Mean	SD	Mean	SD	Effect
Child—DOTS							
activity level	8.29	2.80	9.83	2.67	8.36	3.15	9.35***
rhythmicity	14.00	4.14	14.12	4.29	13.98	4.76	0.04
adaptability	8.39	1.67	7.85	2.56	7.90	1.79	2.09
threshold	3.85	1.48	4.05	1.59	3.78	1.75	0.50
intensity	4.24	2.01	5.02	2.01	5.71	1.81	7.10**
mood	5.71	0.51	5.27	1.14	5.34	1.09	3.49*
attention span	3.02	1.81	2.93	1.81	3.17	1.74	0.32
distractibility	3.68	1.27	3.61	1.67	3.66	1.33	0.04
approach/withdrawal	7.20	1.71	6.49	2.08	6.49	2.03	4.55**
Multivariate F ratio					$F(18, 23) = 4.92$***		
Mother—DOTS							
activity level	6.66	2.74			6.95	2.17	0.53
rhythmicity	15.07	5.32			14.49	4.62	0.48
adaptability	7.02	2.25			6.98	2.41	0.02
threshold	2.24	1.58			2.51	1.85	1.04
intensity	3.00	2.42			3.10	2.15	0.07
mood	5.27	1.00			5.02	1.19	1.97
attention span	3.89	1.89			3.84	1.84	0.02
distractibility	3.29	1.68			3.61	2.42	0.75
approach/withdrawal	6.90	2.07			7.05	2.57	0.17
Multivariate F ratio					$F(9, 32) = 0.53$		
Father—DOTS							
activity level	6.15	2.70			6.90	2.36	3.15
rhythmicity	12.61	5.24			13.46	4.98	2.71
adaptability	8.07	1.68			7.93	1.89	0.28
threshold	3.85	1.75			3.76	1.96	0.15
intensity	2.46	1.88			2.56	1.83	0.13
mood	3.84	1.64			4.56	1.77	1.18
attention span	4.10	1.38			4.17	1.77	0.07
distractibility	3.05	1.34			2.39	1.82	4.83*
approach/withdrawal	7.10	2.26			7.17	2.11	0.06
Multivariate F ratio					$F(9, 32) = 2.22$*		
Infant—IBQ							
activity level			59.90	11.04	70.51	11.94	28.40****
smiling and laughter			64.66	15.66	68.94	10.23	3.28[a]
soothability			31.49	7.44	51.54	6.52	281.96****
distress to limitations			54.51	12.94	69.27	12.78	37.28****
duration of orienting			25.76	6.99	34.98	7.96	41.80****
distress and latency to approach stimuli			25.68	11.31	52.22	11.77	121.03****
Multivariate F ratio					$F(6, 35) = 62.00$****		

NOTE: All time effects are reported with Greenhouse-Geisser adjusted degrees of freedom and probability levels.
a. Trend, $p < .08$.
*$p < .05$; **$p < .01$; ***$p < .001$; ****$p < .0001$.

more smiling and laughter, increased (easier) soothability, greater distress to limitations, increased duration of orienting, and increased distress and latency to approach novel stimuli. Changes in the fathers' temperament scores were limited to a decrease in their distractibility scores.

Comments Concerning
Changes in Temperament Ratings

Any study employing parental report instruments must assume that some degree of confound exists among the complex social and constitutional factors that affect temperament. These data indicate that the birth of a second child and/or the transition period following this event are associated with a number of significant changes in maternal perceptions of both child and infant temperaments. The maternal perceptions of the firstborns' behavioral adjustments following the birth of a sibling as presented above suggest a general pattern of adaptation whereby the child first displays high frequencies of many forms of "regressive" behaviors, then becomes more withdrawn, moody, and anxious by the 4-month postpartum period, and finally becomes less withdrawn and anxious, though more likely to enter confrontations with the ever-more-intrusive younger sibling, by 8 and 12 months postpartum. It is reasonable to assume that the mothers' perceptions of their children's temperaments would be affected by their awareness of and reaction to the behavioral displays exhibited during this potentially trying period of adjustment. Thus one must assume that measures of child temperament taken during this period of familial adjustment do not assess characteristics of the child independent of the setting or maternal responses to that setting. Indeed, these assessments reflect maternal strategies and reactions to handling the child during this period (cf. Rothbart, 1982; Rothbart & Derryberry, 1981).

Certainly, the developmental transition appearing between 7 and 9 months of age for the infants also must play a large role in accounting for the changes detected in these subjects (see Emde, 1977; Kagan, Kearsley, & Zelazo, 1978). The perceived "lack of change" in the mothers themselves warrants further study employing a multitrait-multimethod strategy such as that suggested by Rothbart (1982) and Plomin (1982). One especially interesting measure, if it could be obtained reliably, would be to ask firstborn children to provide descriptions of their and their mothers' behaviors over this period of familial transition and adjustment.

OBSERVATIONS OF FAMILIAL PLAY

Do family interactions change over the transition period?

Multivariate analyses of variance (BMD-P4V) were conducted with parent treated as a within-subject factor, session as a repeated measures factor, and 9 of the 11 target behaviors treated as dependent variables; the variables onlook and off task were excluded because they both represented solitary, noninterpersonal activities and thus were not pertinent in describing parent-child interactions. Moreover, neither type of behavior was observed at a frequency sufficient for analysis. (An initial analysis was conducted with child gender as a between-groups factor; because no main effect or interaction effects involving this factor were detected, the design was simplified by deleting the between-groups component.) A significant overall time effect was noted, $F(36, 2) = 33.66$, $p < .03$, with significant univariate effects found for talk, exploration, show, prescriptive commands, proscriptive commands, and rewards. In each case, less behavior was directed to the child over time, with the largest single decrease occurring between the prepartum and 1-month postpartum sessions.

A significant parent effect was also detected, $F(9, 29) = 2.48$, $p < .03$, with significant univariate differences for declare and redirect, and a trend ($p < .06$) for reward. A comparison of the means for these behaviors indicated that fathers displayed a higher frequency of declarations and redirects, whereas mothers rewarded their children more frequently than did their husbands. In the absence of an overall parent-by-time interaction, $F(36, 2) = 1.12$, $p < .58$, one should exercise caution in considering the significant univariate effects detected for talk, explore, and prescriptive commands. In each case the mothers' rates of displaying these behaviors decreased dramatically from the prepartum to the 1-month postpartum session, and then remained relatively equable throughout the remainder of the study. On the other hand, fathers showed continuity in their rate of displaying these behaviors from the prepartum to the 1-month postpartum session, but then gradually decreased these rates until no significant differences between the parents existed at the 12-month session. The means, standard deviations, and pertinent multivariate and univariate statistics for these parent-to-child behaviors are presented in Table 6.5.

Another analysis was conducted with parent and time treated as within-subject factors and the frequencies of 7 child-to-parent behaviors,

including talk, show, explore, declare, refuse, and prescriptive and proscriptive commands as dependent variables; child-to-parent redirect and
reward behaviors were not included in this analysis due to their insufficient occurrence. (As before, an initial analysis failed to detect an overall
child gender factor or any significant interactions including this factor.)
A significant multivariate time effect was found, $F(28, 10) = 7.98$, $p <$
.0008, with significant univariate effects established for every behavior
except refusals, prescriptive commands, and proscriptive commands. No
single pattern of changes was found to describe these time effects—talking and showing decreased dramatically after the prepartum session, but
then remained rather stable; exploration increased after the initial observation and then remained stable; and declarations were especially frequent at both the 4- and 8-month sessions and less so at the others.

A significant overall parent effect also was detected, $F(7, 31) = 5.69$,
$p < .0003$, with significant univariate effects established for all behaviors
except exploration and declaration. In each of the univariate cases the
child directed more overall behavior to the father than to the mother—
talking, showing, exploration, refusing, prescriptive command, and proscriptive command. In the absence of a multivariate parent-by-time
interaction, $F(28, 10) = 1.05$, $p < .49$, caution should be used in considering the significant interactions detected for the talk and declare variables. The means for these variables indicate an increase in behavior
directed toward father, and a corresponding decrease in that directed to
the mother, from the prepartum to the 1-month postpartum sessions. The
differences between the rates directed toward each of the parents dimin-
ished over the remaining sessions. The means, standard deviations, and
pertinent multivariate and univariate statistics for these child-to-parent
behaviors are presented in Table 6.6.

Comments on Observation Data

The data obtained from the observations of familial interaction during the play sessions indicate that the process of adjusting to the
birth of a second child is a complex phenomenon that might be studied
best from a family systems perspective. Our data replicate the findings of
Dunn and Kendrick (1980) that most children experience with the arrival
of a sibling a decrease in maternal playful attention and interaction. Our
data go further to suggest that this pattern does not necessarily extend to
describe the changes in father-child interaction. If one considers the
significant parent-by-time interaction effects detected on talking and

Table 6.5 Summary of Parent-to-Child Behaviors During Free Play Sessions

	−1 Month		+1 Month		+4 Months		+8 Months		+12 Months		Parent $F(1, 37)$	Time $F(4, 34)$	Parent × Time $F(4, 34)$
	M	SD	M	SD	M	SD	M	SD	M	SD			
Talk											2.28	64.74****	5.50***
mother	34.71	12.34	20.63	8.42	18.00	9.70	17.26	7.75	16.21	6.57			
father	30.53	12.62	28.29	10.73	23.18	12.02	23.92	12.16	15.21	8.53			
Explore											2.57	30.73****	3.45**
mother	15.55	7.76	9.42	7.78	9.03	6.66	7.34	6.52	5.16	3.82			
father	13.39	7.14	12.87	8.60	12.55	10.78	8.79	7.77	6.21	5.67			
Declare											8.69**	2.22	1.27
mother	1.58	1.33	1.45	2.11	1.63	2.32	2.16	3.48	1.34	1.73			
father	2.26	2.16	3.21	2.52	2.76	3.62	2.82	2.80	1.82	2.19			
Redirect											4.90*	1.18	1.00
mother	.55	1.37	.32	.66	.63	2.02	.53	1.08	.21	.47			
father	.53	.80	.87	1.95	.76	1.50	.89	1.41	.45	.92			
Show											2.44	13.58****	.63
mother	3.74	4.16	1.97	2.52	1.45	2.21	1.37	2.75	1.58	2.09			
father	4.47	4.86	2.97	2.97	2.18	2.18	1.42	2.55	1.76	3.35			

MANOVA and ANOVA Statistics

(continued)

Table 6.5 (Continued)

	−1 Month M	SD	+1 Month M	SD	+4 Months M	SD	+8 Months M	SD	+12 Months M	SD	MANOVA and ANOVA Statistics Parent F(1, 37)	Time F(4, 34)	Parent × Time F(4, 34)
Refuse													
mother	.13	.41	.11	.51	.05	.23	.24	1.15	.07	.36	.11	.47	.87
father	.13	.53	.29	1.01	.13	.13	.08	.27	.08	.27			
Prescribe													
mother	6.82	5.28	4.10	4.10	1.74	1.88	2.74	2.91	1.55	1.46	3.30	13.97****	3.90**
father	5.34	6.35	6.90	5.66	3.60	3.78	3.84	4.18	2.55	4.86			
Proscribe													
mother	.71	1.50	.97	1.55	.34	.63	1.00	1.69	.34	.81	.55	3.45*	.99
father	.60	1.22	.95	1.27	.45	1.08	.50	1.06	.34	.58			
Reward													
mother	2.74	2.29	1.87	2.75	1.53	2.25	1.18	1.45	.92	1.10	3.91	8.58***	.95
father	2.08	2.28	1.21	1.60	1.50	2.60	1.16	1.28	.42	.76			
Multivariate F ratios											2.48* (df = 9, 29)	33.66* (df = 36, 2)	1.12 (df = 36, 2)

SOURCE: From R. B. Stewart, L. A. Mobley, S. S. Van Tuyl, and M. A. Salvador, "The Firstborn's Adjustment to the Birth of a Sibling: A Longitudinal Assessment," *Child Development, 58*, 341-355. Copyright 1987 by the Society for Research in Child Development. Reprinted by permission.

NOTE: All contrasts involving the time factor are reported with Greenhouse-Geisser adjusted degrees of freedom and probability levels.

$*p < .05$; $**p < .01$; $***p < .001$; $****p < .0001$.

Table 6.6 Summary of Child-to-Parent Behaviors During Free Play Sessions

| | −1 Month | | +1 Month | | +4 Months | | +8 Months | | +12 Months | | MANOVA and ANOVA Statistics | | |
| | | | | | | | | | | | Parent | Time | Parent × Time |
	M	SD	M	SD	M	SD	M	SD	M	SD	F(1, 37)	F(4, 34)	F(4, 34)
Talk													
mother	16.79	10.26	7.24	5.12	9.66	7.32	9.63	7.10	11.11	5.61	8.51**	11.03****	5.19***
father	15.74	10.80	16.05	7.80	15.26	9.20	15.50	8.69	12.05	7.58			
Show													
mother	1.53	1.83	1.58	3.00	.71	1.18	.74	3.24	.34	.62	6.57*	6.53***	.76
father	2.63	3.09	1.74	2.19	1.34	1.42	.95	1.27	.76	1.46			
Explore													
mother	2.92	3.58	2.60	3.18	2.03	3.12	2.34	3.64	1.76	2.30	4.97*	4.43**	2.31
father	2.60	2.69	4.37	4.05	3.32	3.75	3.32	3.66	2.16	2.15			
Declare													
mother	3.45	3.96	1.87	2.69	2.84	4.16	2.84	3.66	2.10	1.93	3.03	3.13*	3.74**
father	2.68	2.72	4.10	4.32	4.21	4.13	3.97	3.44	2.24	2.14			
Refuse													
mother	.60	.89	.24	.54	.47	.95	.39	.72	.26	.45	10.20**	2.52	1.13
father	.95	1.04	.82	1.41	.89	1.89	1.13	1.60	.37	.67			

(continued)

Table 6.6 (Continued)

	−1 Month		+1 Month		+4 Months		+8 Months		+12 Months		MANOVA and ANOVA Statistics		
											Parent	Time	Parent × Time
	M	SD	M	SD	M	SD	M	SD	M	SD	F(1, 37)	F(4, 34)	F(4, 34)
Prescribe													
mother	.34	.67	.45	1.22	.55	.98	.76	1.00	1.03	1.22	16.15***	2.26	1.66
father	.76	1.08	1.37	1.91	1.29	1.68	.89	1.25	1.24	1.72			
Proscribe													
mother	.16	.44	.13	.31	.08	.27	.05	.23	.13	.41	13.81***	.32	1.24
father	.26	.76	.31	.62	.42	.89	.58	1.41	.29	.61			
Multivariate F ratios											5.69***	7.98***	1.05
											(df = 7, 31)	(df = 28, 10)	(df = 28, 10)

SOURCE: From R. B. Stewart, L. A. Mobley, S. S. Van Tuyl, and M. A. Salvador, "The Firstborn's Adjustment to the Birth of a Sibling: A Longitudinal Assessment," *Child Development, 58*, 341-355. Copyright 1987 by the Society for Research in Child Development. Reprinted by permission.
NOTE: All contrasts involving the time factor are reported with Greenhouse-Geisser adjusted degrees of freedom and probability levels.
*$p < .05$; **$p < .01$; ***$p < .001$; ****$p < .0001$.

exploration in the play sessions (with due caution given the absence of a significant MANOVA effect), one might interpret these results in a family systems framework by noting that the fathers may be adjusting to changes in the needs of the family. Specifically, the presence of the infants at the play sessions and the limited time and resources of the mothers may have decreased the fathers' or mothers' ability to interact with their firstborns. Whether or not they sensed this, the fathers increased their relative contribution to the total amount of interaction involving the firstborns, if only by keeping their rates of interaction high when their wives were decreasing theirs. Similarly, the firstborns increased the frequency of talking and exploration with the fathers over repeated play sessions, such that by the 12-month session the rates of mother-to-child and father-to-child interactions did not differ significantly from the rates of child-to-parent interactions.

7

Summary
and Discussion

No attempt will be made in this summary to integrate all the results presented in the preceding three chapters. Instead, some of the more interesting findings will be highlighted through a demonstration of how they illustrate the McCubbin and Patterson (1982, 1983) Double ABCX model of family crisis and the Family Adjustment and Adaptation Response process described in the Chapter 1. As mentioned previously, the Double ABCX model provides a means for describing (a) the additional life stressors and strains prior to and following a crisis-producing event, (b) the range of outcome of family processes in response to a pileup of stressors associated with this event, and (c) the intervening factors that influence the course of family adaptation. The FAAR model describes family adaptation to change as a function of the pileup of demands, family resistance, and adaptive resources, and the family's perception and appraisal of the situation. The FAAR process has been conceptualized as involving two distinct phases, the initial Adjustment Phase and a subsequent Adaptation Phase, which is, in turn, divided into Restructuring and Consolidation subphases.

This organizational scheme was first utilized when the results of this project were presented to the parents of our sample after the initial data analysis procedures had been completed. Parents attending this series of presentations were quite willing to make comments concerning our interpretations of various findings. The research assistants who had conducted the interviews and observations of the families attended these presentations and were responsible for recording, via written notes and audiotape, parental comments and questions but not the identities of the parents. None of the parents appeared to be concerned about this recording; indeed, some of them recorded the sessions themselves. Although I am well aware of the unscientific nature of anecdotal statements collected at public meetings, some of these comments are presented here to supplement this presentation; they provide a richness to the data and the analyses not often found in studies of this kind.

The data suggest that the study of the transition to parenthood should not be restricted merely to the adjustment following the birth of a first child. Just as it has been suggested that much of the crisis associated with the birth of the first child is a result of the role strain experienced by the spouses (see Rollins & Galligan, 1978), so also the birth of a second child may be conceptualized as an event demanding further role definition not only by both parents, but by the firstborn child as well. The data indicate that this event (a) offered fathers the opportunity to redefine both their marital and parental roles, and that many fathers assumed greater responsibility for the actual performance of child-care activities after this transition point; (b) was perceived by many mothers not just as the birth of a second child but, more important, as the birth of what would most likely be their last infant; and (c) demanded that the firstborn child adapt to changes in his or her role in the family and to new patterns of interaction with the parents. Furthermore, the adjustment to the birth of a second child involves both a remarkable commonality of experience for both parents and different sets of factors and responses for mothers, fathers, and firstborn children. Throughout the preceding presentation of the statistical analyses, my commentary has focused upon both the differences between and the commonalities among mothers and fathers in their respective adjustments to the birth of a second child. The repetition of this theme surely has provided evidence that focusing upon either concordance or discordance alone would not provide a useful means of describing this transition process.

PILEUP OF DEMANDS

Much of the transition to parenthood literature, especially the earlier studies, has assumed a "universalist" position in exploring the degree to which parents in general perceive the event to be a crisis. More recent studies have adopted a "contextualist" position to emphasize the differences in mothers' and fathers' reactions to parenthood (e.g., Belsky, Gilstrap, & Rovine, 1984; Belsky, Lang, & Huston, 1986; Belsky, Spanier, & Rovine, 1983; Cowan et al., 1985). This contextualist position might be generalized further to suggest that parents in different life circumstances might have different perceptions of the stresses associated with the birth of a second child. Our data clearly indicate that the birth of a second child constitutes a family-life transition event that is differentially perceived as stressful by both mothers and fathers. Indeed, our data indicate that not all mothers necessarily perceive the event in the same manner, thereby indicating that the "context" of perception demands consideration of more than just gender.

Considering the stressors associated with the Self domain of the Parenting Stress Index, both parents reported higher levels of depression at the 4-months postpartum assessment than at any other time, and increased perceptions of role restriction at each postpartum session. Although the amount of stress associated with having a realistic attitude about children did not change over time when analyzed at the absolute (i.e., mean) levels reported by the parents, the number of mothers and fathers obtaining scores on this subscale within the "high stress" classification did increase with each subsequent assessment.

Wives reported higher levels of stress than did their husbands on each of the following four subscales of the Self domain: depression, sense of role restriction, difficulty in the spousal relationship, and personal health. The stress associated with a sense of role restriction and difficulty with the spousal relationship increased significantly between the 1- and 4-month postpartum assessments, and then remained high until the end of our data collection period. Moreover, when these data were transformed to indicate the frequency of parents reporting clinically "high" levels of stress it was revealed that more of the mothers than might be expected experienced high levels of stress associated with role restriction and health problems, while fewer than expected experienced "high" stress associated with social isolation. On the other hand, more of the fathers than might be expected experienced "high" levels of stress associated with social isolation and the problems of having unrealistic attitudes about children, while fewer than expected experienced "high" stress associated with role restriction. In short, many but by no means all of the mothers sensed role restriction but not social isolation; the fathers sensed social isolation, but not role restriction. Stressors of this type would be expected to be especially salient for fathers who recently have taken on greater responsibility in caring for the firstborns and may be experiencing increased tension and conflict similar to that experienced by mothers, especially primiparous mothers, in traditional families (cf. Hoffman, 1983; Russell & Radin, 1983).

A recent study by Ruble, Fleming, Hackel and Stangor (1988) offers some insight for interpreting these changes in the marital relationship following the birth of a child. Ruble et al. (1988) used cross-sectional and longitudinal samples of primiparous mothers to assess changes in their marital relationships associated with the birth of the child. They learned that the division of labor, both child-care and household responsibilities, was particularly important for the wives, and that feelings of well-being and depression were related to husbands' participation in household chores. More important, Ruble et al. discovered that women whose expectations concerning the division of child-care and household chores had been violated tended to have more negative feelings at the postpartum assessments. The most dramatic difference between expectation and actual division of labor occurred with child care. Very few of the pregnant women (12% and 16% of the cross-sectional and longitudinal samples, respectively) expected to be doing much more of the child care than their husbands. Instead, most (55% and 45%) assumed that they would do somewhat more than their husbands, or that they would divide child-care responsibilities equally (33% and 39%). At the postpartum assessment more than 40% of the women reported a large discrepancy in the child-care division of labor, with themselves being responsible for more of these duties than had been expected. Specifically, Ruble et al. state that women who found themselves doing relatively more of the child-care or household tasks than they had expected reported more negative feelings about their husbands' involvement in child care and about the effect of the newborn on the marital relationship. You might recall that Entwisle and Doering (1981) also reported that many of the new mothers in their study had unrealistic expectations concerning childbirth and parenting, and that these unrealistic expectations made the mothers vulnerable to disappointments. Ruble et al. (1988) conclude that, although the violations of expectations had some negative effects, these effects were not overly strong or pervasive.

You might recall that LaRossa and LaRossa (1981) found that equity-based negotiations tended to involve less conflict between the spouses. If one is willing to assume that the majority of the mothers Ruble et al. studied were employed at least on a part-time basis outside the home, then it appears that these mothers had expectations for what is termed a "parallel marriage," where tasks are performed on an equitable or at least negotiable and mutually acceptable basis (cf. Ross, Mirowsky, & Huber, 1983). Making such an assumption is not so unusual or radical today, especially given the urban areas (New York, Toronto, Seattle) from which Ruble et al. drew their samples. Once the assumption is made that the couples have attempted to establish an equity-based division of labor, other questions arise—Did this equitable arrangement fail to materialize, or do husbands and wives differ in what they consider to be equitable? Are the husbands aware of the violation of these expectations? Does their awareness that they are not doing their fair share affect them? Researchers must be careful not only to clarify the distinction between equity and equality when considering divisions of labor, but to consider that husbands and wives may differ sharply on what is perceived to be equitable, or on what the consequences of not being equitable may mean. We have no doubt concerning the Ruble et al. (1988) conclusion that the violation of expectations is associated with negative consequences, such as the heightened depression, sense of role restriction, or difficulties with the spouse reported by the mothers of our sample, but wish to argue that the meaning of the violation needs to be explored more carefully.

The decline in maternal stress associated with health matters may well be trivial and an artifact of using the Parenting Stress Index with pregnant women of the middle and upper-middle classes, since this scale includes items assessing the number of visits to a doctor. Still, this change over time was experienced only by the mothers and thus suggests a further distinction between maternal and paternal adjustments to the birth of a second child—that mothers show a change with time that fathers lack. Whether fewer visits to a doctor represents a positive, neutral, or negative change may be debatable; comments from the mothers in our sample suggest that it was a welcome change if only because they no longer needed to drag the firstborn along with them to the obstetrician's office.

The mothers' increased sense of role restriction appears quite meaningful, however, given the finding that the women who had not returned to work by 4 months postpartum were more depressed, reported more difficulties with their spouses, and sensed greater social isolation than did the mothers who had returned to work. This finding points to the importance not only of making the distinction between mothers and fathers, as more recent studies focusing on the transition to parenthood have done, but also of being aware that neither all mothers nor all fathers need respond to the birth of a second child, and the adjustments this entails, in a singular, gender-specific manner. In particular, the mother's choice concerning her involvement in the paid work force outside the home, and her subjective evaluation concerning that choice, needs to be understood to define the context of her transition.

The firstborn child was the most common source of stress reported by both mothers and fathers throughout the course of this study. It was particularly interesting to note the absence of both main effects for parent, as well as any interaction term including this factor in the analysis of Child domain stressors, thereby suggesting a commonality of experience among the parents within this area. Specifically, mothers and fathers reported relatively the same levels of stress to be coming from comparable sources. Most of Child domain stress appeared to be associated with the immediate perception that the child's behavior following the birth of a sibling was unacceptable, the gradually increasing perception of the child as being moody and having problems in adaptability, the decreasing parental perception of the child as a source of positive reinforcement, and the unacceptable state of the activity level, distractibility, and demandingness of the child. When analyzed in terms of categorically "high" levels of stress, increases were noted in the numbers of mothers and fathers reporting the child as a stressor on the moodiness, adaptability, and positive reinforcement subdomains. Moreover, most of the incidents of "high" parental stress were found with subdomains in the Child domain.

The data from both mothers and fathers revealed that stress associated with the Infant domain, though rather low overall, increased over time. Specifically, problems associated with the infant being perceived as too demanding, too easily distracted, and not being a satisfactory source of positive reinforcement were detected with both parents. When these data were reanalyzed to assess the presence of "high" stress, it was discovered that more than the expected number of parents found the infants' inability to adapt to their environments and to provide adequate positive reinforcements to be problematic, while fewer than expected parents experienced "high" stress associated with demandingness and distractibility.

The parents are not the only ones who experience a pileup of demands following the birth of a second child; the firstborn child appears to experience a pileup of unfulfilled demands of his or her own making, as the child makes attempts to reobtain lost interaction with, or attention from, the mother. As discussed in Chapter 6, a significant association was detected between the type of regressive problem exhibited by the child and the time relative to the birth of the sibling. We labeled this association the PTR effect, and interpreted it as the firstborn's search for a successful strategy to reobtain maternal attention. In a sense, the report of these behavioral problems on the part of the firstborn child can be considered as indicative of the child's perceived stress. Furthermore, if one considers the information derived from the observations of family interaction, then an indication of how the child attempted to mitigate this stress is obtained. We noted during the early postpartum observations of family interaction that the child appeared to ignore the father's overtures to interact, but continued to elicit interactions with the mother. Eventually, the child discovered or accepted the fact that the father was a potential substitute for the mother, and by the 8- and 12-month postpartum sessions the father and child began to interact on a more reciprocal basis. The child's shift from the mother to the father thus can be seen to represent a search for new resources, the bB term in the McCubbin and Patterson model, as the child attempts to cope with the now divided attention of the mother.

Two issues repeatedly arose during the presentations of these findings and interpretations to the parents who had participated in the study. On a number of occasions, parents asked whether the higher levels of stress experienced by the mothers had influenced any of the other reports provided by these mothers. Specifically, it was asked whether the mothers who felt a greater burden due to the pileup of demands, as evidenced in their higher perceived stress scores, reported more problems of adjustment in their firstborn children or more negative changes in the perceptions of firstborn temperament. Although the hypothesized effect would be a logical one to expect, it was not found with the current set of data; indeed, if we had detected such an effect it would have been reported in one of the preceding chapters.

One mother in particular was not satisfied with this "lack of effect" finding, and, as she readdressed the question, it became evident that she had a slightly different issue in mind. You may recall from the analyses presented in Chapter 4 that mothers were partitioned into three groups based on whether they were "back-to-work," "still-at-home," or "homemakers" at the 4-month postpartum assessment. You also may recall that our analyses revealed that the still-at-home group experienced the greatest sense of social isolation, and in general appeared to be more stressed than the back-to-work mothers. Two things were interesting about the mother who wanted to continue the discussion of what she called the "burdened mother effect"—first, she stated that even though she had previously agreed with our homemaker designation, she now rejected our use of the term in describing her activities, and instead preferred to be described as a "professional mom." Second, she rejected our description of the still-at-home group and instead suggested that these mothers might be described more accurately as being "stuck-at-home."

This comment stirred a lively discussion among the other mothers in the audience, as some other mothers implied, not too subtly, that the "burdened, stuck-at-home mothers" were treating their firstborn children as scapegoats because they wanted to return to work rather than be full-time mothers. These accusations were pointedly challenged by a comment indicating that the spokeswoman had not obtained her degrees so that she could "become June Cleaver and bake cookies all day," and that if she could find good day care, she would return immediately to her career. Those interested in conducting further research into the ramifications of transition to parenthood at the time of the firstborn's birth or the family's subsequent transition at the birth of a second child would be well advised to consider the employment choice of the mothers as a potentially important between-groups factor. The mothers in our sample did not represent a single, homogeneous group. Our mothers included "professional moms" who professed to be quite happy and satisfied with their role; "two-career women" who had been successful in coordinating their roles of wife, mother, and professional; and a more stressed third group who openly admitted that they wanted to return to their careers outside the home but could not because of the difficulties of arranging alternative care for their two children.

The second issue typically raised in these discussions with the parents focused on the fact that fathers appeared to experience less stress than did their wives. One father in particular commented that if we had asked him questions about his relationship with his boss, his job security, or his chances for promotion, then we would have found that he too was experiencing high levels of stress. This father continued to point out that he had not been especially concerned with these issues until his first child had been born, but that the firstborn's birth had made him suddenly and keenly aware of his "responsibilities" to his family. Other fathers then added that, following the births of their first children, they too had devoted most of their attention to their careers so as to ensure financial security for their families. At the time of their second children's birth they felt the need to balance their careers with their desires to be more active in their families. A number of the fathers emphasized that they and their wives had planned that the second child also would be the last, so this too was their final opportunity to get involved with young children.

In short, these fathers argued that they had lost the opportunity to be "daddies" at the time of the first child's birth and infancy because they had decided that job security was more immediately important, but that now they were struggling to find a balance between career and parenthood. One father summarized the issue by pointing out that "fatherhood" had always struck him as being a biological, legal, and economic matter, while being a "daddy" somehow involved emotional commitment and loving interaction. To fathers such as these, the family was perceived as the goal rather than the source of stress. On the other hand, the career, the boss, and the deadlines were all seen as the primary roots of stress in their lives because these things interfered with the establishment of a balance between career and family life. When this group of parents heard about one father's closing interview statement that "it took only one child to make my wife a mother, but two to make me a father," the fathers gave it wholehearted endorsement. Equally important, the mothers also agreed that this statement summarized their perceptions of their husbands' transitions. The fathers who profess to support such a statement appear to reflect the social norm in defining their roles primarily in terms of being "providers" for their families, but this definition is accepted with reservations because these men wanted to be "daddies" rather than just "fathers." Future investigations of the sources and roles of stressors during family transitions should consider how the transitions might affect this salient "provider" role for the fathers and consider a wider range of potential stressors than utilized in our study.

COPING WITH THE PILEUP OF DEMANDS

The parents' method of coping with the pileup of demands associated with the birth of a second child was assessed with reference to changes in their division of labor for household and child-care tasks, and their utilization of and satisfaction with various sources of support. Like the parenting stress data already discussed, the Who Does What? Index data also provided a further example of commonality of experience for mothers and fathers during the restructuring of parental role responsibilities as the families adjusted to the birth of a second child. Although a consistent bias was detected for each parent to overestimate her or his own relative contribution to the performance of household tasks, to underestimate the contribution of the spouse, or both, it is interesting to note that mothers and fathers were in agreement when the structures underlying these tasks were considered. Specifically, mothers and fathers agreed that certain tasks were primarily mothers' responsibilities (washing clothes, fixing meals, caring for children when they were ill), that others were primarily fathers' responsibilities (providing family income, doing yard work), and that some tasks were shared (playing with and putting children to bed, paying bills). Moreover, the parents agreed in their reports of the changes in this structure over time by indicating an awareness both of the fathers' overall increased participation in terms of the mean level of responsibility for tasks and of the increase in task performance as a family group activity rather than chores for an individual.

The two analyses of the Who Does What? data indicate both that the fathers became more responsible for various household and child-care tasks when this responsibility was reported in terms of mean ratings and that the mothers appeared to maintain "control" of the tasks at a more fundamental, or structural, level. A cursory glance at Figures 5.1, 5.2, and 5.3 (in Chapter 5) quickly indicates that most of the responsibility for most of the household and child-care tasks lies with the mothers. Indeed, that was the immediate reaction of the parents attending our discussion sessions until one parent, a father, pointed out that "providing the family income" and "washing the family laundry" should not be directly compared. Interestingly, these two items are at opposite poles with respect to the Mother-Father dimension, and are relatively equal in their position along the Individual-Family dimension. This father continued his argument by noting that the relative importance of these items, assessed in terms of either the amount of time necessary to accomplish each or the ease with which the family might have the task performed by another source, were vastly different: "I can do the laundry, or I can pay someone to do it for us, but my wife cannot earn my salary, and we cannot find someone else to provide it for us."

This father's point is an interesting one—it would be far easier to find someone else to do the laundry than it would be to find someone else to provide family income, it certainly takes longer to work at the career primarily responsible for providing family income than it does to do the wash, and it is doubtful, at least in the case of their particular family, that his wife would obtain a salary equal to his if she were to become employed full-time outside the home. On the other hand, it does not make much sense to compare doing the laundry with having a full-time job. The maintenance of a home involves a number of tasks, some of which are included on the Who Does What? Index; collectively these tasks require a great deal of time, and, certainly when combined with the requirements of caring for two preschool-aged children, should be conceptualized as being a full-time position. After these points were made, the father clarified his position by pointing out that "providing the family income" was but one of the 13 household tasks included on the Who Does What? Index. He continued by noting that he could just as easily list 10 or 12 things he did at work in order that income would be obtained and instead list "housework" as a single item. In short, this father appeared to be reacting to the impression given by the figures in Chapter 5 that the wives were responsible for the lion's share of the tasks while the husbands could claim responsibility for only a few.

Of course this father was correct in arguing that one should not simply count the household tasks and report that the fathers primarily are responsible for only 4 (income, yard work, and household and automobile repairs) out of the 13. Although combining tasks to create a general "housework" item would create a sort of graphic equality in the presentation of mother and father responsibilities, our data indicate that such a procedure would not be advisable. For one thing, the results would be trivial because the graph would merely present the traditional arrangement whereby wives are responsible for housework and child care while husbands provide income. Further, the fact that the responsibility for some tasks is shared by husbands and wives (seeing that the bills are paid, making social arrangements, caring for a crying child) would be ignored. Three major arguments opposing the suggestion for a more refined breakdown of the "providing the family income" category were made: (a) All the fathers could have been involved in household tasks, while few of the wives would even have the opportunity to be involved in the day-to-day activities of their husbands; (b) the diversity among the various occupations held by the fathers would make it impossible to generate such a list; and (c) the focus of the project was primarily on family life and family functioning, not career activities.

The discussion evoked by his point was more revealing of maternal and paternal perceptions of the structure of their division of labor. As the father in question continued to explain his position, he indicated that he "*helped* his wife out whenever he could around the house" and that he "*baby-sat* the kids so that she could get out to play golf." I asked how many of the other fathers "baby-sat the kids" and nearly all present indicated that they did. When the women were asked how many of them "baby-sat the kids" so that their husbands could play golf the mothers filled the room with laughter. None of the mothers would describe her own child-care activities as "baby-sitting" because to the mothers "baby-sitting" is an activity performed temporarily by a hired helper rather than a parent. Fathers, on the other hand, appeared to be relatively comfortable using the term to describe their own child-care behavior.

Aside from this interesting discovery of a semantic distinction between maternal and paternal "baby-sitting," the father's original point warrants further consideration. You may recall from the discussion of the LaRossa and LaRossa research project and their conflict sociological model presented in Chapter 2 that a distinction was made between the qualitative and quantitative conceptions of time. Specifically, it was pointed out that LaRossa and LaRossa had found that the couples they studied based their negotiations to establish a division of labor on issues of *equity*, a parity of opportunity and constraints in terms of a qualitative conception of time, rather than *equality*, a parity of activities in terms of a quantitative conception of time. The fathers' primary responsibility in providing the family income not only requires a large amount of time in a quantitative sense, but it also affords the father the opportunity to develop a secure and unrestricted sense of role identity (the fathers' lower sense of stress due to a restricted role). On the other hand, we already have seen that many of these fathers wanted to establish a more satisfactory balance between their careers and their families, and that they perceived as desirable an increase in time spent doing some, but by no means all, household or child-care tasks.

Two issues arose during the discussion with the parents concerning changes in their division of labor. The first focused on why there had been a change at all. Were the fathers aware that their wives were experiencing higher levels of familial-based stress, and were they assuming more responsibility for the performance of tasks as a way to alleviate some of this stress? When this question was posed to the parents, the fathers immediately, but jokingly, agreed that the alleviation of their wives' burdens was indeed their primary motivation. One mother retorted that her husband started doing more around the house only because she "made him do it, or else!" A father then explained that he "helped out by getting the kids their baths and getting them to bed" so that his wife would get out of her "housewife and mother role" and make the transition to "wife and lover." This statement immediately drew a wide range of supportive and denunciatory comments from the other parents.

The reasons the fathers gave for their increased activity were varied; what remains an issue is why both mothers and fathers see the father's role as one of "helper" rather than "partner." When this question was presented, a number of mothers stated that their spouses were good "helpers" if told what to do and when to do it, but that their husbands did not seem to know, or perhaps did not want to know, when to do tasks on their own. The parents attending the discussion sessions were quite interested in DeVault's concept of invisible work and readily admitted that this factor was a major contributor to their consistent differences in assigning ratings on the Who Does What? Index. Indeed, a number of fathers acknowledged that they were "reasonably proficient in the kitchen if only someone else would plan the menu." It appears that the role of the father as a helper rather than as a partner is, in part, based on his lack of experience in organizing and coordinating the day-to-day activities of the home. Interestingly, many of the fathers expressed what appeared to be a genuine interest in the "invisible" aspects of maintaining a home. In particular, some indicated that they found the organization and planning necessary for grocery shopping and menu planning to be more complex than they had imagined.

The second issue concerning increased involvement on the part of the fathers focuses upon the resources they utilized to support this change in behavior. Initial differences between the parents were noted on two of the three indices of social support, Community/Neighborhoods and Family/Friends, and one of the two indices of satisfaction with parenting, Degree of Pleasure in Child. In each case the mothers reported more satisfactory support networks and a greater sense of pleasure in their children. Although different processes of transition and adjustment appear to have been adopted by mothers and fathers, it is interesting to note that these initial differences were not present at the 12-month postpartum assessment except for that of the Family/Friends index, and even here the magnitude of this difference had been reduced.

The patterns of changes reported by mothers and fathers for their satisfaction with parenting and their use of various support networks varied dramatically. For mothers, the parenting role satisfaction and degree of pleasure in children appeared to be amazingly stable over the course of this project, with the exception of one dramatic decline at the 8-month postpartum session. This time of assessment reported changes in situations since the 4-month session, and thus probably represents the increased stress experienced by the mother as she accommodated to having a more active and/or crawling infant. It also may represent a reaction to an apparent decline in support received from Family/Friend sources, which was at its peak at the 1- and 4-month sessions. It seems reasonable to suggest, at least in this culture, that mothers may have more support from extended family members or friends immediately after the birth of a child than 8 months thereafter. That mothers may be seeking additional support during this subphase of accommodation is evident in the fact that their scores for support from community sources or neighbors increased between the 4- and 8-month sessions.

The paternal pattern of adjustment during the year following the birth of a second child is one of continued increases in the levels of parental role satisfaction and degree of pleasure derived from children, as well as increases in the support received from both Community/Neighbor and Family/Friend networks. Moreover, fathers reported increases in the support they received from their spouses at the 4-month postpartum session, indicating that their transitions into their roles as more active fathers had been facilitated by assistance from their wives. At the 12-month session, the absence of meaningful differences between maternal and paternal scores for satisfaction with parenting and for the three sources of support suggest that the different patterns of adjustment over the year result in a convergence of perceived parental situation.

The manner in which these support or parental satisfaction factors were useful in mitigating the effects of stress also varied widely between mothers and fathers. Higher levels of stress were found when the mother lacked satisfaction with her role as a parent or failed to find pleasure in her children. With the exception of support derived from Family/Friends being associated with lower maternal scores on the Self domain stressors, social support networks did not appear to function as well in decreasing the mothers' levels of perceived stress as did either of the subdomains of the Satisfaction with Parenting Scale. While a greater reduction in uncertainty was obtained by predicting Self domain stress from support and/or satisfaction measures, the inverse relationship existed for Child domain stressors and these support/satisfaction sources. That is, higher levels of stress in the Self domain would be predicted if the mother possessed lower levels of satisfaction and/or support, and higher levels of stress in the Child domain would be predictive of, rather than predicted by, lower levels of satisfaction and/or support.

Each of the three sources of social support appeared to play a role in lessening the stress experienced by fathers. With regard to stressors of both the Child and Self domains, support from the spouse was combined with that from Family/Friends, as well as with satisfaction with one's role as a father and the degree of pleasure derived from the children, to lessen perceived stress. A greater reduction in uncertainty was found for predicting the Child domain stress levels from these support/satisfaction measures, thus supporting the buffer hypothesis, but no conclusive results were obtained for the Self domain stressors. Support to fathers from Community/Neighborhood sources was more closely associated with stressors of the Infant domain, and here again the reduction of uncertainty did not differ appreciably with the direction of prediction.

In short, mothers derived much of their support for coping with stress from an internal sense of satisfaction with being parents and from the degree of pleasure derived from interactions with their children. Fathers, on the other hand, appeared to draw most of their support for their roles from external groups such as friends, neighbors, or their wives. You may recall from the discussion of the Entwisle and Doering (1981) project presented in Chapter 2 that young fathers were described as being "expected to measure up to fathering standards they have no role model for" and as "expected to be a different kind of father from their own father" (p. 256). Given the absence of clear role models, it seems logical that support from friends and neighbors would be especially helpful to fathers, while their wives would be strengthened by a socially stable identity as "mothers." Furthermore, given the finding from Pedersen and Robson (1969) that the father's support for his wife is directly related to her initial competence in caring for the firstborn child, it is interesting that now support from the wives would be important in assisting the husbands to develop their own child-care skills.

The lack of clarity with regard to an optimal direction for predicting levels of stress from support/satisfaction measures, or vice versa, demands careful consideration. As briefly indicated in Chapter 4, redundancy or the reduction of uncertainty is often defined as the variance one canonical variate extracts from the variables in the opposing set. Redundancy answers the question: If I knew the score on a canonical variate from one set of variables, how much would my uncertainty regarding the other set of variates be reduced? (cf. Stewart & Love, 1968; Tabachnick & Fidell, 1983.) If one knows which set of variates can be best considered the independent variables and which the dependent, then the question of which redundancy index to consider becomes obvious, but such is not the case with these data. If one adopts the systemic concept of circular rather than linear causality, then the entire argument surrounding the designation of independent and dependent factors becomes mute. Still, it is logical to assume that the parent who possesses a sufficiently strong network of social support, or a sufficiently strong and rewarding self-identity, would in effect be protected (i.e., buffered) from experiencing high levels of stress.

The presentation of these points to the parents did not produce as much discussion or as heated an interchange as did previous issues. Both mothers and fathers appeared to be in agreement that, as a concept, "motherhood" is more clearly and adequately defined in this society than is "fatherhood." A couple of the fathers indicated that they wished that their employers had offered "paternity leaves" when their children were born, though they doubted that such a practice ever would be established. Many of the fathers acknowledged that their wives had been extremely helpful and supportive of their efforts to become more involved in child care. This support and involvement appeared to be focused upon the fathers' care of their firstborn children, with most mothers and fathers indicating that the care of the infant remained primarily within the mother's purview.

In the McCubbin and Patterson (1982, 1983) Double ABCX model of familial crisis this realization of the need for further support resources is represented by the cC term, with the new resources being represented by the bB term. The maternal and paternal changes over time in the sources of support variates suggest that the parents did seek additional external support over the course of this transition period. The changes parents made in their divisions of labor concerning household and child-care tasks also might be viewed as representing the bB term, in that the fathers' increased involvement in the family was being developed as a new resource. Although unwarranted given the relatively small sample of this project, future research in this area of family development and adjustment should consider the possibility of fitting recursive models of causality between perceived stressors and sources of support/satisfaction at more points along the time period (see Rogosa, 1980).

COHERENCE

Family coherence, the cC factor in the McCubbin and Patterson model, represents the family's subjective appraisal of their situation. Despite the levels of maternal and paternal stress, and the child's search for a strategy to reobtain parental attention, our data reveal that the transition at the birth of a second child is viewed as a positive growth experience by the families involved. We already have indicated that both mothers and fathers felt that the birth of the second child was somehow instrumental in the husband's assumption of a more active and involved role as father. This increased activity was noted both in the increased mean responsibility ratings for various household and child-care tasks and in the mean rates of father-to-child and child-to-father interaction in the family play situations. In particular, the migration of some of the father's household and child-care tasks away from the isolated pole and toward the family interaction pole suggests that the father-firstborn relationship becomes more intricate during these restructuring and consolidation phases. Furthermore, the analysis of the fathers' reports of the highlights of the previous week clearly indicated that they were becoming more focused on events within the family rather than on their careers as they adjusted to the addition of the second child and to their subsequent increased interaction with their firstborns.

One of the fathers raised another interesting question that has bearing on this discussion of familial coherence. The question focused upon what the mothers were doing as the fathers were increasing their involvement with the family in general, and the firstborn in particular. Before addressing this question directly, it is useful to recall that maternal reports indicated that only very low levels of stress associated with the Infant domain were experienced. In fact, maternal stress in the Infant domain was so homogeneously low that it was impossible to conduct the canonical correlation procedure relating stress in this domain to maternal sources of support and satisfaction. The comment from the self-proclaimed "professional mom" that the so-called stuck-at-home mothers were treating their firstborns as scapegoats due to their own inability to balance their career desires and mothering responsibilities needs to be considered again: Why are the firstborns, but not the infants, considered a source of stress? This question was posed directly to the mothers attending the discussions of this project, and most indicated, as they had during the data-collection phases of the project, that the second-born child was "special" because it would also be their last baby. When these mothers were then asked what they were doing as their husbands became more involved in caring for the firstborn, most indicated that, in part, they were enjoying the experience of caring for their last baby. As might be expected, a few jokingly indicated that they were very busy teaching their husbands how to care for the firstborn child, though there is certainly some truth to that statement. Interestingly, even though these mothers reported that in the ideal situation their husbands would contribute more toward the care of the infant, most also admitted to having the paradoxical sense of not wanting to share with anyone their brief time with this last infant. A few of the mothers even suggested that their husbands' relative lack of skill in caring for the infants provided them with a perfectly acceptable excuse to keep the infants to themselves.

One of the simplest examples of a subjective sense of coherence was found in the discovery that the only parents who wanted to have a third child were those who had two children of the same sex. This finding might be interpreted as an inverse index of the satisfaction on the parts of those parents who got "one of each," in that these parents were satisfied in having obtained an ideal or complete family. Moreover, finding that virtually all the firstborn children wanted to have another sibling, preferably one of the opposite sex of their second-born sibling, suggests not only that the desire for "one of each" extends beyond parents, but also that these firstborns are not so consumed by sibling rivalry as to want to avoid the situation again.

FINAL COMMENTS ON THE APPLICATION OF SYSTEMS THEORY IN THE STUDY OF FAMILY TRANSITIONS

The purpose of this project has been to apply the principles of general systems theory to the study of the family in transition. In doing so, we have conceptualized the family as an open system possessing properties of self-stabilization and adaptive self-organization so as to maintain various essential functions. Moreover, we have assumed that the family system is affected by circular patterns of causality, where "effects" often are seen to feed back into the system, becoming "causes" of future outcomes. This approach has been more precisely operationalized by utilizing McCubbin and Patterson's (1982, 1983) Double ABCX model of family crisis (presented as Figure 1.2, in Chapter 1) and their conceptualization of the Family Adjustment and Adaptation Response process as a theoretical foundation for our observations. Although this model has proven to be extremely useful in organizing the wide range of variables and effects studied in this project, a number of suggestions might be made prior to any further research efforts in this area.

First, more and earlier assessments of parental stress should be seriously considered. The final trimester before delivery appears to be a time when many families already have become aware of the crisis event, the a factor in McCubbin and Patterson's model, and already have begun to cope with this event by various means. Consideration should be given to the possibility of supplementing the assessments of parenting stress by including items specifically addressing the issues of job-related stress, including difficulties in obtaining acceptable day care or other scheduling problems. Doing so would provide a means of adequately reflecting the effects of this mesosystem on the family and thus would provide a more thorough description of the potential pileup or aA factor of the model.

The use of indices of social support should be modified to consider independently the types of support (esteem, information, companionship, or instrumental support) derived from each major ecological level, the satisfaction with each of these levels, and the changes in the parents' intent in seeking or maintaining these resources. For example, the current study was limited in not being able to clarify whether the paternal increases in social support scores were due to their receiving more support from the various sources or their becoming more aware and appreciative of—that is, satisfied with—the support already present. The refinement of the measures of support thus would provide a clearer distinction between the "perception of stress," or cC, and the "existing or new resources," or bB, aspects of the model.

Finally, some form of causal modeling or path analysis should be considered to assess the circular nature of causality that appears to govern the relationships among the various stressors and the social support measures. While it is logical to assume that social supports may act as buffers against stress, this relationship should not be constrained to a simple linear form. Indeed, with the adoption of a longitudinal design, one would expect the well-functioning family to respond to higher levels of stress by seeking additional sources of support. If this is true, then one may be more accurate in predicting levels of social support from the stresses experienced rather than the inverse. Using the Labouvie (1974) terminology for developmental causal models, a recursive-nonrecursive, within-between distal model would serve as a logical starting point, though one need not expect mothers and fathers to follow the same paths throughout the adjustment and adaptation processes. Our data suggest that maternal stress might be buffered by the prior existence of a sufficient support network and a satisfactory identification with and acceptance of the parenting role, while for fathers a more probable path in alleviating stress might be found in the search for additional sources of support once higher levels of parenting stress have been experienced. (For an introduction to the logic and procedures of structural equations modeling, interested readers should see Bentler, 1980, 1985; Kerlinger, 1986, chap. 36; Labouvie, 1974; Lavee, 1988.)

The results of this project clearly indicate that the study of familial adjustment following the birth of a second child represents a potentially rich opportunity for exploring the dynamic interaction and interdependence of subsystems within the family unit and the network of support groups surrounding the family. No longer should we consider the transition to parenthood to be a single life event experienced by mothers and fathers coincidentally, and uniformly, at the birth of the first child.

Appendix A:
Brief Summary of Subdomains of the Parenting Stress Index

Total score: This score is assumed to be of primary importance in guiding professional judgments as to whether or not professional intervention might be necessary or appropriate for a given parent-child system (range, 137-762; high score, 365).

Child and Infant domains: High scores in these domains are associated with children who display qualities that make it difficult for parents to fulfill their parenting roles (range, 54-268; high score, 133).

child adaptability/plasticity: The parenting task is made more difficult by virtue of the child's inability to adjust to changes in his or her physical or social environment. Behavioral characteristics associated with high scores include overreaction to changes in sensory stimulation, avoidance of strangers, difficulty in becoming calm once upset (range, 12-59; high score, 32).

acceptability of child's behavior to parent: The child possesses physical, intellectual, and emotional characteristics that do not match the parent's hoped-for child. Typically, the child is not as attractive, intelligent, or pleasant as the parent had expected or hoped (range, 7-35; high score, 16).

child demandingness/degree of bother: The parent experiences the child as placing many demands upon him or her. The demands may come from diverse sources such as crying, frequent demands for attention, or a high frequency of minor problems. This source of stress is magnified when the parent is overly committed to being a model parent (range, 13-65; high score, 33).

child moodiness: The child is often unhappy or depressed, cries frequently, and does not display signs of happiness (range, 6-30; high score, 14).

child distractibility/activity: The child displays many of the behaviors found in the Attention Deficit Disorders with Hyperactivity, DSM-III 314.01, such as overactivity, restlessness, distractibility, and short attention span (range, 9-45; high score, 29).

child as a source of reinforcement for parent: The interaction between parent and child fails to produce good feelings in the parents about themselves; that is, the child is not perceived as a source of positive reinforcement (range 7-34; high score, 14).

Self (Parent) domain: High scores in the Self domain suggest that the sources of stress and potential dysfunction of the parent-child system may be related to dimensions of parental functioning (range, 71-353; high score, 194).

parental depression, unhappy, guilt: The presence of significant depression in the parent suggests that the parent finds it difficult to mobilize the energy necessary to fulfill parenting responsibilities; withdrawal behaviors and general inability to act with assertiveness are frequent concomitants (range, 16-80; high score, 43).

parental attachment: Either the parent does not feel a sense of emotional closeness to the child or the parent has a real or perceived inability to read and understand the child's feelings and or needs accurately (range, 10-49; high score, 25).

restrictions imposed by parental role: The parents involved experience the parental role as restricting their freedom and frustrating them in their attempts to maintain their own identity (range, 8-40; high score, 29).

parental sense of competence: The parent is lacking in practical child development knowledge or possesses a limited range of child management skills. Parents who find parenthood overwhelming due to feelings that it is more difficult than they had anticipated tend to score high on this source (range, 16-80; high score, 43).

social isolation: The parent is socially isolated from his or her peers, relatives, and other emotional support systems; spouse may be distant or lacking in support for the other's parenting efforts (range, 7-35; high score, 20).

realistic attitude about children: The parent is lacking in objectivity when he or she thinks about or interacts with his or her child. Typically, the parent engages the child in an overprotective yet rejecting relationship in which discipline is, at times, inappropriate (range, 5-25; high score, 15).

relationship with spouse: The parent is lacking the emotional and active support of the other parent in the area of child management. Stress here may be related to an overly strict sex-role definition or may appear as a symptom of a dysfunctional marital relationship (range, 5-25; high score, 17).

parent health: Deterioration in parental health that may be either the result of stress or an additional stressor in the parent-child system (range, 4-19; high score, 12).

Situational/Demographic domain: This score represents a composite of objectively reportable situational and demographic stressors that the research literature has found to be related to dysfunctional parenting behaviors and to the onset of physical health problems in the individual exposed to multiple stressors from this domain (range, 12-141; high score, 48).

situational stress: Characteristics of the socioeconomic circumstances of the family—such as income, employment, education level, and size of family—that are known to be associated with high family stress (range, 12-60; high score, 37).

stressful life events: Particular major common life events that require adaptation and the expenditure of considerable energy, and that have been associated with stress and physical health problems (range, 0-81; high score, 14).

Appendix B:
Brief Summary of
Temperament
Dimensions

Rothbart's Infant Behavior Questionnaire (IBQ)

activity level: child's gross motor activity, including movement of arms and legs, squirming, and locomotor activity (range, 0-119)

distress to limitation: child's fussing, crying, or showing distress while (a) waiting for food, (b) refusing food, (c) being in a confining place or position, (d) being dressed or undressed, (e) being prevented access to an object toward which the child is directing her or his attention (range, 0-133)

duration of orienting: child's vocalization, looking at, and/or interaction with a single object for extended periods of time when there has been no sudden change in stimulation (range, 0-77)

smiling and laughter: smiling or laughter for the child in any situation (range, 0-105)

distress and latency to approach of sudden or novel stimuli: child's distress to sudden changes in stimulation and child's distress and latency of movement toward a novel social or physical object (range, 0-112)

soothability: child's reduction of fussing, crying, or distress when soothing techniques are used by the caretaker of the child (range, 0-77)

Lerner et al.'s Dimensions of
Temperament Survey (DOTS)

activity level: general degree of mobility as reflected in the frequency and tempo of movement, locomotion, and other activity; from highly active to inactive (range, 12-24).

rhythmicity: extent to which sleeping, resting, eating, elimination, and other body functioning is regular and predictable; from regular to irregular (range, 23-46)

approach/withdrawal: type of first reaction a child has when encountering a new situation such as a different person, place, or toy; from approach to withdrawal (range, 9-18)

adaptability: extent to which initial withdrawal response to a new situation becomes modified over time; from adaptive to nonadaptive (range, 10-20)

intensity: typical intensity of the child's reaction to internal states or environmental situations; from intense to mild (range, 8-16)

threshold: strength of the stimulus needed to cause the child to respond; from high threshold to low threshold (range, 10-20)

mood: typical behavior patterns related to a general quality of mood; from pleasant to unpleasant (range, 6-12)

distractibility: difficulty or ease with which the child's ongoing activity can be interrupted; from high to low (range, 5-10)

persistence of attention: extent to which the child remains engaged in an activity and/or returns to the activity after interruption; from high to low (range, 6-12)

References

Abidin, R. (1979). *Parenting Stress Index: Clinical interpretation of scores.* Charlottesville: University of Virginia, Parenting Research Project.

Abidin, R. (1983). *The Parenting Stress Index: Research update.* Charlottesville: University of Virginia, Parenting Research Project.

Ainsworth, M. (1973). The development of infant-mother attachment. In B. Caldwell & H. Ricciuti (Eds.), *Review of child development research* (Vol. 3). Chicago: University of Chicago Press.

Ainsworth, M., Blehar, M., Waters, E., & Wall, S. (1978). *Patterns of attachment: A psychological study of the strange situation.* Hillsdale, NJ: Lawrence Erlbaum.

Ainsworth, M., & Wittig, B. (1969). Attachment and exploration behavior of one-year-olds in a strange situation. In B. M. Foss (Ed.), *Determinants of infant behaviour* (Vol. 4, pp. 233-253). London: Methuen.

Alexander, M. (1971). *Nobody asked me if I wanted a baby sister.* New York: Dial.

Alexander, M. (1979). *When that baby comes, I'm moving out.* New York: Dial.

Altmann, J. (1974). Observational study of behavior: Sampling methods. *Behaviour, 49,* 227-267.

Anderson, J. (1972). Attachment behaviour out of doors. In N. Blurton Jones (Ed.), *Ethological studies of child behaviour* (pp. 199-216). London: Cambridge University Press.

Ashby, W. R. (1956). *An introduction to cybernetics.* London: Chapman & Hall.

Ashby, W. R. (1960). *Design for a brain.* London: John Wiley.

Ashby, W. R. (1962). Principles of the self-organizing system. In H. Foerster & G. Zopf (Eds.), *Principles of self-organization* (pp. 255-278). New York: Pergamon.

Awalt, S. (1981). *Transition to parenthood: Predictors of individual and marital stability and change.* Unpublished doctoral dissertation, University of California, Berkeley.

Baltes, P., Reese, H., & Nesselroade, J. (1977). *Life-span developmental psychology: Introduction to research methods.* Monterey, CA: Brooks/Cole.

Barnett, R., & Baruch, G. (1987). Determinants of fathers' participation in family work. *Journal of Marriage and the Family, 49,* 29-40.

Bartlett, M. (1947). Multivariate analysis. *Journal of the Royal Statistical Society, 9,* 176-197.

Baruch, G., & Barnett, R. (1981). Fathers' participation in the care of their preschool children. *Sex Roles, 7*(10), 1043-1055.

Baruch, G., & Barnett, R. (1986). Consequences of fathers' participation in family work: Parents' role strain and well-being. *Journal of Personality and Social Psychology, 51*(5), 983-992.

Bassoff, E. (1984). Relationships of sex-role characteristics and psychological adjustment in new mothers. *Journal of Marriage and the Family, 46,* 449-454.

Beauchamp, D. (1968). *Parenthood as crisis: An additional study.* Unpublished manuscript, University of North Dakota.

Belsky, J. (1979). The interrelation of parental and spousal behavior during infancy in traditional nuclear families: An exploratory analysis. *Journal of Marriage and the Family, 41*, 62-68.

Belsky, J. (1980). A family analysis of parental influence on infant exploratory competence. In F. Pedersen (Ed.), *The father-infant relationship: Observational studies in a family context* (pp. 87-110). New York: Praeger.

Belsky, J. (1981). Early human experience: A family perspective. *Child Development, 17*(1), 3-23.

Belsky, J. (1984). The determinants of parenting: A process model. *Child Development, 56*, 407-414.

Belsky, J. (1985). Exploring individual differences in marital change across the transition to parenthood: The role of violated expectations. *Journal of Marriage and the Family, 47*, 1037-1044.

Belsky, J., Gilstrap, B., & Rovine, M. (1984). The Pennsylvania infant and family development project, I: Stability and change in mother-infant and father-infant interaction in a family setting at one, three, and nine months. *Child Development, 55*, 692-705.

Belsky, J., Lang, M., & Huston, T. (1986). Sex typing and division of labor as determinants of marital change across the transition to parenthood. *Journal of Personality and Social Psychology, 50*(3), 517-522.

Belsky, J., Lang, M., & Rovine, M. (1985). Stability and change in marriage across the transition to parenthood: A second study. *Journal of Marriage and the Family, 47*, 855-865.

Belsky, J., & Rovine, M. (1984). Social-network contact, family support, and the transition to parenthood. *Journal of Marriage and the Family, 46*, 455-462.

Belsky, J., Rovine, M., & Taylor, D. (1984). The Pennsylvania infant and family development project, III: The origins of individual differences in infant-mother attachment: Maternal and infant contributions. *Child Development, 55*, 718-728.

Belsky, J., Spanier, G., & Rovine, M. (1983). Stability and change in marriage across the transition to parenthood. *Journal of Marriage and the Family, 45*, 553-566.

Belsky, J., Taylor, D., & Rovine, M. (1984). The Pennsylvania infant and family development project, II: The development of reciprocal interaction in the mother-infant dyad. *Child Development, 55*, 706-717.

Belsky, J., & Volling, B. (1987). Mothering, fathering, and marital interaction in the family triad during infancy. In P. Berman & F. Pedersen (Eds.), *Men's transitions to parenthood* (pp. 37-63). Hillsdale, NJ: Lawrence Erlbaum.

Belsky, J., & Vondra, J. (1985). Characteristics, consequences, and determinants of parenting. In L. L'Abate (Ed.), *Handbook of family psychology and therapy* (pp. 523-556). Homewood, IL: Dorsey.

Belsky, J., Ward, M., & Rovine, M. (1986). Prenatal expectations, postnatal experiences, and the transition to parenthood. In R. Ashmore & D. Brodinsky (Eds.), *Thinking about the family: Views of parents and children* (pp. 119-145). Hillsdale, NJ: Lawrence Erlbaum.

Bentler, P. (1980). Multivariate analysis with latent variables: Causal modeling. *Annual Review of Psychology, 31*, 419-456.

Bentler, P. (1985). *Theory and implementation of EQS: A structural equations program.* Los Angeles: BMDP Statistical Software.

Berenstain, S., & Berenstain, J. (1974). *The Berenstain Bears' new baby.* New York: Random House.

Berman, P., & Pedersen, F. (1987). Research on men's transitions to parenthood. In P. Berman & F. Pedersen (Eds.), *Men's transitions to parenthood* (pp. 217-242). Hillsdale, NJ: Lawrence Erlbaum.

Bernard, J. (1974). *The future of marriage*. New York: World.

Berrien, F. (1968). *General and social systems*. New Brunswick, NJ: Rutgers University Press.

Berscheid, E. (1986). Mea culpas and lamentations: Sir Francis, Sir Isaac, and "The slow progress of soft psychology." In R. Gilmore & S. Duck (Eds.), *The emerging field of personal relationships* (pp. 267-286). Hillsdale, NJ: Lawrence Erlbaum.

Bertalanffy, L. von (1968). *General systems theory*. New York: Braziller.

Bishop, Y., Fienberg, S., & Holland, F. (1975). *Discrete multivariate analysis*. Cambridge: MIT Press.

Black, D., & Sturge, C. (1979). The young child and his siblings. In J. Howells (Ed.), *Modern perspectives in the psychiatry of infancy* (pp. 262-283). New York: Brunner/Mazel.

Boulding, K. (1956). Toward a general theory of growth. *General Systems Yearbook, 1*, 1-6.

Bowlby, J. (1969). *Attachment and loss: Vol. 1. Attachment*. New York: Basic Books.

Bowlby, J. (1973). *Attachment and loss: Vol. 2. Separation*. New York: Basic Books.

Braiker, H., & Kelley, H. (1979). Conflict in the development of close relationships. In R. Burgess & T. Huston (Eds.), *Social exchange in developing relationships* (pp. 135-168). New York: Academic Press.

Brazelton, T. B., Koslowski, B., & Main, M. (1974). The origins of reciprocity: The early mother-infant interaction. In M. Lewis & L. Rosenblum (Eds.), *The effect of the infant on its caregiver* (pp. 49-76). New York: John Wiley.

Bretherton, I., & Ainsworth, M. (1974). Responses of one-year-olds to a stranger in a strange situation. In M. Lewis & L. Rosenblum (Eds.), *The origins of fear* (pp. 131-164). New York: John Wiley.

Bronfenbrenner, U. (1979). *The ecology of human development: Experiments by nature and design*. Cambridge, MA: Harvard University Press.

Buckley, W. (1967). *Sociology and modern systems theory*. Englewood Cliffs, NJ: Prentice-Hall.

Burke, W., & Abidin, R. (1980). Parenting Stress Index (PSI): A family systems assessment approach. In R. Abidin (Ed.), *Parent education and intervention handbook* (pp. 516-527). Springfield, IL: Charles C Thomas.

Burr, W. (1972). Role transitions: A reformulation of theory. *Journal of Marriage and the Family, 34*, 407-416.

Burr, W. (1973). *Theory construction and the sociology of the family*. New York: John Wiley.

Carter, E., & McGoldrick, M. (1980). The family life cycle and family therapy: An overview. In E. Carter & M. McGoldrick (Eds.), *The family life cycle: A framework for family therapy* (pp. 3-20). New York: Gardner.

Cattell, R. (1966). The scree test for the numbers of factors. *Multivariate Behavioral Research, 23*(1), 245.

Clarke-Stewart, A. (1978). And daddy makes three: The father's impact on mother and young child. *Child Development, 44*, 466-478.

Cohen, S., & Wills, T. (1985). Stress, social support, and the buffering hypothesis. *Psychological Bulletin, 98*(2), 310-357.

Coverman, S., & Sheley, J. (1986). Change in men's housework and childcare time, 1965-1975. *Journal of Marriage and the Family, 48*, 413-422.

Cowan, C., & Cowan, P. (1981). *Conflicts for partners becoming parents: Implications for the couple relationship.* Paper presented at the American Psychological Association Symposium on Research on Families, Los Angeles.

Cowan, C., & Cowan, P. (1985). *Parents' work patterns, marital and parent-child relationships, and early child development.* Paper presented at meeting of the Society for Research in Child Development, Toronto.

Cowan, C., & Cowan, P. (1987). Men's involvement in parenthood: Identifying the antecedents and understanding the barriers. In P. Berman & F. Pedersen (Eds.), *Men's transitions to parenthood* (pp. 145-174). Hillsdale, NJ: Lawrence Erlbaum.

Cowan, C., Cowan, P., Coie, L., & Coie, J. (1978). Becoming a family: The impact of the first child's birth on the couple's relationship. In W. Miller & L. Newman (Eds.), *The first child and family formation* (pp. 296-324). Chapel Hill, NC: Carolina Population Center.

Cowan, C., Cowan, P., Heming, G., Garrett, E., Coysh, W., Curtis-Boles, H., & Boles, A. (1985). Transitions to parenthood: His, hers, and theirs. *Journal of Family Issues, 5*(4), 451-482.

Cowan, P., & Cowan, C. (1983). *Quality of couple relationships and parenting stress in beginning families.* Paper presented at the biennial meeting of the Society for Research in Child Development, Detroit, MI.

Cox, M., Owen, M., Lewis, J., Riedel, C., Scalf-McIver, L., & Suster, A. (1985). Intergenerational influences on the parent-infant relationship in the transition to parenthood. *Journal of Family Issues, 5*(4), 543-564.

Crnic, K., Greenberg, M., Ragozin, A., Robinson, N., & Basham, R. (1983). Effects of stress and social support on mothers of premature and full-term infants. *Child Development, 54*, 209-217.

Crouter, A., Perry-Jenkins, M., Huston, T., & McHale, S. (1987). Processes underlying father involvement in dual-earner and single-earner families. *Developmental Psychology, 23*(3), 431-440.

Darlington, R., Weinberg, S., & Walberg, H. (1973). Canonical variate analysis and related techniques. *Review of Educational Research, 48*, 511-515.

DeVault, M. (1985, August). *Housework: Keeping in mind what's out of sight.* Paper presented at the annual meeting of the American Sociological Association, Washington, DC.

Dickie, J. (1987). Interrelationships within the mother-father-infant triad. In P. Berman & F. Pedersen (Eds.), *Men's transitions to parenthood* (pp. 113-143). Hillsdale, NJ: Lawrence Erlbaum.

Dixon, W., et al. (1983). *BMDP: Biomedical computer programs, P-series.* Los Angeles: University of California Press.

Doering, S., & Entwisle, D. (1975). Preparations during pregnancy and ability to cope with labor and delivery. *American Journal of Orthopsychiatry, 45*, 825-837.

Doering, S., Entwisle, D., & Quinlan, D. (1980). Modeling the quality of women's birth experience. *Journal of Health and Social Behavior, 21*, 12-21.

Dunn, J., & Kendrick, C. (1980). The arrival of a sibling: Changes in patterns of interaction between mother and first-born child. *Journal of Child Psychology and Psychiatry, 21*, 119-132.

Dunn, J., & Kendrick, C. (1982). *Siblings: Love, envy, and understanding.* Cambridge, MA: Harvard University Press.

Dunn, J., Kendrick, C., & MacNamee, R. (1981). The reaction of first-born children to the birth of a sibling: Mothers' reports. *Journal of Child Psychology and Psychiatry, 22*, 1-18.

Duvall, E. (1977). *Marriage and family development.* New York: Lippincott.

Dyer, E. (1963). Parenthood as crisis: A restudy. *Marriage and Family Living, 25*, 488-496.

Easterbrooks, M., & Goldberg, W. (1984). Toddler development in the family: Impact of father involvement and parenting characteristics. *Child Development, 55*, 740-752.

Emde, R. (1977). Two developmental shifts in infant biobehavioral organization: Two months and seven-nine months. In *Qualitative transitions in behavior during infancy.* Symposium presented at the meeting of the Society for Research in Child Development, New Orleans.

Entwisle, D., & Doering, S. (1981). *The first birth: A family turning point.* Baltimore: Johns Hopkins University Press.

Fein, R. (1978). Consideration of men's experiences and the birth of a first child. In W. Miller & L. Newman (Eds.), *The first child and family formation.* Chapel Hill, NC: Carolina Population Center.

Feiring, C., & Lewis, M. (1978). The child as a member of the family system. *Behavioral Science, 23*, 225-233.

Feldman, S. (1987). Predicting strain in mothers and fathers of 6-month-old infants: A short-term longitudinal study. In P. Berman & F. Pedersen (Eds.), *Men's transitions to parenthood* (pp. 13-35). Hillsdale, NJ: Lawrence Erlbaum.

Feldman, H., & Rogoff, M. (1968, September). *Correlates of changes in marital satisfaction with the birth of the first child.* Paper presented at the annual meeting of the American Psychological Association.

Field, T., & Reite, M. (1984). Children's responses to separation from mother during the birth of another child. *Child Development, 55*, 1308-1316.

Fienberg, S. (1977). *The analysis of cross-classified categorical data.* Cambridge: MIT Press.

Flavell, J. (1985). *Cognitive development* (2nd ed.). Englewood Cliffs, NJ: Prentice-Hall.

Freud, A. (1965). *Normality and pathology in childhood.* New York: International Universities Press.

Glenn, N., & McLanahan, S. (1982). Children and marital happiness: A further specification of the relationship. *Journal of Marriage and the Family, 44*, 63-72.

Gold, D., & Andres, D. (1978). Relations between maternal employment and development of nursery school children. *Canadian Journal of Behavioral Science, 10*, 116-129.

Goldberg, W., Michaels, G., & Lamb, M. (1985). Husbands' and wives' adjustment to pregnancy and first parenthood. *Journal of Family Issues, 5*(4), 483-504.

Green, J. (1980). *The relationship of stress to infant-mother attachment.* Unpublished doctoral dissertation, University of Virginia, Institute of Clinical Psychology.

Gronseth, E. (1978). Work sharing: A Norwegian example. In R. Rapoport & R. Rapoport (Eds.), *Working couples.* St. Lucia, Queensland: University of Queensland Press.

Grossman, F. (1987). Separate and together: Men's autonomy and affiliation in the transition to parenthood. In P. Berman & F. Pedersen (Eds.), *Men's transitions to parenthood* (pp. 89-112). Hillsdale, NJ: Lawrence Erlbaum.

Grossman, F., Eichler, L., & Winickoff, S., with Anzalone, M., Gofseyeff, M., & Sargent, S. (1980). *Pregnancy, birth, and parenthood.* San Francisco: Jossey-Bass.

Grossman, F., Pollack, W., & Golding, E. (1988). Fathers and children: Predicting the quality and quantity of fathering. *Developmental Psychology, 24*(1), 82-91.

Gutmann, D. (1975). Parenthood: A key to the comparative study of the life cycle. In N. Datan & L. Ginsberg (Eds.), *Life span developmental psychology: Normative life crises* (pp. 167-184). New York: Academic Press.

Guttman, L. (1968). A general nonmetric technique for finding the smallest coordinate space for a configuration of points. *Psychometrika, 33*, 469-506.

Haley, J. (1986). *Uncommon therapy.* New York: Norton.

Hansen, D., & Hill, R. (1964). Families under stress. In H. Christensen (Ed.), *Handbook of marriage and the family.* Chicago: Rand McNally.

Hansen, D., & Johnson, V. (1979). Rethinking family stress theory: Definitional aspects. In W. Burr, R. Hill, I. Reiss, & I. Nye (Eds.), *Contemporary theories about the family* (Vol. 1). New York: Free Press.

Harris, M. (1968). *The rise of anthropological theory: A history of theories of culture.* New York: Cromwell.

Henchie, V. (1963). *Children's reactions to the birth of a new baby.* Unpublished master's thesis, University of London, Institute of Education.

Hertzog, C., & Rovine, M. (1985). Repeated-measures analysis of variance in developmental research: Selected issues. *Child Development, 56*, 787-809.

Hill, R. (1949). *Families under stress.* New Haven, CT: Greenwood.

Hill, R. (1958). Generic features of families under stress. *Social Casework, 49*, 139-150.

Hill, R. (1971). Modern systems theory: A confrontation. *Social Science Information, 72*, 7-26.

Hill, R., & Aldous, J. (1969). Socialization for marriage and parenthood. In D. Goslin (Ed.), *Handbook of socialization theory and research* (pp. 885-950). Skokie, IL: Rand McNally.

Hill, R., & Rodgers, R. (1964). The developmental approach. In H. Christensen (Ed.), *Handbook of marriage and the family.* Chicago: Rand McNally.

Hinde, R. (1982). Attachment: Some conceptual and biological issues. In C. Parkes & K. Stevenson-Hinde (Eds.), *The place of attachment in human behavior.* New York: Basic Books.

Hobbs, D. (1965). Parenthood as crisis: A third study. *Journal of Marriage and the Family, 27*, 367-372.

Hobbs, D. (1968). Transition to parenthood: A replication and extension. *Journal of Marriage and the Family, 28*, 723-731.

Hobbs, D., & Cole, S. (1976). Transition to parenthood: A decade of replication. *Journal of Marriage and the Family, 30*, 413-417.

Hoffman, L. (1963). Parental power relations and the division of household tasks. In F. Nye & L. Hoffman (Eds.), *The employed mother in America.* Chicago: Rand McNally.

Hoffman, L. (1977). Changes in family roles, socialization, and sex differences. *American Psychologist, 32*, 644-657.

Hoffman, L. (1978). Effects of the first child on the woman's role. In W. Miller & L. Newman (Eds.), *The first child and family formation.* Chapel Hill, NC: Carolina Population Center.

Hoffman, L. (1979). Maternal employment: 1979. *American Psychologist, 34*, 859-865.

Hoffman, L. (1983). Increased fathering: Effects on the mother. In M. Lamb & A. Sagi (Eds.), *Fatherhood and family policy* (pp. 167-190). Hillsdale, NJ: Lawrence Erlbaum.

Homans, G. (1950). *The human group.* New York: Harcourt, Brace & World.

Hood, J., & Golden, S. (1979). Beating time/making time: The impact of work scheduling on men's family roles. *Family Coordinator, 28*, 575-582.

Huston, T., & McHale, S. (1984). Sex role strain in marriage: A longitudinal study of the impact of having a child on the topography of the husband-wife relationship. In S. Duck

& R. Gilmore (Eds.), *Key issues in interpersonal relationships*. Hillsdale, NJ: Lawrence Erlbaum.

Huston, T., & Robins, E. (1982). Conceptual and methodological issues in studying close relationships. *Journal of Marriage and the Family, 44*, 901-925.

Isabella, R., & Belsky, J. (1985). Marital change during the transition to parenthood and security of infant-parent attachment. *Journal of Family Issues, 5*(4), 505-522.

Janis, I. (1958). *Psychological stress*. New York: John Wiley.

Jenkins, B. (1982). *Stress in mothers of regular and special nursery school children*. Unpublished manuscript, Rutgers University.

Jones, M. (1960). *Practice as a process of simplification*. Pensacola, FL: U.S. Naval School of Aviation Medicine.

Kagan, J., Kearsley, R., & Zelazo, P. (1978). *Infancy: Its place in human development*. Cambridge, MA: Harvard University Press.

Kantor, D., & Lehr, W. (1975). *Inside the family*. San Francisco: Jossey-Bass.

Karmel, M. (1983). *Thank you, Dr. Lamaze*. New York: Harper & Row.

Kaye, K. (1985). Toward a developmental psychology of the family. In L. L'Abate (Ed.), *Handbook of family psychology and therapy* (pp. 38-72). Homewood, IL: Dorsey.

Kazak, A., & Marvin, R. (1984). Differences, difficulties, and adaptation: Stress and social networks in families with a handicapped child. *Family Relations, 33*, 67-77.

Kelley, H. (1979). *Personal relationships*. New York: John Wiley.

Kelley, H., & Thibaut, J. (1978). *Interpersonal relations*. New York: John Wiley.

Kendrick, C., & Dunn, J. (1980). Caring for a second baby: Effects on the interaction between mother and firstborn. *Developmental Psychology, 16*, 303-311.

Kerlinger, F. (1986). *Foundations of behavioral research* (3rd ed.). New York: Holt, Rinehart & Winston.

Kotelchuck, M. (1972). *The nature of the child's tie to his father*. Unpublished doctoral dissertation, Harvard University.

Kotelchuck, M. (1976). The infant's relationship to the father: Experimental evidence. In M. Lamb (Ed.), *The role of the father in child development* (pp. 329-344). New York: John Wiley.

Kreppner, K. (1986). *Phases in family socialization after the birth of a second child*. Paper presented at the Fifth International Conference on Infant Studies, Los Angeles.

Kreppner, K. (1987). *Changes in family interaction patterns after the arrival of a second child*. Paper presented at the meeting of the Society for Research in Child Development, Baltimore.

Kreppner, K., Paulsen, S., & Schuetze, Y. (1982). Infant and family development: From triads to tetrads. *Human Development, 25*, 373-391.

Kruskal, J. (1964). Multidimensional scaling by optimizing goodness of fit to a nonmetric hypothesis. *Psychometrika, 29*, 1-27.

Labouvie, E. (1974). Developmental causal structures of organism-environment interactions. *Human Development, 17*, 444-452.

Lafiosca, T. (1981). *The relationship of parent stress to anxiety, approval, motivation and children's behavior problems*. Unpublished doctoral dissertation, University of Virginia, Institute of Clinical Psychology.

Lamb, M. (1977). Father-infant and mother-infant interaction in the first year of life. *Child Development, 48*, 167-181.

Lamb, M., Pleck, J., Charnov, E., & Levine, J. (1985). Paternal behavior in humans. *American Zoologist, 25*, 883-894.

LaRossa, R., & LaRossa, M. (1981). *Transition to parenthood: How infants change families.* Beverly Hills, CA: Sage.

Laszlo, E. (1972). *Introduction to systems philosophy: Toward a new paradigm of contemporary thought.* New York: Harper & Row.

Lavee, Y. (1988). Linear structural relationships (LISREL) in family research. *Journal of Marriage and the Family, 50*, 937-948.

Lavee, Y., McCubbin, H., & Olson, D. (1987). The effects of stressful life events and transitions on family functioning and well-being. *Journal of Marriage and the Family, 49*, 857-873.

Lavee, Y., McCubbin, H., & Patterson, J. (1985). The Double ABCX model of family stress and adaptation: An empirical test by analysis of structural equations with latent variables. *Journal of Marriage and the Family, 47*, 811-825.

Lawrence, E. (1982). *The relationship between husband supportiveness and wife's adjustment to motherhood.* Unpublished doctoral dissertation, University of Virginia, Institute of Clinical Psychology.

Legg, C., Sherick, I., & Wadland, W. (1974). Reactions of pre-school children to the birth of a sibling. *Child Psychiatry and Human Development, 5*, 233-261.

LeMasters, E. (1957). Parenthood as crisis. *Marriage and Family Living, 19*, 352-355.

Lerner, R., & Bush-Rossnagel, N. (1981). *Individuals as producers of their own development.* New York: Academic Press.

Lerner, R., Palermo, M., Spiro, A., & Nesselroade, J. (1982). Assessing the dimensions of temperamental individuality across the life span: The Dimensions of Temperament Survey (DOTS). *Child Development, 53*, 149-159.

Levenson, R., & Gottman, J. (1983). Marital interaction: Physiological linkage and affective exchange. *Journal of Personality and Social Psychology, 45*, 587-597.

Levy, J., & McGee, R. (1975). Childbirth as a crisis. *Journal of Personality and Social Psychology, 31*, 171-179.

Lingoes, J. (1966). New computer developments in pattern analysis and nonmetric techniques. In *Uses of computers in psychological research: The 1964 IBM symposium of statistics* (pp. 1-22). Paris: Gauthier-Villars.

Lingoes, J. (1973). Smallest space analysis I: An IBM-7090 program for Guttman-Lingoes smallest space analysis. In J. Lingoes (Ed.), *The Guttman-Lingoes nonmetric program series.* Ann Arbor, MI: Mathesis.

Lingoes, J. (1979). New computer developments in pattern analysis and nonmetric techniques. In J. Lingoes, E. Roskam, & I. Borg (Eds.), *Geometric representations of relational data* (pp. 349-370). Ann Arbor, MI: Mathesis.

Loyd, B., & Abidin, R. (1985). Revision of the Parenting Stress Index. *Journal of Pediatric Psychology, 10*(2), 169-177.

Main, M., & Weston, D. (1981). The quality of the toddler's relationship to mother and father: Related to conflict behavior and readiness to establish new relationships. *Child Development, 52*, 932-940.

Marascuilo, L., & Levin, J. (1983). *Multivariate statistics in the social sciences.* Monterey, CA: Brooks/Cole.

Marvin, R. (1977). An ethological-cognitive model for the attenuation of mother-child attachment behavior. In T. Alloway, L. Krames, & P. Pliner (Eds.), *Advances in the study of communication and affect: Vol. 3. Attachment behavior* (pp. 25-60). New York: Plenum.

Marvin, R., & Stewart, R. (1990). A family systems framework for the study of attachment. In M. Greenberg, D. Cicchetti, & M. Cummings (Eds.), *Attachment in the preschool years: Theory, research and intervention*. Chicago: University of Chicago Press.

McCall, R. (1977). Challenges to a science of developmental psychology. *Child Development, 48*, 333-344.

McCubbin, H., Joy, C., Cauble, E., Comeau, J., Patterson, J., & Needle, R. (1980). Family stress and coping: A decade review. *Journal of Marriage and the Family, 42*(4), 855-870.

McCubbin, H., & Patterson, J. (1982). Family adaptation to crises. In H. McCubbin, A. Cauble, & J. Patterson (Eds.), *Family stress, coping, and social support* (pp. 26-47). Springfield, IL: Charles C Thomas.

McCubbin, H., & Patterson, J. (1983). The family stress process: The Double ABCX model of adjustment and adaptation. In H. McCubbin, M. Sussman, & J. Patterson (Eds.), *Social stress and the family: Advances and developments in family stress theory and research* (pp. 7-37). New York: Haworth.

McHale, S., & Huston, T. (1984). Men and women as parents: Sex role orientations, employment, and parental roles with infants. *Child Development, 55*, 1349-1361.

McHale, S., & Huston, T. (1985). The effect of the transition to parenthood on the marriage relationship. *Journal of Family Issues, 6*(4), 409-434.

Mederer, H., & Hill, R. (1983). Critical transitions over the family life span: Theory and research. In H. McCubbin, M. Sussman, & J. Patterson (Eds.), *Social stress and the family: Advances and developments in family stress theory and research* (pp. 39-60). New York: Haworth.

Menaghan, E. (1982). Assessing the impact of family transitions on marital experience. In H. McCubbin, A. Cauble, & J. Patterson (Eds.), *Family stress, coping, and social support* (pp. 90-108). Springfield, IL: Charles C Thomas.

Miller, G., Galanter, E., & Pribram, K. (1960). *Plans and the structure of behavior.* New York: Holt, Rinehart & Winston.

Miller, J. (1965). The organization of life. *Perspectives in Biology and Medicine, 9*, 107-125.

Minuchin, P. (1985). Families and individual development: Provocations from the field of family therapy. *Child Development, 56*, 289-302.

Minuchin, S. (1974). *Families and family therapy.* Cambridge, MA: Harvard University Press.

Moore, T. (1969). Stress in normal childhood. *Human Relations, 22*, 235-250.

Nadelman, L., & Begun, A. (1982). The effect of the newborn on the older sibling: Mothers' questionnaires. In M. Lamb & B. Sutton-Smith (Eds.), *Sibling relationships: The nature and significance across the lifespan* (pp. 13-38). Hillsdale, NJ: Lawrence Erlbaum.

Neugarten, B., & Hagestad, G. (1976). Aging and the life course. In R. Binstock & E. Shanas (Eds.), *Handbook of aging and the social sciences*. New York: Van Nostrand Reinhold.

Olson, D., McCubbin, H., Barnes, H., Larsen, A., Muxen, M., & Wilson, M. (1983). *Families: What makes them work*. Beverly Hills, CA: Sage.

Olson, D., Sprenkle, D., & Russell, C. (1979). Circumplex model of marital and family systems: I. Cohesion and adaptability dimensions, family types and clinical applications. *Family Process, 14*, 1-35.

Parke, R. (1979). Perspectives in father-infant interaction. In J. Osofsky (Ed.), *Handbook of infancy* (pp. 549-590). New York: John Wiley.

Parke, R., & Anderson, E. (1987). Fathers and their at-risk infants. In P. Berman & F. Pedersen (Eds.), *Men's transitions to parenthood* (pp. 197-215). Hillsdale, NJ: Lawrence Erlbaum.

Parke, R., Hymel, S., Power, T., & Tinsley, B. (1980). Fathers at risk: A hospital-based model of intervention. In D. Sawin, R. Hawkins, L. Walker, & J. Particuff (Eds.), *Exceptional infant: Vol. 4. Psychosocial risks in infant-environment transactions.* New York: Brunner/ Mazel.

Parke, R., & O'Leary, S. (1975). Father-mother-infant interaction in the newborn period: Some findings, some observations, and some unresolved issues. In K. Riegel & J. Meascham (Eds.), *The developing individual in a changing world: Vol. 2. Social and environmental issues.* The Hague: Mouton.

Parke, R., Power, T., & Gottman, J. (1979). Conceptualizing and quantifying influence patterns in the family triad. In M. Lamb, S. Suomi, & G. Stephenson (Eds.), *Social interaction analysis: Methodological issues* (pp. 231-252). Madison: University of Wisconsin Press.

Parke, R., & Tinsley, B. (1984). Fatherhood: Historical and contemporary perspectives. In K. McCluskey & H. Reese (Eds.), *Life-span developmental psychology: Historical and generational effects.* Orlando, FL: Academic Press.

Parsons, T. (1951). *The social system.* New York: Free Press.

Parsons, T., & Shils, E. (1951). *Toward a general theory of action.* Cambridge, MA: Harvard University Press.

Pedersen, F. (1975, September). *Mother, father and infant as an interactive system.* Paper presented at the annual meeting of the American Psychological Association.

Pedersen, F., Anderson, B., & Cain, R. (1977). *An approach to understanding linkages between the parent-infant and spouse relationships.* Paper presented at the biennial meeting of the Society for Research in Child Development, New Orleans.

Pedersen, F., & Robson, K. (1969). Father participation in infancy. *American Journal of Orthopsychiatry, 39,* 466-472.

Pedersen, F., Yarrow, L., Anderson, B., & Cain, R. (1978). Conceptualizations of father influences in the infancy period. In M. Lewis & L. Rosenblum (Eds.), *The social network of the developing infant.* New York: Plenum.

Pedersen, F., Zaslow, M., Cain, R., & Anderson, B. (1980). *Caesarean birth: The importance of a family perspective.* Paper presented at the International Conference on Infant Studies, New Haven, CT.

Pedersen, F., Zaslow, M., Cain, R., Suwalsky, J., & Rabinovich, B. (1987). Father-infant interaction among men who had contrasting affective responses during early infancy: Follow-up observations at 1 year. In P. Berman & F. Pedersen (Eds.), *Men's transitions to parenthood* (pp. 65-87). Hillsdale, NJ: Lawrence Erlbaum.

Pepper, S. (1942). *World hypotheses.* Berkeley: University of California Press.

Petty, T. (1953). The tragedy of Humpty Dumpty. *Psychoanalytic Study of the Child, 8,* 404-422.

Piaget, J. (1970). *Structuralism.* New York: Basic Books.

Pleck, J. (1976). *Men's new roles in the family: Housework and child care* (Working paper). Wellesley, MA: Wellesley College Center for Research on Women.

Pleck, J. (1981, August). *Changing patterns of work and family roles.* Paper presented at the annual meeting of the American Psychological Association, Los Angeles.

Plomin, R. (1982). The difficult concept of temperament. A response to Thomas, Chess, and Korn. *Merrill-Palmer Quarterly, 28*(1), 25-33.

Pollack, W., & Grossman, F. (1985). Parent-child interaction. In L. L'Abate (Ed.), *The handbook of family psychology and therapy* (pp. 586-622). Homewood, IL: Dorsey.

Power, T., & Parke, R. (1984). Social network factors and the transition to parenthood. *Sex Roles, 10*, 949-972.

Radin, N. (1981). Childrearing fathers in intact families: An exploration of some antecedents and consequences. *Merrill-Palmer Quarterly, 47*, 489-514.

Radin, N. (1982). Primary caregiving and role-sharing fathers of preschoolers. In M. Lamb (Ed.), *Nontraditional families: Parenting and child development*. Hillsdale, NJ: Lawrence Erlbaum.

Ragozin, A., Basham, R., Crnic, K., Greenberg, M., & Robinson, N. (1982). Effects of maternal age on parenting role. *Developmental Psychology, 18*, 627-634.

Rapoport, R. (1963). Normal crises, family structure and mental health. *Family Process, 2*(1), 68-80.

Robertson, J., & Robertson, J. (1971). Young children in brief separation: A fresh look. *Psychoanalytic Study of the Child, 26*, 264-315.

Rogosa, D. (1980). Causal models in longitudinal research. In J. Nesselroade & P. Baltes (Eds.), *Longitudinal research in the behavioral sciences: Design and analysis* (pp. 263-302). New York: Academic Press.

Rollins, B., & Galligan, R. (1978). The developing child and marital satisfaction. In R. Lerner & G. Spanier (Eds.), *Child influences on marital interaction: A life-span perspective* (pp. 91-105). New York: Academic Press.

Ross, C., Mirowsky, J., & Huber, J. (1983). Dividing work, sharing work, and in-between: Marriage patterns and depression. *American Sociological Review, 48*, 809-823.

Rossi, A. (1968). Transition to parenthood. *Journal of Marriage and the Family, 30*, 26-39.

Rossi, A. (1977). A biosocial perspective on parenting. *Daedalus, 106*(2), 1-31.

Rossi, P., Sampson, W., Bose, C., Jasso, G., & Passel, J. (1974). Measuring household social standing. *Social Science Research, 3*, 169-190.

Rothbart, M. (1981). Measurement of temperament in infancy. *Child Development, 52*, 569-578.

Rothbart, M. (1982). The concept of difficult temperament: A critical analysis of Thomas, Chess, and Korn. *Merrill-Palmer Quarterly, 28*(1), 35-40.

Rothbart, M., & Derryberry, D. (1981). Development of individual differences in temperament. In M. Lamb & A. Brown (Eds.), *Advances in developmental psychology* (Vol. 1, pp. 37-86). Hillsdale, NJ: Lawrence Erlbaum.

Ruble, D., Fleming, A., Hackel, L., & Stangor, C. (1988). Changes in the marital relationship during the transition to motherhood: Effects of violated expectations concerning the division of household labor. *Journal of Personality and Social Psychology, 55*(1), 78-87.

Russell, C. (1974). Transition to parenthood: Problems and gratifications. *Journal of Marriage and the Family, 36*, 294-302.

Russell, G. (1978). The father role and its relation to masculinity, femininity and androgyny. *Child Development, 49*, 1174-1181.

Russell, G. (1982). *The changing roles of fathers*. St. Lucia, Queensland: University of Queensland Press.

Russell, G., & Radin, N. (1983). Increased paternal participation: The fathers' perspective. In M. Lamb & A. Sagi (Eds.), *Fatherhood and family policy* (pp. 139-165). Hillsdale, NJ: Lawrence Erlbaum.

Sameroff, A. (1983). Developmental systems: Contexts and evolution. In W. Kessen (Ed.), *Handbook of child psychology* (Vol. 1). New York: John Wiley.

Sarason, I., Johnson, J., & Siegel, J. (1978). Assessing the impact of life changes: Development of the Life Experiences Survey. *Journal of Consulting and Clinical Psychology, 46*, 932-946.

Shereshefsky, P. (1973). Summary and integration of findings. In P. Shereshefsky & L. Yarrow (Eds.), *Psychological aspects of a first pregnancy* (pp. 237-251). New York: Raven.

Shereshefsky, P., Liebenberg, B., & Lockman, R. (1973). Maternal adaptation. In P. Shereshefsky & L. Yarrow (Eds.), *Psychological aspects of a first pregnancy* (pp. 165-180). New York: Raven.

Shereshefsky, P., & Yarrow, L. (Eds.). (1973). *Psychological aspects of a first pregnancy.* New York: Raven.

Siegel, P., Hodge, R., & Rossi, P. (1975). *Occupational prestige in the United States.* New York: Academic Press.

Simmel, G. (1950). *The sociology of George Simmel* (K. Wolff, Ed.). New York: Free Press.

Sollie, D., & Miller, B. (1980). The transition to parenthood as a critical time for building family strengths. In N. Stinnet & P. Knaub (Eds.), *Family strengths: Positive models of family life* (pp. 149-169). Lincoln: University of Nebraska Press.

Spanier, G. (1976). Measuring dyadic adjustment: New scales for assessing the quality of marriage and similar dyads. *Journal of Marriage and the Family, 38*, 15-38.

Spence, J., & Helmreich, R. (1978). *Masculinity and femininity: Their psychological dimensions, correlates, and antecedents.* Austin: University of Texas Press.

Spock, B., & Rothenberg, M. (1985). *Baby and child care.* New York: Dutton.

Sprey, J. (1979). Conflict theory and the study of marriage and the family. In W. Burr, R. Hill, F. Nye, & I. Reiss (Eds.), *Contemporary theories about the family: Vol. 2. General theories/theoretical orientations* (pp. 130-159). New York: Free Press.

Sroufe, A., & Waters, E. (1977). Attachment as an organizational construct. *Child Development, 48*, 1184-1199.

Stern, D. (1974). Mother and infant at play: The dyadic interaction involving facial, vocal and gaze behaviors. In M. Lewis & L. Rosenblum (Eds.), *The effect of the infant on its caregiver* (pp. 187-214). New York: John Wiley.

Stewart, D., & Love, W. (1968). A general canonical correlation index. *Psychological Bulletin, 87*, 245-251.

Stewart, R. (1977). *Parent-child interactions in a quasi-naturalistic setting.* Unpublished master's thesis, Pennsylvania State University.

Stewart, R. (1982). *Familial preparation for the birth of the second child.* Unpublished manuscript, developed for parental education workshops.

Stewart, R., & Amaranth, P. (1983). *Assessing inter- and intra-observer reliability for sequential data: A comparison of Pearson and kappa correlational procedures.* Unpublished manuscript, Oakland University.

Stewart, R., & Marvin, R. (1984). Sibling relations: The role of conceptual perspective-taking in the ontogeny of sibling caregiving. *Child Development, 55*, 1322-1332.

Stewart, R., Mobley, L., Van Tuyl, S., & Salvador, M. (1987). The first-born's adjustment to the birth of a sibling: A longitudinal assessment. *Child Development, 58*, 341-355.

Stewart, R., Van Tuyl, S., Mobley, L., Salvador, M., & Walls, D. (1986). *The transition at the birth of a second child: Sources of parental stress and support.* Paper presented at the Conference on Human Development, Nashville, TN.

Stewart, R., Van Tuyl, S., & Vala-Rossi, M. (1983). [Sibling relations: Parental reports of adjustment, rivalry, and caregiving.] Unpublished data, Oakland University.

Stewart, W. (1977). A psychosocial study of the formation of the early adult life structure in women (Doctoral dissertation, Columbia University, 1977). *Dissertation Abstracts International, 38*, 381B-382B.

Stryker, S. (1964). The interactional and situational approaches. In H. Christensen (Ed.), *Handbook of marriage and the family*. Skokie, IL: Rand McNally.

Tabachnick, B., & Fidell, L. (1983). *Using multivariate statistics*. New York: Harper & Row.

Taylor, M., & Kogan, K. (1973). Effects of birth of a sibling on mother-child interaction. *Child Psychiatry and Human Development, 4*, 53-58.

Thibaut, J., & Kelley, H. (1959). *The social psychology of groups*. New York: John Wiley.

Thomas, A., & Chess, S. (1977). *Temperament and development*. New York: Brunner/Mazel.

Trivers, R. (1974). Parent-offspring conflict. *American Zoologist, 14*, 249-264.

Vernon, D., Foley, J., Sipowicz, R., & Schulman, J. (1965). *The psychological responses of children to hospitalization and illness: A review of the literature*. Springfield, IL: Charles C Thomas.

Veroff, J., Douvan, E., & Kulka, R. (1981). *The inner American*. New York: Basic Books.

Waldron, H., & Routh, D. (1981). The effects of the first child on the marital relationship. *Journal of Marriage and the Family, 43*, 785-788.

Walker, A. (1985). Reconceptualizing family stress. *Journal of Marriage and the Family, 47*, 827-837.

Walker, K., & Woods, M. (1976). *Time use: A measure of household production of family goods and services*. Washington, DC: American Home Economics Association.

Weiss, J. S. (1981). *Your second child*. New York: Summit.

Wente, A., & Crockenberg, S. (1976). Transition to fatherhood: Lamaze preparation, adjustment difficulty, and the husband-wife relationship. *Family Coordinator, 25*, 351-357.

Author Index

Subject Index

About the Author

Robert B. Stewart, Jr., is an Associate Professor of Psychology at Oakland University in Rochester, Michigan. He received his doctorate degree in human development and family studies, with a minor in applied statistics, from the Pennsylvania State University in 1979. Throughout his professional career, he has focused his attention on the systemic study of family interactions, first by comparing mother-infant and father-infant interactions in home and laboratory settings, and later by studying the role of the firstborn child as a subsidiary attachment figure for the infant. It was this work on sibling attachment relations that led him and his colleagues to initiate their studies of early sibling interactions and relationships, including the role of the older sibling as a teacher for the younger, a detailed analysis of the cognitive prerequisites necessary to enable the older child to act as a subsidiary attachment figure for the infant, and finally a longitudinal analysis of the firstborn child's adjustment following the birth of a sibling.

NOTES

NOTES

NOTES